Straight up and Dirty

Straight up and Dirty

Stephanie Klein

EBURY
PRESS

5 7 9 10 8 6 4

This edition published in 2007

Published in 2006 by Ebury Press, an imprint of Ebury Publishing

Ebury Publishing is a division of the Random House Group

First Published by HarperCollins Publishers (USA) Inc. in 2006

Text © Stephanie Klein 2006

Stephanie Klein has asserted her right to be identified as the author of this Work in
accordance with the Copyright, Designs and Patents Act 1988

The Random House Group Limited Reg. No. 954009

Addresses for companies within the Random House Group can be found at
www.randomhouse.co.uk

A CIP catalogue record for this book is available from the British Library

The Random House Group Limited makes every effort to ensure that the papers used
in our books are made from trees that have been legally sourced from well-managed
and credibly certified forests. Our paper procurement policy can be found on
www.randomhouse.co.uk

Mixed Sources
Product group from well-managed
forests and other controlled sources
www.fsc.org Cert no. TT-COC-2139
© 1996 Forest Stewardship Council

Printed and bound in Great Britain by Cox & Wyman Ltd, Reading, Berkshire

ISBN 9780091908997

FOR MY FATHER

TELL THE TRUTH
or someone will tell it for you

Contents

AUTHOR NOTE | 1

one A PAIR AND A SPARE | 3

two STAGING LOVE | 29

three CEREAL MONOGAMY | 57

four PACK ANIMALS | 77

five RED WINE WITH FISH | 101

six THE ORAL SEX SOUTH BEACH DIET | 121

seven CELERY AND FUNNEL CAKE | 137

eight MOVING THE FURNITURE | 151

nine THE RUNS | 173

ten CONTROL ALT DELETE | 191

eleven THERE'S NEVER JUST ONE COCKROACH | 207

twelve THE BUTTERFLY EFFECT | 233

thirteen SOMEBODY LANGUAGE | 241

fourteen MANUAL FOCUS | 257

fifteen RED | 271

ACKNOWLEDGMENTS | 289

Author Note

STRAIGHT UP & DIRTY. STRAIGHT UP.

In writing this memoir, I have recalled conversations as I've remembered them; they are not meant to be verbatim dictations of my life. They are my voice, recounting what happened to me and retaining the feeling and sentiment of what occurred. As a result, my relationships are more properly portrayed for the impact they had on me; some people might sound wittier, others less obtuse. In no case have I made anyone appear to be someone they weren't to me. It's my story. My perception. My experiences. And I was true to them. I compressed timelines and created composites of minor people in the book for narrative flow in a limited number of instances, and I changed names and other identifying details, including occupations, throughout to protect the privacy of others. There is a trust between a writer and the reader, a trust I hold dear. So make no mistake, this is a work of nonfiction, despite how straight up or dirty I am in the telling of it.

one

A PAIR AND A SPARE

IT WAS APRIL FOOL'S DAY, 2003—FOURTEEN DAYS FROM TAX time—and the biggest joke of a day. I sat on the floor of his closet, my head between the hems of his pants. His suede loafers made imprints on the backs of my thighs. I'd bought him those herringbone pants at a Zanella sample sale, that reversible leather belt, and all those fine sweaters and tailored shirts. I'd shop with an index card of his sizes so he wouldn't need to return things. I wanted to make him happy.

He'd said pleats were outdated and told me to return them, but you can't return samples, so they remained, tags intact, toward the back of his closet. I could touch the grain of his wooden shoe trees, finger his cashmere sweaters, and cry into his shirts. I still had his things. His smell was still there, but he was a stranger.

The ties were the hardest part to leave. I'd bought more than a handful of them for him in Paris, when he'd proposed marriage to me at the Eiffel Tower in June of 1998. Charvet, Ferragamo, and Hermès were all he'd wear. I didn't know from any of it. Unlike him, I wasn't raised on a diet of designer. So I made an effort by introducing him to Etro ties, hoping he'd tell people I'd turned him onto something new. But he didn't like Etro—he liked what he knew. "I'm sorry Stephanie, but your taste, uh . . ." he said shaking his head in disproval, "it's from hunger."

"What the hell does that mean?"

"You know how when you're starving you'll eat anything?"

"Yeah."

"Well," then he closed the lid on the tie box and pushed it toward me as he said, "you're looking at anything."

My twenty-eight-year-old husband Gabriel Rosen never pretended to be a retrosexual. I mean the boy was a hardcore metrosexual before its emergence in the lexicon. He always knew from hair product and thread count. Then he joined a new gym and never missed a tanning appointment. For the five and a half years we'd been together, I'd occasionally joke when he revealed his chest at the beach: "Oh look, you decided to wear a Gap sweater." Back then, he was too fixated on his bald spot and Propecia to ever contemplate hair removal. But suddenly, after two and a half years of marriage, his Palm calendar included laser sessions for his arms, chest, and back. A foreign cologne hung heavy in the air, clinging to his new Prada button-down. His new shirt wasn't red, but the flag was. The signs were there, an article straight from a woman's magazine:

- JOINS A GYM
- VISITS A TANNING SALON
- SPORTS A NEW HAIRSTYLE
- WEARS HAIR PRODUCT AND COLOGNE MORE OFTEN
- PURCHASES VARIOUS NEW AND DIFFERENT CLOTHES
- SUDDENLY AND INEXPLICABLY CHANGES HIS CLOTHING STYLE

He wasn't gay. He was cheating. I didn't say adultery. I didn't say sex. I said cheating as in living as if I weren't in his life.

WHEN I CONFRONTED GABE, HE SWORE. NOT "SHIT" OR "oh, fuck." He swore, "*Nothing . . . happened.*" In his pause between "Nothing" and "happened" he was devising the next lie. "Nothing," I would later discover, consisted of movie premieres, courtside seats at Madison Square Garden, Bungalow 8, text messages, late night phone calls, meeting her friends, and a string of missed electronic pages. "Happened" was a forty-three-year-old socialite. If recklessness were currency, he could have purchased all of Prada. When tax season approached, he had nothing left to expense. I'd already written him off. Dependents: 0.

Enough with his designer closet; none of it was mine anymore. I needed to finish packing. As I sat cross-legged on our hardwood floor, I smelled packing tape and was surrounded by brown. Brown packing boxes, brown shadows cast on barren walls, left only with brown rusted picture hooks and sun rings, revealing what was no longer there. Depleted from a day of instructing movers which boxes would go to storage and which would go to my new smaller apartment across town, I sat alone. All I had were the keys I'd need to turn in and the last wheel of brown tape in my hands. I sealed my last box, the Gabe box—full of vacation itineraries, smiling photographs, our certificate of marriage, old tax returns, printed e-mails, and folded notes signed with xxx's, ooo's, and *Always*. The box was leaving the Upper East Side and heading for storage. I was heading to the Upper West without any of it. I closed the door behind me.

"I HAVE TO START MY WHOLE LIFE OVER. AGAIN."

"Please, your life was for shit before," I could almost hear my younger sister Lea say over the phone in my new apartment a week later. Instead she responded, "Oh, stop. Starting your life over is a good thing; it's an opportunity." Lea spoke in semicolons.

"Don't do that. Don't bring up the whole door-window thing."

"Well it's true; it's a makeover. I know it doesn't feel like it now, Stephanie, but this is a blessing in disguise."

She went there, like everyone else, reaching into their heavy bags searching for the appropriate cliché to smack on my condition: betrayed. I wanted time to fast-forward, so I could awake happy and over it. So I ate Benadryl and cried into the buttery neck of my shorthaired furkid Linus.

"You get to redecorate and cut your hair. You get to go and buy new clothes. Oooh, and new bedding. I need to hurry up and get married, so I can get divorced too. You're so living *A Fashion Emergency*; I should send them a tape."

"Lea, I'm serious."

"Wait—Steph, have you seen the show? It's sooooo good; you can get a free wardrobe."

Lea, if not reminded she's still talking, can easily talk the shit out of a livestock auctioneer. "Seriously, enough with your pity party over there. I bet you're still in that white bed wearing yesterday's clothes. Have you even walked Linus?"

Linus curled himself into a small bean beneath the down comforter. Even when I'd tease him with my "Wanna go for a walk. Huh? Do ya?

Huh?" he'd only lift his head temporarily, then go back to sleep. He knew it was only a tease. We weren't going anywhere. We were both depressed.

"He's sleeping."

"Stephanie, it's not like you're some housewife. You're a goddamn vice president at a big advertising firm. You're a talented web designer, have all these friends, you're thin and gorgeous, and you're the one sitting in bed? Excuse me, but it could be a lot worse. You could've had children. Shit, you could be me, fat and friendless, living in your father's basement."

Despite the clichés, I loved Lea just then for making me laugh. If I'd heard one more person use "life" and "journey" in the same breath, I would've thrown her down a flight of stairs and hoped the wind got knocked out of her. If that didn't work, there was always suffocation. According to Gabriel, The *Was*band, I was always good at that.

Lea knit clichéd quotes into a tight weave of sickening. "Winding roads," "stay in the moment," "when a door shuts," and something to do with a train. I told Lea to stay out of my way and get off her fucking Bikram yoga mat. For the love of God, no one wants to hear it. "You only live once." Jesus, she served packaged clichés as small and saccharine as Sweet'N Low.

And they helped. I hate saying it, but it's true.

"Ah, he was an asshole anyway." Okay, that really helped.

Of course, Gabe wasn't my *whole* life, but when you're in the thick of it, you don't know from rational—you know from drama. I did have my own friends, my own salary, my health, and TiVo: all the important things we're likely to take for granted. Still, when it hit that I'd now have to date again, I panicked. Dating meant nightclubs, heels, and black. It meant, "No, thank you. Really, I'm full." It meant matching bras and underwear. Clothes with the word *MICRO* used to describe them.

I had to shed my identity as "wife." Lily Pulitzer clothes fell into abandoned clumps on the floor beside my patent leather driving shoes. My diamond wedding band and engagement ring were relegated to a box atop my closet. Sometimes I'd take it down and slip the rings back on. I'd sob softly, wishing I could keep the life I thought I had. Then I'd remove the rings and push the box further back in the closet. Even my hands were different. It's something you don't think about, but at least there was new room for a gold Panther ring on my middle finger. All the better to say "fuck you" with.

It was time to move on, and moving on meant dating. Because until you date again, people will hiccup lines about getting back on horses. So you invest in an Agent Provocateur whip and a subscription to an online dating service.

Exactly one month after deciding to refer to The Husband as The Wasband, I thought I was ready to date. Time spent without concrete plans was time anxious. If another man wanted me, I was valuable. I was esteemed, no matter that it wasn't *self*-esteem. You can't be picky when you're up to your armpits in drama. I'd have plenty of time to mourn and autopsy the death of my marriage. I know, assbackward thinking on my part. But we can cover that later.

Dating meant "a pair and a spare," which had nothing to do with balls or a tire. My phone therapist, who lived in Queens, introduced me to the method early on. A therapist in Queens quickly becomes a phone session therapist for a Manhattanette who has no time to leave her borough. "Always date at least three men at once," she instructed in a nasal whine, "because it will prevent you from latching on to the wrong relationship out of neediness." Okay, so first I had to find *one*, never mind three. "Okay, okay, find one, but be on the lookout for two and three. If you're out to dinner with another man it will help you deal when runner-up number one doesn't call." Already, we were dealing with a man who wouldn't call, and I wasn't even dating yet. Just kill me now.

So now you get to meet them: the men I *rodated* over the next three months.

OUR FIRST INTRODUCTION HAPPENED ONLINE. DID YOU hear that? 'Cause I sorta whispered it. I am twenty-nine, divorced, and live in Manhattan, New York. A stranger lives in Manhattan, Kansas, has a lazy eye, a lazy mustache, and wants to marry me. This is online dating, and this is my profile:

> I don't like long walks—I cab it. Hiking to me sounds like a fate worse than death, yet I love the *idea* of camping. It has to be the food. Second, who doesn't like to travel? And why does everyone say they like "curling up" with a good book? I love Milkduds in my popcorn and cold air. Movies are a given. I don't like chocolate, but I love cream cheese frosting and when autumn arrives in tweeds and hand-knit scarves. Artichokes with drawn butter. A new toothbrush. A gin martini, straight up and dirty. Grapefruit-scented lotion in summer. Rose oil in winter. Insanely high thread-count sheets year-round. The girl can cook and dress. And please, dear God, enough with the jeans-to-evening-gown cliché. Yawn. I'm skilled with chopsticks, but I prefer to eat sushi with my hands. I have so much passion, I assure you, you'll be floored. I can bait my own hook, but I'll count on you for back scratches, letting me eat the fries off your plate, and definitely good bedtime stories. Flowers from Takashimaya certainly don't hurt, especially when sent to the office, but I've learned romance is about sacrifice and compromise . . . about lemon water in the middle of the night.

About my match:
You don't pronounce dog "dawg," lounge in Sean John velour, and you know jewelry belongs on a woman, not your neck. If you want to cook me dinner on the second date, you're cheap. You don't refer to yourself in the third person or drink anything pink. You do eat carbs but will never Blackberry over dinner. You would never say, "the bomb," or "nizzle," but an occasional "bi-atch" for good measure is okay. If you always order chicken teriyaki at Japanese restaurants, I'm not the girl for you. I need someone with a sense of adventure, even if that means a spicy tuna roll. LOL would never be used in any of your communications with me. You live in Manhattan and ideally live alone. You've ex-

perienced pain at one point in your life, have evolved communication skills, and want to find a partner. You're intelligent, tender, and audacious with an enduring sense of character. You know when to swallow pride, grab me, and fight for it. An emotionally available man who doesn't acquiesce because it's easier than confrontation has a spot beside me. Men with mommy and daddy issues or who manage their anger with drugs or alcohol need not apply. A robust sexual drive is essential, really, no seriously, I mean it. Enjoy photography, listening to music, with me by your side, sipping wine from your glass (preferably, you'll be the one creating the music with your acoustic guitar? My God, nothing is sexier). Holding my hand and kissing me on the street is a have-to. It's all about passion. I crave it and give it, good. A good first date would include honesty and alcohol. And, most of all, be armed with attention span, an appetite for everything, and an open mind to chick flicks and music that might as well be a TBS afternoon movie. Oh, and you can't mind that my toy fox terrier, Linus, sleeps under the covers with me and licks my face.

Who knew I needed to specify, Manhattan, *New York*. I know there's a stigma to online dating. When people manage to get beyond date numero tres, they spend cuatro creating a how-we-met story over shared appetizers and white wine. I didn't care about stigma. I already had one: Divorcée. "Oh, come on. Do you really buy that?" Do I buy it? No, I get it for free. One guy actually hung up the phone on me when he learned I was divorced. He played the technotard card, asking me to hold while he answered his call-waiting. "Ooops," he could say if I ever bothered to call him out on it, "uh, this whole call-waiting thing." Right, he's a technosexual crackberry who Palms at the dinner table, but he somehow doesn't know the first bit about using the flash button? Oh, gigabyte me.

It was a newsflash to me that dating as a pre-thirty divorcette was as bad as having herpes. And now, along with a perfume atomizer, a curiously thick stack of business cards, and plastic poop bags for my furkid Linus, I get to tote around the stigma of being a divorcée in my diminutive Marc Jacobs clutch. Dating-engine-minded men uncheck "divorced" in their online search preferences for a mate.

That April, I sorted match.com profiles with an open mind. So he looked like Al Borland from *Tool Time* . . . so that could be cute in a "let's cuddle in matching flannel" kind of way. I was done with hot. Hot was The *Was*band. Hot didn't exactly take. I was looking for someone just good looking enough to get me aroused. Excess leads to torment.

The date with The Tool was set. We talked on the phone for hours, and I of course conjured up the wrong image of this cuddly man. My Mister Tool Time would "fix" things. I wasn't shy about my recent past. Details were shared with a stranger—a stranger whom I hoped would be a brilliant replacement. He was emotionally available and compassionate. He seemed evolved and to possess excellent communication skills. He had feelings beyond anger because the ref made a bad call.

It was unseasonably freezing for April, but I felt beautiful in my new cream coat and cashmere wrap as I waited in the cold watching my breath disappear as if it were smoke. Exhale. As the bearded man approached, all I could think was "uncle." He was not my uncle, but he was asexual in an uncle sort of way. My shoulders fell; I smiled harder to conceal my disappointment. I imagined his kitchen cabinets filled with microwavable soups for one. He was the kind of man who liked cats, both the animal and the musical. We exchanged an awkward cheek kiss and walked to Payard Patisserie. I downed two glasses of pinot.

That's better.

Okay, let me make the most of this. He did go to Columbia, was a banker and a film critic. There were things to say. I hadn't anticipated what happened next.

"So Stephanie, thanks for meeting me." His body seemed built to lift heavy things, but his nervous voice conveyed that he hired someone to install his window screens. "I've been sad lately, see, and, well. Ya know. Well, tomorrow is my birthday, and I have no one to go out with. Will you please have dinner with me?"

Freeze-frame there for a sec.

I'm on a pseudo-date with The Tool right then, and I'm not feeling him. And now, in my emotionally tender state, I have to commit to another date? No way, right? I have plans, would love to, sorry. Wrong. "Of course I will." I was rubbernecking with my mouth agape, as I saw my Saturday night pass me by. I really needed a good twelve-step. The man knew I was into sushi. It said so in my profile, so he promised a spectacular sushi dinner. It was his birthday. How could I cancel on the poor guy's birthday?

When he called the next day, it was too fast.

"I'll pick you up in my car and take us there. Be ready at seven-thirty."

Click. He emphasized *my car* the way someone refers to his vacation home, Swiss account, or private jet. A car doesn't necessarily warrant a tone. If there were time to e-mail, I'd send "unsubscribe."

I had him pick me up at my friend Hannah's apartment on the Upper East Side. I needed wine. Hannah had converted her armoire into storage for her French reds ending in "Pape." Hannah had a married sugar daddy, nineteen years her senior, who shipped her wine, clothing, and shoes from Europe on a regular basis. The wine was helping. "It's sushi for chrissake. How bad can it be? You know there's more to a man than his looks." Hannah said as she twisted her wrist, her new gold bangles clinking.

The Tool and I buzzed west in his red flag. Flag, Ferrari, same diff. Okay, now his Ferrari warranted a tone. Where can he be taking me? Fujiyama-Mama? My mind reeled through Zagat pages. Haru? There's a Haru on the East Side. Then it became clear when we neared the West Side Highway. "Are we going to New Jersey?" Instinctively, I gripped the door handle.

Okay, so if he were cute, the gesture of bad sushi with a great Manhattan skyline view would have been romantic in a whimsical, clumsy way. "How creative is he? He put so much thought into our date. What effort . . ." Friends would swoon. When you're not into the guy, it's: "Can you even believe he took me to JERSEY for sushi?!" Friends shake their heads and repeat "Jersey" in a whisper.

Thankfully, the fates were aligned, and our waiter was new—he didn't know to stagger the entrée from the appetizers. All at once, our food arrived. Thank you, maestro. God love you. During our meal, however, The Tool asked to see my hand. He wanted to hold it, I knew. To avoid this, and to give him an out, I offered, "Why, you want to tell my fortune?"

"No," he countered, "I want to hold it."

I'm certain I flinched. But just to clear up any perceived misconceptions, I whispered, "I'm sorry, I'm just not comfortable with that." You could hear the buzz as the anvil dropped off the cliff. Splat.

After dinner he suggested a stroll on the pier. Clearly, the table rejection wasn't enough pain. He'd sprung back into action. He was Wile E. Coyote in the next scene. It was freezing out, and had I been into the guy, I would have walked slowly, clinging to him. I would have hardly noticed my fingers had no feeling. "No, I really just want to get home. I'm exhausted." I might have actually pushed out a convincing yawn.

He dropped me off. I unrolled my scarf, entered my apartment, flung my handbag onto the floor, and began to cry. This is what's out there? This is what's left now that I've squandered my time away with a two-and-a-half-year starter marriage? No wonder women learn to look the other way. And this was only the beginning.

Teary-eyed I leaned before the mirror. I knew I had to face the shit out of this, and facing it meant moving forward. It meant hideous dates and misleading men, but as pathetic as any date could ever be, nothing would be more pathetic than running backward. I couldn't go back to Gabe. "He lied to you and didn't know your worth. He was a boy. You will find a man, Stephanie." I was suddenly a self-help book, chanting in the mirror. I didn't believe what I was saying. Gabe was a handsome, wealthy, educated charmer, a Jewish urologist. I worried I'd never do better. I worried I would have to settle.

Being married to a liar is settling. Being alone might be unsettling, but it's temporary, a yellow ribbon woven through a rope of hair. At least you've got the hope of a healthy relationship in the future to keep you company. See, I'm good once I'm *in* a relationship. I'm good with "afraid," "hurt," and "frustrated" over "McFucker Coward Bastard Go Die." I've honed my communication skills to a very sharp point. I know to not bring up the past, mention his bald spot, or use "you always." I'll even give him the last word. I will too. The problem? My knuckles turned white in every relationship once I realized it was over. I'd latch on to "wrong" because the wrong relationship was better than "alone"; it was better, even, than dating. I stayed because I feared Tool Time moments.

I lay in bed, too tired to peel off the too-good-for-you outfit. I stared at the phone. My friend Dulce (yes, as in *de leche*) would cheer, "You should learn to make yourself happy first." She'd whine, "You know you won't find it as long as you're looking for it." I knew I couldn't call her. I'd want to throw the phone . . . or worse, hang up and dial an ex.

Before marrying Gabe, I kept a string of ex-boyfriends on the back burner. We'd meet for lunch and chat on my office phone. Exes were "in case." They were my mother in the middle of the night. My pacifier. But I'd outgrown my baby shoes. They're in bronze on my grandfather's dresser beside my graduation photo. I worried I hadn't graduated, not really. Because I should have learned strength and "what you deserve" in school. I remembered a + b = c, but I didn't remember how I got there, to divorce. Yet, there I was, fully dressed, lying in bed, trembling every time I looked in the mirror trying to smile. How can this be it? How did it get to this point?

It was fear. Fear was governing my decisions. Until I faced what terrified me, I'd cozy up to unhealthy, and I'd never find happiness. But I didn't know this then. When I heard, "You need to face alone, work on your neediness, and not date for at least a year." I'd agree aloud, shaking my head. Yeah, right. There was no way I'd not date for a year.

Clothed in bed, I realized I was the one suffering from an anvil injury. "It's time to stand on your own" is what I ought to have said to the mirror. I should have unsubscribed from all of it. Instead, I updated my online profile: Love Manhattan Sushi. Disdain for dining in Jersey. Ix-nay on the eard-bay.

IT WAS MY SIXTH DATE WITH DAVID MINETTI SINCE MEET-ing at Compass, a neighborhood restaurant with killer Parmesan bread-sticks. There was no beard, no Jersey, and he was definitely not an uncle. Admittedly, The Tool made for great starter conversation on my initial date with David. Worst-date-ever scenarios give everyone hope. "Well at least I'm not that bad." David was the third "try" in "try and try again."

So here I was, date six, but I'd been too lazy the day prior for necessary dating errands. So I scrambled and raced through appointments. As a single woman, I'm concerned with the bottom line . . . my bikini line. I know the men I date are playing the field. Mine might as well be mowed. Bikini waxing is as essential as a firm handshake at an interview. You're not going to get any type of job if you're not buttoned-up once you've been unbuttoned.

Prior to arriving at the salon, I shot down three Advil to ward off the inevitable swelling. Helga (yes, Helga) was running late. I dug through my heavy Celine bag for the to-do list. Helga told me to undress in room five. Relax, this isn't *Porn Stories* by Klein. Not yet. In the room, there was a cold doctor's chair, the metal kind with a short *pleather* back, that's hardly a back, more like a strolling stool with a Tootsie Roll for back support. The chair was sandwiched between a massage table and an over-flowing trash pail. Admittedly, it wasn't the J Sisters Salon. Still, it wasn't some hole-in-the-wall nail place tampering in waxing and tanning. The "massage table" was also the kind you see in doctor's exam rooms—with the white translucent paper attached to a roll covering the table for sanitary reasons. Except that day, the paper was flecked with baby powder and stained with oil and yellow wax. The stuffed garbage container screamed "Used," filled with balls of translucent paper and cloth strips covered in thick yellow wax with short black hairs poking through the yellow lines. I walked outside my room and summoned Helga with,

"Um, I don't think the room is ready."

Helga tidied up the room somehow. She Russian-shuffled, like a housekeeper making her way under the sink for a rag. I was extended a polite half-smile and told to get undressed and lie down. She left the room. There was no robe. I was torn. Did she mean take off my underwear completely? Usually, I left it on, but since I was going Brazilian, I figured, well, when in Brazil . . . so I flicked off my heels, wiggled free from my jeans, and dropped the slingshot. I got on the doctor's table, paper cringing and crinkling with me as I waited.

Helga rubbed powder into her hands like a gymnast. With her hands fanned, she spread the powder onto my exposed skin, along my inner thighs, sprinkles on my mound. She proceeded to dip a thick popsicle stick into hot wax, allowing the excess to drip off, then blew on the stick, with the expertise of a daily soup drinker. Spread it on thick, pushed cloth atop the wax, and smoothed out the fabric with the palm of one hand, then tap tap tap, she slapped the cloth and then ripped it off. Okay, this had been done before; this is old territory.

We get to the lips. My God, the lips. I had to stretch against where she was working, so the skin would be taut, so the fabric would catch and lift the wax. I was touching myself, holding inner parts, labia minora, grabbing my thighs. It was not, I assure you, as fun as it sounds. I told her to leave a square of hair on the top only, smaller than a Triscuit, larger than a Wheat Thin. I made sure, though, the square was not connected to anything. It was floating almost, like a buoy. I couldn't believe I was going to let her rip the hair from the top bridge of my inner lips. Then as soon as I felt the warmed wax approaching what felt like it had to be my clitoris, I thought, oh my God, is it too late? Is there any way I can change my mind? I exhaled and became religious in prayer.

"Zat's a good gurl. Very good gurl." I believed it had to be over. She had even taken out pointed tweezers and a magnifying glass to lift the strays. Nope. "Okay, now onto stomach. Zat's it. Okay, hold here, sweetie. Can you pull zees apart?" Helga asked me to spread my ass cheeks to her. She then began to dig—I mean really dig, the way you look for loose change in a slim evening clutch—with her probing warm popsicle stick. "Clean as a vistle. All done," she chanted as she spread warm baby oil over my swollen hoo-hoo, legs, and ass crack. Done. Thank the good Lord; there was more cleaning to do. I hoped David was worth all this new religion.

At home I realized my armpits smelled fine, but my apartment was a mess. I began with the bedside table—it speaks volumes. It's like your choice of shoes. I rearranged my bedside table book arrangement, placing the French soapbox filled with condoms to the top of the stack. Some might check the book titles for anything scary: *Father Hunger, Overcoming Overeating, The Needy and Greedy*, and be quick to shove them in the sock drawer. But since I'm frighteningly open, I left them on display. A vase with Gerber daisies, a carafe of drinking water, my eye mask, and the pill were now somehow orderly. Dusting wouldn't hurt. I was naked cleaning my apartment. I couldn't decide what to wear, but I knew I couldn't even think wardrobe until the apartment was tidy. I wouldn't invite him in unless the place was representative of the me I wanted to be.

Random bits of mail were shoved in a bag, DVDs in their sleeves, fuck music cued in the player. Fresh-cut flowers arranged in the living room, beside the bed, and yes, even in a Tiffany tissue vase, compliments of my wedding registry, in the bathroom beside the matches. I was ready for a sleepover. Well almost. I was running late.

Late meant Frizz-Ease and a hair clip. It meant one eye shadow, no time for a duo. It meant brushing my teeth and washing my *vaja*. There was no time for a shower and full makeup. See, there's an attitude to being put together in a hurry—it's a good one. All women should know how to do this. Febreze, fresh flowers, Frizz-Ease, a quick vagina cleaning, some sexy unmentionables, and you're ready. Okay, some gloss out the door. Oh, yeah, perfume, but how French whore . . . I'd skip it. Okay, maybe I'd add a little.

Sometimes, you like the guy a lot, or you want to because he's thoughtful and a gentleman. David was that "sometimes." On our previous dates, our evenings would end with waitstaff clearing throats and glancing at watches. We'd outstay our welcome, chatting on until 1 A.M. without noticing the time. When he walked me home, he'd insist on buying Gray's Papaya hot dogs for Linus. This was his power move. Show her you're into her dog and you're guaranteed rank in the pair and spare lineup.

I really wanted to be into him—he was great on paper. Management Consultant, Ivy grad, lived alone and had a terrace, parents still married. David liked wine, my hair, and yes, even my dog. That whole half-stand thing when he pushes himself up from the table is overblown. I hear women add it to the retelling of their dates. They do it because they think it's what other women will respond to. He did it, but who cares? He'd e-mail often, everything from articles concerning the re-org of my parent company, to town histories about Sag Harbor because he knew I'd have a share house there in the summer. His links to Citysearch write-ups on 5 Ninth, a hip new restaurant in the Meatpacking District, were much more impressive than any half-stand number. He could even kiss, although he improved once I put him on a regimented tongue-training program. Someone had to cure him from the world of small bird peck circles. Finally, he learned to hold my face with both hands, definitely shows you're into it, and stick it in properly. I know. I'm a martyr.

SO WHY? WHY COULDN'T I BE INTO MISTER GREAT ON PAPER?

Because you don't fuck paper.

Still, if there were a promise of a passionate sex life, it would all change. So enough talk. I needed to test his action.

"He's showed such restraint, particularly when faced with three-hundred-dollar perfume quite literally made for a queen," my friend Hannah told me when I complained I'd yet to size up one Mr. David Minetti. On our previous dates, he had walked me home, offering me his arm, and when we turned corners, he ensured he was on the outside, near the curb. Kissing him was delicious. Inviting him up seemed cheap. I was with a gentleman now, and it's hard to really fuck a gentleman. Inviting him up felt too "this will never last."

But, I'm here to report that after five dates of just rubbing up against each other, David Minetti finally, albeit timidly, touched my triangle.

Five dates is a really long time to go before sizing a guy up. I was nervous I'd be disappointed, so I avoided it at all costs when we'd made out previously. I got bold and decided to go for it.

Minetti. His last name even sounds like it means "small penis" in Italian. You know he's doing the best with what he's got; you feel it in the stubble of his pubes. You're certain he's trimming to make it look bigger. He must know he's little. But he doesn't have a fancy car or fancy voice. He's genuine, and it's sad because you can't move past it.

I'd done it once before. Gabe was a roll of quarters, and I'd spent too many nights wishing I could feel it in my stomach. In the same way you can't imagine the taste of butter on your dry baked potato, you can't fantasize the feeling of weight in your hands. Unfortunately, it's not like the pimple on your face—it doesn't feel bigger than it actually is. Been there, done a past life of that. Lesson learned.

This is one you just can't compromise away. The careless leaving-the-seat-up thing is a nonissue. There's therapy for a bad temper. Get a maid to deal with the socks. But a lifetime with a penis made of kibbles and bits is a deal-breaker. I'm just not willing to live with sexual disappointment again.

Skip to the next paragraph if you're squeamish. So I was jerking him off because I wanted it to be over, but not so much that I was willing to go down on him. I'd had too much and not enough to drink because I wasn't drunk at all, but instead, completely dehydrated. I'd no saliva to work onto my palms. I punctuated any forward motion with a stop at the bedside water carafe. Meanwhile, what the fuck, any time he got excited he completely abandoned me. He stopped rubbing me and was all about his pleasure. What, you can't do two things at once? I so pegged him for a multitasker. Then he proved me wrong. He could, as it turned out, make verbal requests while he got jerked off. "Higher, please." He said it as if he were politely asking for some ketchup. *Please?!* And I was thinking, higher? I mean there's so little there to work with, he had to be kidding. I'd worked with bigger mushrooms in my salads.

Then he brought me toilet paper to wipe his mess off my stomach. Toilet paper never works. It gets wet and drags the mess around. Give me a fucking proper towel, the "spankerchief," and then, *please*, finish me off. So he did. He tried going down on me, using just his tongue. Men don't get this. When going down on a woman, there's more to it than tongue. I needed a helping hand, or two.

Screw this. I yanked him up toward me, so his face was now beside mine. "Here," I said as I slapped his hand over mine. I began to masturbate, pressing his palm over mine, so he'd learn how I liked it. I so didn't need him there. That's the worst kind of sex, when the guy adds nothing. He could have attempted to talk dirty. That would have at least been something. Somehow, though, I sensed his idea of talking dirty was telling me he had a cock.

I knew it would be the first and last time I'd orgasm with this man. It wasn't just the size of his member. It was the "please." Who says "please" in bed? I mean, unless you're on your knees and your partner has you begging for it, "please" has no place in pleasing me. I like 'em dirty. Let him go be polite someplace else. I wanted him to leave. It was 2 A.M., and he liked me, so I couldn't ask. He'd be hurt, and I'd seem rude. So I put on the new Guster CD and told him, "Shh, no talking."

Just before falling asleep I giggled.

Mushrooms.

I WAS WEARING TURQUOISE, DESPITE THE CHILL OF spring. Turquoise is for tanned skin, open-toed shoes, and girls with braids and bandanas. It's not the making of spring. Besides, I was too lazy to shampoo that day—my hair was twisted, frayed ribbons. My makeup was leftovers. As I waited for my friend Smelly to meet me for a drink, I sidled up to the MOBar in the Mandarin Oriental Hotel, and asked for a wine list. They were without a list and had only extended a verbal blur of choices.

"You know what? Even easier, do you have anything from South Africa, New Zealand, or Germany?" Negative. The female bartender poured me a taste of some white wine. I tasted oak and felt myself star-

ing for longer than appropriate at her overflowing breasts. "I don't mean
to be a pain, but anything unoaked? Do you have something other than
Chardonnay?" I know what I sounded like. I didn't care. I wanted what I
wanted—go ahead, say it.

"I hear they've got a nice Sancerre," I like to believe were the words
the man beside me offered. In truth, though, I can't remember his first
words to me, or if we even talked about wine. Somehow, though, he
ended up paying for mine. Pleasantries were not exchanged. We didn't
talk about the weather or about jobs. We talked about his day, and he presented me with the proof. His day's activities were wrapped in shiny black
cardboard boxes and nestled into a Thomas Pink bag. The boy could
shop.

"Well, you might as well show me what you've got in there, cause
Jeez, you'll have no chance of dating me if I hate your taste." I can't believe I used the word "Jeez." Now, there's no subtext here. This isn't *Pulp
Fiction*—it wasn't his soul in there. I approved of more than just the
shirts. I don't know if it was his shoulders, his voice, or those liquidy
overcast eyes. I was lost. Our banter was truncated upon the arrival of
Smelly, my old college roommate. Her younger identical twin brothers
lent me her childhood nickname, "Smell Adele, go to Hell," in lieu of
Adele, despite the fact that she now considers "hell" a swear word and
smells only of Quelques Fleurs and Aveda lipstick. Introductions were
made; my attention shifted. The wine kept coming.

I don't understand how any woman can be seen in stockings and
sneakers, even if it is a commute. There is absolutely no excuse for this. I
told Smelly just this after she complained to me about her blisters. She
was wearing Pumas with a skirt, and she responded with a wrinkled smile
and raise of her glass. After we covered work, wardrobe, and weekend
plans, I realized he might have to leave. I might have to leave. As Smell
excused herself to make a phone call outside, I dug in. In my handbag, I
found one of my business cards. I turned to him and smiled. He smiled.
I pushed the card to him as if it were a bill. "Just in case I need to go, or
you need to abscond, I wanted to give you this. It was nice not quite

meeting you." It wasn't the wine.

"Abscond, huh? I hope this doesn't mean you'll be departing for the evening. I still want to talk." I think that was a blush.

"I'm not leaving." What I meant, of course, was "I'm not going anywhere without you."

Smelly had to return to her office, kiss, kiss, I'll call you tomorrow. He asked if I would join him for dinner. We were, after all, in a hotel bar, beside a hotel restaurant, and I was, after all, hungry. Okay, let's face it, had I just eaten a full-course tasting menu at Danube, I would have feigned starvation to break bread with this man. Suddenly, he was ready to leave. "You didn't think we'd eat here, did you?"

We were in a cab headed south. Blue Ribbon. Oysters were slurped. Even more wine, something unoaked and perfect. He asked about work, and when I mentioned "artist," he did what all men do. "Oh, have I seen your work anywhere?" It's their way of asking if it's a job or a hobby.

I didn't falter. "Not yet. I'm still working on my craft." Then I smiled knowing exactly what someone who calls her hobby her craft sounds like: affected. I didn't care. "Web designer in advertising" seemed too nerd, skullcap, canvas shoes. "Artist" seemed to cover me better, and I suddenly felt powerful in my conviction. It was as if we were in candlelight, surrounded by our favorite colors. The streets of Manhattan were flecked with gold, never mind moonlight. It was rapture.

We were in a cab headed north, and he was headed south. My pants were pulled to my ankles. I assumed he tipped the driver well. We'd arrived at his apartment, and suddenly we were past his doormen and in his elevator. I was going home with this guy. I'd never in my life done anything like this. I crossed my ankles, read the *Times* on Sunday, and enunciated the *t* in the word *bottle*. I wasn't the type of lady who accompanied a gentleman home upon first meeting. This wasn't a bend in the rule—it was a snap. This behavior was reserved for girls with daddy issues, plagued with low self-esteem, for women who wore leather hotpants.

The view from his thirty-second-floor apartment was panoramic. He was an adult: I saw it in the lack of futon. His chestnut paneling and saffron accents were as impressive as his ability to use area rugs to help define the massive space. It was surprisingly nonbachelor-padesque, save for the black leather sofa near the office area. Still, it wasn't fur or synthetics. It was comfortable and impressive. Then, he suddenly had to excuse himself. There I was, standing in his adult apartment, this man I met only a few hours ago, and he had to get something from the doorman. Dry cleaning, some FedEx, condoms? I didn't know what was going on, only that I had to leave.

I knew if I pressed the down arrow in the hall, there was a chance the elevator would arrive with him in it. I took the stairs down a level to prevent our crossing. On the thirty-first floor, I pressed Down, then floated past his doormen. They told me he'd just gone up. "Oh, yes, fine. It's okay, he knows," I spouted with the flip of my hands. I said it as if we'd discussed it already, with authority.

I was in a taxi at a red light, my forehead in my hand. What the hell am I doing? I'm not this girl. I have a doggie at home wondering where I am. This guy won't take me seriously. I won't even be a real option. You can't have sex with the ones you really like, or it's over before it even starts. Men. Chase. Things. Men like the hunt. Right? I stared into the yellow glow of the taxi driver's identification window and wondered how many one-night stands Mohammed had. BOOM.

He was there, pounding his palms on the taxicab window, his tie loosened and hanging open. He was undone and fixed with passion. His blond, barely-there eyebrows said "please" for him.

"Please, don't go."

"This isn't me. I don't do this."

"It doesn't have to be. Please, take my hand. Let's go upstairs. We'll figure it out." He was calm when he said it, patient and loving. He did, after all, come outside to get me. Okay, it was drama. It was wonderful.

When I took his hand, I had the this-is-it's. This is the making of movies, tissues, and piped-in music. He took my hand, and I knew. I knew I didn't want to let go, knew I could have a future with him. I knew all this before knowing his middle name or if he drank coffee at night. I was in *like*, and I didn't care anymore about tomorrow. I just wanted that moment.

In an instant, all my clothes were off. We were naked on his living room rug, where he was massaging me with oil. He kneaded my muscles, pulling my shoulders, following each muscle into the next, like hands over a braid. "Turn over." I knew where this was going, and for once, I would "enjoy the journey." More massage oil. After plunging his hands into me, he whispered, "You know, I do have a bed." I rocked my body in pleasure and frustration, but I let him take my hand and lead me to his room.

"I'm not having sex with you," I warned. Now, just for the record, if a woman says this to you, she means intercourse, not oral sex. "I mean it." I *did* mean it. He believed me and sought an alternative. In a snap, he left the room and returned with a bottle of lotion. Trying to squirt some body lotion into his hand, he stood naked above the bed. The bottle was empty. Splatters of white lotion speckled his hand.

"Damn it. I'm out of Astroglide, too." Here's a tip, men. Try to leave "Astroglide" out of your speech with any women you've any interest in fucking or seeing again. Nix it from your vocab. "Astroglide" translates to "Sketchy Perv." Defeated, he left the room again. He returned with Pam Cooking Spray. Red cap, aerosol spray. You know the one. You use it to cook eggs, fry up some onions, render some bacon. You don't spray it on your dick.

He shook it and then sprayed. He used his free hand to rub it in, or rub one out. More spray. I smelled butter. At that moment, I simply could have asked for the check, terminating the evening, but I decided to carry on with our meal. Alas, the "you only live once" cliché resonated. He masturbated over my face. I might have licked his balls, but he might have been too soused to climax. Through his childlike squeals, I learned he was caught a little off guard by my finger up the ass maneuver. "Do you mind quieting down? I'm. Working. Here!"

When we were finally tired out, we lay on his bed beside each other, naked, no sheets. We talked about his family, his sister, his mother. As I sit here recounting it, I have enhanced memory. I remember details about his life, the way a fascinated second grader knows things about the paramecium. His mother had red hair and was married twice, bringing her son to her second marriage. "Linus," he said, "can be your equivalent to our relationship." Soon, the sun came through his bedroom windows. Thin stripes of it marked his wooden floor. It was 6 A.M., and I had to go home. I nearly busted into a jog toward his living room to collect my clothes. Being naked in daylight before a stranger ranks right up there with someone discovering your period panties.

"Wow," I exclaimed. I looked at the floor, our clothes strewn about, abandoned like the clothes of lovers, and then I saw the empty bottle of "massage" oil. Colavita Extra Virgin Olive Oil.

He answered, "Yeah, it's a great view, isn't it?" Wide-open windows surrounded me. I stood naked in bewilderment. The man had tossed my salad . . . at least he did it without Astroglide.

HE HADN'T JUST MOVED SOUTH IN THE CAB THAT NIGHT. Turns out the following week he moved south again. To frickin' Southeast Asia. I went north, to Gristedes for a pint of Rocky Road and self-esteem.

How was I to keep three bachelors in rotation when I couldn't even find one with lasting potential? Forget the spare—I couldn't even rally a pair together. It was depressing. I went through all the dating hurdles and always ended up alone anyway. All of my girls heard me dramatize my dates, twirling squeals of excitement around a core of disbelief. And when I was down to a drought, I'd have to pick myself up, go shopping for a $125 tank top to show off my shoulders, and start all over again. Enjoy the journey? Yeah, I'd enjoy "Lovin', Touchin', Squeezin'" myself, in my pajamas, on a night off, thank you very much.

two

STAGING LOVE

ABOVE ALL OTHER OCCASIONS, A WEDDING IS AN EVENT where people get insulted and remember, in remarkable detail, how they were slighted many years later. "How could you sit me at a table with that one?" "Could you have seated me any closer to the kitchen?" and "I can't believe I wasn't invited with a date." And my personal favorite, the one I ingested after each meal with my ex-nag-in-law, "You've made it perfectly clear you want to do it all yourself, and you don't want my help."

No one is ever satisfied, including the newlyweds. They're too tired from a night of having to try to remember names to have good sex. Everyone loses. People should elope, then have a big party to celebrate. Riiiiight, because in-laws would never *dream* of taking that personally. Instead, they'd create a *nightmare* for you until death do you part.

An invitation to my cousin Electra's wedding arrived in the mail. She was marrying a third. Not a third of her worth or a third time's a charm guy, but William Trevor Rand III. Upon reexamination of the weighty embossed envelope, I saw it, right there, in black and ecru: and guest. I drummed my nails on the coffee table. Shit. Shit. Shit. It was my first family wedding since my split with Gabe, and now I had to find my second to attend a "third wedding." Having to endure the love orgy that is a wedding was bad enough, but now I needed not just a date, but a *proper guest*. You know, someone I'd need to offer things to, like fresh hand soap, a cold beverage, or, say, the chance to hold back my hair at the end of the night while I vomited champagne. This would be swell. Something to really look forward to, you know, like a Pap smear.

I had to factor in what I like to call "Grate Expectations." It's the double-edged sword of function dating. One side of the sword is devoted to the guests: expectation. If you're invited with a date, people expect you to bring one. The invitation should've said, "black tie and date optional" because procuring a date to a wedding is no small task. The flip side of the dagger belongs to my date: he couldn't grate the guests with his incessant declarations of his love for me. What he showers me with in private is one thing, but really, telling anyone who will listen how "fond" he is of me vexes people into stiff smiles and sprints toward the loo. "She's really a great lady, isn't she?" Then you conjure images of a panting Odie, jumping through the hoops Garfield tells him to. This isn't dating, it's babysitting. This wouldn't do.

My date would have to endure abandonment when family summoned me. I'd apologize too often about deserting him, so he'd have to deal with that too. He couldn't dance the whole time, or not dance the whole time. He'd need the ability to make me feel beautiful and wanted, to touch my arm, to stare at me and get caught doing it, then produce a wry smile. My guest would understand my anxieties and make me laugh at them, knowing that for a girl like me, who was once married, alcohol and vows might make me . . . oh, I don't know, want to throw myself in front of a meat truck. He couldn't smell or have a small penis in case I got drunk and wanted to fool around. And I would get drunk, like you read about in medical textbooks beside photos of damaged livers.

Okay, so I was asking for more than a date, I suppose. I was looking for a worn-in love, the kind where he'd know to introduce himself to someone because he could read my expression of memory loss. A love like I thought I had with Gabe.

The last wedding I'd attended had been with Gabe. We were running late, something we did remarkably well together. We sat in Long Island Expressway traffic with the car windows down and the radio up. He asked me to give him singing lessons. We sang along to The Barenaked Ladies' "What a Good Boy." When Gabe got to the "bear with me, bear with me, be with me tonight" lyrics, he squeezed my hand and looked at me, finishing his last choral note in a smile. And I remember thinking,

"My God, this is it. This is really it. I get to be with this man for the rest of my life." I felt so lucky. I sang and smiled, and—not at all shocking for me—I even cried a little. "You have such a beautiful voice, Stephanie," he said. I adored hearing him say my name. I felt loved when it came from his mouth.

Later that night, after the wedding reception, I became ill from too much wine. Gabe stayed up late with me, in the dark of our bathroom, so I wouldn't have to be sick alone. "I'll do whatever I can to always take care of you," he'd whispered. "Stephanie, you're my girl, and I love everything about you. Even when you make us late to a wedding, no matter how much warning time I give you." I looked up from the toilet bowl and squinted at him. "Yes, I even love when you make your mean face. And I love how excited you get about stuff, even the stuff I have no interest in, like in the museum the other day." I had dragged him through the sweltering Museum of Natural History because I wanted to draw some of the animals.

"Ugh, how can you be telling me all of this when I'm like this, all nasty and on the floor, sick like this?"

" 'Cause we're family, and I get to see you like this and be this close to you, and I just realized that I'm excited about the fact that I get all of this, all of you, the woman who lets her mail pile up higher than the kitchen table but still complains that I don't throw out my magazines fast enough. Speaking of mail, you know what I love most?" I shook my head. "I love, and never repeat this because it's huge, that your e-mail subject lines are historically all better than mine." This made me laugh because we constantly tried to one-up each other in funny. "I know you're not going to believe me, but you look so pretty sitting there." I did believe him.

We fell asleep watching *My Fair Lady* until the room stopped spinning, which is exactly what I shared with his friends the following afternoon. Upon hearing me tell them that he'd spent the morning repeating, "The rain in Spain stays mainly in the plain," Gabe rolled his eyes, jokingly denied it, and pulled me to him and whispered that he was going to kill me.

I'd kill to have a date like that again for Electra's wedding. But finding a wedding date is like finding a valentine: if you have to *find* one, it doesn't count. Certainly, I've heard of wearing a dress on loan, but borrowing, or dare I say, buying a man is so provincial, yet it was still suggested.

"I saw an ad in the back of a magazine," my sister half-joked over the phone.

"Don't even finish that statement."

"I'm just sayin.' At least you know he specializes in shiatsu in case things get out of hand at the wedding."

"Lea, shiatsu is a form of massage, not a martial art."

"I know." No she didn't.

"What are you reading that crap for?"

"Oh come on, everyone reads them. They're funny as shit. The swinger ads are the best. One actually said they were looking for a hairy nut finder."

"What does that even mean?"

"I don't know, but that's funny as shit." Then she snorted.

I was approaching the maximum spending limit on the AmEx as it was, thanks to the outfits I'd purchased to reclaim the esteem that was ripped from me on the recent litany of bad dates. And since the only feasible option appeared to be paying for a date, I decided to do the ever practical, and oh so dismal: I RSVP'd for one.

"Are you sure you want to stag it?" Electra asked over the phone days later, "because there really won't be any single men at my wedding. Well, no one over twelve who you aren't related to, anyway."

"Yeah, I'm sure. Besides, I can spend time with the fam for a change."

"Good, because I'm sitting you with Fay and Yiya then. I don't know who else to put at their table." Yiya is my eighty-six-year-old Puerto Rican grandmother. Fay is her older sister. Undoubtedly, they'd be wearing muumuus and walkers and want to talk to me about sex. If I weren't related to them, I'd have taken bets on Spanglish Tourette's syndrome.

"Yeah, okay, whatever you want." I decided to be accommodating. Certainly, my cousin already had to manage a handsome share of "this wedding is about me" demands.

"Ugh, thank you," she exhaled. "You have no idea how impossible everyone is being about the simplest things."

I had more than an idea—I had an inexhaustible memory.

BEFORE THE INVITATIONS TO MY WEDDING HIT THE printer, announcing our marriage on August 28, 1999, Gabe panicked, using the words, "not ready yet." To this day, my unworn wedding gown hangs in a thick plastic garment bag, in a basement, appropriately enough where everyone stores their pasts. Lucky for my cousin—because she enslaved me to the stately position of bridesmaid, I was forced to wear the appropriated dress for the job and could not wear my white wedding gown as a nod to her "something new." Okay, not that I would. No one ever has an occasion to wear her formal wedding dress again, even if it has never been worn. So now, the only one left to insult was Electra's mother, my aunt, who would later lecture, "You and Lea should have had the dresses altered with my girl. It's a bridesmaid dress, not a bachelor party." I didn't give a gnat. I wasn't about to schlep to Long Island just to use her "girl." Who the hell even says that? And last I checked, Manhattan was known to have some stuff. You know, like a fashion district and directories of A-list clothing geniuses.

I convinced Lea to haul her bridesmaid dress into the city with promises of a free meal, a sleepover chick-flick fest, and an unadulterated make-out session with my dog. She wants to violate the laws of nature with Linus.

"I'm serious, Steph. We're talkin' the big bad vows, and I claim him now," she cautioned as she wiggled free from her sweat-soaked clothes at a midtown dressmaker's studio. "I have dibs. When the laws change, that little nugget is *mine* to have and to hold."

"Yes, dear. Can you zip this atrocity of a top for me, please?" We were crammed in an airless, makeshift dressing room composed of a curtain and exposed brick wall.

"You think I'm kidding. I'm going on eBay later and ordering him the doggie bowtie and top hat in preparation. God, I wish I could marry him."

I was wearing my way-too-tight navy pants, trying to stretch them out for their eventual date debut. There wasn't room for panties in there, even my slingshots, so I warned Lea, "I'm nekked in Tahiti down there, so watch out for my red fire-crotch."

"Please, more like firecracker. That thing looks like a dog treat."

"Ew, stop looking!"

"Whatever, mine's a burning bush. Boys can hear the voice of God in there. Go ahead, make a wish!" She cackled.

I wished I didn't have to be a bridesmaid. The problem wasn't really the ill-fitting dress. It was me. I needed alterations. I'd already done this, been the bridesmaid and the bride. Walking down an aisle felt like walking backward. I had to stop feeling sorry for myself. So what if I looked like a chunk? No one was going to be looking at the back fat that would protrude from my top as I ambled down her aisle. This was Electra's day. Not everything had to be about Stephanie and her broad-beamed bod. What was wrong with me?

I'll tell you precisely what was wrong: when you look like shit it quickly becomes all about you. Bridesmaids complain for a reason, and it has so little to do with taffeta and everything to do with demure. Bridesmaid dresses might be garish but, I assure you, they're always prudish. It was a Saturday evening in late June. The rest of the guests would be grandstanding their go-go calves and cleavages. The last thing I wanted to be wearing was a yellow floor-length gown named "Provenance Squash" with nary a breast in sight. I looked like an egg yolk.

Lea and I stood side by side, staring at our reflections.

"Oh, Steph, this is bad." She turned to the side and extended her stomach. "So bad. I look like a knocked-up Perdue roaster."

"I have two words for you Lea: Open. Bar."

THE GROOM'S MOTHER WAS GREETING GUESTS BY THEIR first and last names, as if she'd studied the seating chart for months. She was heavier than I'd expected a mother of a III to be. From across the church, she looked like a shrub of a woman, the kind with a meaty laugh who, if given the opportunity, would lift Bob Barker upon meeting him. She'd win the brand-new car and make it to the showcase showdown. Everyone would want her to win. As I got closer, she looked more like a woman who had a one-night stand with a disco ball. Was that glitter eye shadow?

"Oh my, Stephanie Klein, your hair is just Love. Ly." She sounded like she'd swallowed a southerner. "Where ever did you get these magnificent curls?" She gripped one and pulled it toward her nose, inhaling deeply. "Just Love. Ly." She had puppet mouth when she spoke, moving her face only by way of her enormous mouth. It seemed like a hinge that kept her head together. "You know, I just love Electra's curls too. You girls have great genes. I can't wait for those two to give me some grandbabies. My husband and I just love Electra."

I didn't know what to say, only that I suddenly wanted to squeeze her. Maybe it was her voice or her disarming casual manner, but I loved Electra's mother-in-law to be. "It's true honey. Did you know we were never close to our William until Electra came into his life?" I wanted to borrow her eye shadow. I wanted anything this woman had to give. "She's a blessing I tell you, a God's honest blessing. He is lucky to have found her. We all are, you know." I didn't know. I didn't know women like this existed.

I thought all mothers-in-law lived up to their dreaded clichés. Mine was certainly no exception. Accustomed to one-upmanship, Gabe's mother, Romina Rosen, was a cliché and a half. On the whole, a woman isn't keen on her mother-in-law if she's controll*ing*, disapprov*ing*, or interfer*ing*. Romina was a triple major in the *ing*s and took extra night classes in calculat*ing* just for kicks. The woman was a hate nerd.

Everyone called Romina "Rome" because she told them to. "Just call me Rome." She'd say it the same way each time, with her head tilted. Then came the haughty laugh, open-mouthed, without the slightest hint of hand raised in a modest reaction. She gave it up too easily, laughing at everything without investment. "Yes, that's right. *ROME*," she'd say loudly as if speaking to a foreigner. "*Rome,* like the city. You know, in Italy." Okay, Rome, 'cause no one but you knows where Rome is. And as far as insults went, she coated hers in sugar and hoped I'd swallow them by the spoonful.

Suggesting I "play house for a while longer instead of getting married" was her way of curing the hiccups between us. "I mean, what's the rush, Stephanie?" Rush? Gabe and I had been engaged and living together for a year and a half at that point. "I'm just saying, it's very lonesome being a doctor's wife. He can't even support you." I try to see it as independent, not lonesome. Oh, and by the way, "playing house" is something I did when I was four, you crotch rot.

Did I ever wonder how I'd put up with her for the rest of my life? God, yes. But I loved Gabe, so I became an actress, sucked it up, bit my tongue, and smiled. For his sake. "I'm not marrying Rome," I told myself. When she became particularly infuriating, I'd invoke a loving memory with Gabe, hold it in my mind, and remind myself that we were in love, and that love would transcend all, even Rome.

In regard to our upcoming wedding, once Rome heard Gabe utter "not ready yet," she threw the dreaded mother-in-law cliché into high gear, revving things beyond "cold feet" and landing full-throttle on the "she wasn't right for you anyway" gear. "Don't worry about Stephanie's lost deposit money, we'll take care of everything. If you're not ready, Gabe, you shouldn't get married." That's what parents do—they want to save their children pain, from repeating their mistakes. Gabe's father Marvin concurred. He had, after all, divorced after a very brief marriage, while he was in law school, before committing his life to Rome. They only wanted the best for their son. It's what any parent wants. "We'll give Stephanie back the money she lost, so don't even factor that into your decision." I would've said the same thing to my own child, except I would have followed through and done some reimbursing.

Electra's ceremony was a flood of fragrant yellow roses, punctuated with a hint of stephanotis, flowers I'd considered for my own wedding. I felt anxious seeing them there along the aisle between the tapered candles and flowing gauze. It all should have been mine, but mine was canceled.

Gabe somehow thought he could cancel a wedding without canceling us. So he slid into "postponed" mode, claiming he just needed more time to figure himself out.

"I promise we'll do it soon, just not now. I'm not ready now. I want us—"

"You never should have proposed to me if you weren't ready. And now you want to postpone the wedding and somehow keep us intact?"

"No really, I know I want to spend the rest of my life with you, Stephanie. Really, soon, I promise."

"Soon isn't good enough."

Here's what I've learned about "soon"; it's short for "someday." We make space in our lives for what matters, now. Not in promises and soons, but on mantels with sterling frames, in shelves we clear to make room for our now. Everything else is talk. I didn't want to share space with someone who didn't want his someday now.

I MOVED IN WITH SMELLY WHILE I SEARCHED FOR A NEW apartment.

I also took up residence in the self-help aisles of bookstores. I needed something to make me feel better, some book, a phrase, words to get me through. I purchased a breakup book for lesbians and read it in a taxicab on my way to work. It was the first morning I'd spent not waking up in *our* bed. Gabe and I didn't have *our* anymore except for our broken engagement. It was raining. I pulled my knees to my chest as we drove down Fifth Avenue. *We* was me, alone in the backseat, a cab driver taking me to work. We were stopped at a red light in front of the Met. It was too early for lines, just staff sweeping in yellow ponchos, a man pushing a pretzel cart, opening his red umbrella. Pigeons hiding beneath benches. I wanted to ditch work and sit at The Stanhope to drink tea and half-sleep it, upright. Maybe I'd meet a foreigner who'd offer me a tissue or a tea sandwich. Maybe I'd meet a mother who'd offer me her son. I wanted to heal; if a new prospect were in the picture, I was certain I'd heal faster. I know better now. Now, I'd just stick to the tea.

I bought the book because surviving a breakup as a lesbian is the same as enduring the ending of any serious relationship. Despite the years we'd been together, as man and woman, because we weren't married, it somehow counted less to everyone else. It shouldn't have. When it's divorce, people pay attention and know it's a big deal. But when you're gay, too many people diminish the severity of what you're dealing with. They don't understand your partnership was as profound as any marriage. The book understood how hard this was for me, how acute my pain was.

"It's a breakup. They happen all the time," Smelly said, hoping to soothe me. With a trivial flip of the hand, my reality was fanned aside as I was told, "You'll be back at it in no time," as if that were the good, healthy thing to do. It made me feel like a lesbian and anything but gay.

"He's an idiot," Smelly added, "and has a lot of growing up to do." Oh God, please don't whip out the "his loss, you're so much better off" speech. It's what's done. Lines are drawn, sides are taken. I didn't know where I belonged. I wanted to hate him.

In the years we'd been together, he'd spent nights making promises in whispers and sighs: "I'll never leave you." Signed his letters with "always" and "forever."

It still amazes me how fast everything important can be undone. In a phone call, a text message, an e-mail, an instant message conversation. Weddings that took months of planning can be called off. Engagements broken. A phone call to a moving company and real estate agent and you're as good as gone. Complicated relationships, where promises and truths were shared in dark theaters, through a bar with his hand on her back, in the backseat of cabs, in the rain when he shared his umbrella, can unbutton in a beat. It saddens me how a lifetime of promises that mean everything to us can be unraveled faster than something as trivial and maddening as fine tangled thread.

I wanted to feel angry with him. I was too focused on being victimized. Had I taken the time to let myself get to anger, perhaps I would have realized I ought to have been angry with myself. I knew he wasn't ready to marry me, but he asked on bended knee, so I answered. Yes. His asking was good enough. It shouldn't have been.

Give him time, space, move out and see what happens. Check, check. I cried to realtors. I cried on the subway. I cried in the shower. Strangers offered me tissues. I'd ride the subway wondering how people went on with their lives, how they functioned. What it was like not having to remind myself to breathe or eat. How appreciative I became of the smallest gestures. Someone helped me with a bag, and I thanked her as if she'd rescued me from sudden death. The smallest consideration was amplified in the wake of grave disappointment. I wanted to find normal again.

"WILLIAM IS MISSING," I HEARD SOMEONE WHISPER OUTside the bridal suite. Was the groom detained, running late, what? All I heard was "missing." I began to pace and clutch my stomach. I knew this feeling all too well. Yanked my cuticles. I wanted to save Electra from it. I'd just bitten the nail polish off my index finger when I heard Electra's voice.

"Whatever," she said when someone else mentioned it to her, "he'll be here." She was examining her eyelashes in the mirror without a wrinkle of concern. I didn't know how she did it.

"How can you be so calm?" I asked, surveying her face for concealed signs of anxiety.

"Because."

"Because? That's your answer? Because?"

"Because I know he loves me and that we're meant to be. I just know. Completely." I was in awe of her.

WHEN WE'RE MISSING, PEOPLE LOOK FOR US. IT'S THE ENtire philosophy behind playing it cool. When someone is gone, we imagine the best for them and the worst for us. "I bet he doesn't even miss me," I'd said, once I moved out of my apartment with Gabe. "I bet he's fucking playing golf while I'm sitting here with eye compresses." Often-times, our imaginations are crueler than reality. We'll whine to our friends, using words like *depressed* and *miss* interchanged with *sooooo much*! Then they'll sling an "if it's meant to be" your way because that's what friends do . . . remind us that life exists beyond our own tortured selves.

"If it's meant to be, Stephanie," Smelly had cheered while I searched for a new apartment. I wanted to pull out her blond hair and see how she'd manage bald. "Meant to be" allows for lazy. The idea of destiny al-leviates anxiety; it comforts us. We stop believing that we had ownership, that we could have done something to change the outcome. It's lazier than The Clapper.

You have to live life with unanswered questions—there isn't always an answer for "Why?" In my case, people panted sentences, and rounded them off with "there's a reason for everything." Doors slam, windows open suddenly, and "meant to be" flies in and sticks like marmalade on the sill of your life. People want to wrap lessons around things and tie them with ribbons of hope. "It will make you stronger." We tell ourselves things and convince ourselves to make sense of the senseless. We feel bet-ter when we have concrete answers to grip, even if they're wrong. They're ours, something to hold onto, like a ledge. The problem with ledges, of course, is eventually you fall from them. After I'd been living with Smelly for three weeks, Gabe did just that: he hit rock bottom and wanted me back at all costs.

Everything changed when I'd remained strong and refused to return his phone calls. He showed up with the words I wanted to hear. "Call the rabbi. I'll marry you right now. My life is miserable without you, Stephanie. Please come home." He was terrified of losing me, and that fear of loss would keep him faithful till death us do part.

Or not.

He should have wanted to marry me because he wanted me, not be-cause he was afraid of loss. But he let fear govern his decision, which usu-ally leads to regret. Our best decisions are made from a place of joy—they should be things we're eager to do. Hearing the peace and liquid strength in Electra's voice, I realized that. She didn't use "meant to be" as an excuse. She didn't use it at all. It was just fact, her deepest sense of right. Despite William's tardiness to their wedding, she never doubted what her senses told her. She knew it was meant to be, and fear had no place in her marriage to William.

I know this now, but when I was with Gabe, I was too busy convincing myself he was just a boy afraid of an idea. I believed his "not ready yet" came from his fear of his parents' reaction. Deep down he wanted me to be his partner, but he was just frightened of what others would think of his decision. I didn't think it was the other way around—that really he didn't want to be married yet, but he was afraid of disappointing me, of losing me. Because when he did lose me, when I stayed with Smell, he felt lost. He came to me with "I choose you. You are what I want!" And I took his hand, thinking we could face his fears together. I would be his partner in that. I thought he'd get over his fear of marriage once we were actually married, and he learned people were actually supportive. It was just the *idea* that scared him. That had to be it, because really, what would change? We'd still be living in our apartment, have the same friends, do the same things. Only once we married, it would no longer be just between the two of us. Now there would be family to support us, to help us honor the vows we'd made to each other.

Or not.

THE CHURCH WAS OVERFLOWING WITH FAMILY, AND William was where he belonged, at the front of the church, beside Electra's brothers and the other groomsmen, waiting for the love of his life to arrive. She was an aisle's distance away, and as I walked down it in front of her, tears began to slip down my face. I didn't care who saw. William's face was eager and flooded with joy. I didn't know how many wedding dates they'd tried to set, only that this one was meant to be. They would be okay.

After our August wedding was canceled, Gabe and I tried just being us for a while, in our apartment, ordering in burgers, watching movies in bed. We were going to be okay, but things with his parents were not.

I had put down the wedding deposit money my family had given me. When Gabe wanted to call off the wedding, his parents told him it was okay, that he should follow those feelings and not worry about the money I'd lose.

"We'll reimburse her," they had promised. "So don't even factor that into your decision." But when the decision he finally made was to marry me, they changed their story. "We'll get her back the money she lost only once she moves out." I couldn't believe they actually said it aloud.

"But we're setting a new wedding date," Gabe countered.

"Yeah, well, IF you actually get married, then we'll reimburse her the money we'd promised. You called off the wedding, so now do something about it."

Gabe assured me we would get married, "as soon as my father checks his work schedule. He promised to give me a list of dates. Don't worry about the money and repaying your family. Sweetheart, I promise everything will be okay."

We aimed to marry in December. Burgundy calla lilies, red bruneas, Black Beauty roses, accented with hints of pale pink pepperberries. Mugs of hot cocoa with s'mores wrapped in parchment for the guests' journeys home. Bridesmaids in dark chocolate satin. Gabe told his parents the new date and, surprisingly, they were fine with it. Everything was back on schedule. Venues were free, the florist was available. Done and done. Until it was undone, yet again.

Gabe never told his parents the new wedding date—he'd lied to me. His parents had phoned, throwing around the words *grapevine* and *disappointed* on our answering machine.

"What the fuck, Gabe! Why wouldn't you tell them?" I was pacing and cutting the air with my hands. "I mean, what were you thinking?" I felt sick.

"Stephanie, I was going to, really. I just didn't want to hear it. I knew they'd be pissed, and I just thought if I waited until the right time. I don't know." Gabe was really good at "I don't know."

"What are you afraid of?" I turned quiet.

"I'm not afraid." He took my hands. "I just have studying to do, and I really don't need to hear it from them. You know how they are. It has nothing to do with my feelings for you, sweetheart." I wasn't so sure. I wanted to believe it, to believe he wasn't afraid of us but of them and what they thought of us.

"Is this something you even want to do?"

"Yes. I'm going to fix this, baby."

"No, I mean, getting married. Is this something you even want anymore?" I held my breath as I waited for his answer.

He pulled away. "Jesus, would you stop with your Psych 101? I'm not talking about this with you anymore."

"What, that's it? You've said your piece, and now you're done?"

"You really want to know what I think?" Whenever anyone begins a sentence like this, I look for something to hold. "Fine. You are fucking retarded! That's what I think. I swear to God, Stephanie, you're fucking Rainman! All you do is repeat yourself. You must work with a bunch of morons because you talk to me like I'm a fucking idiot."

"Stop screaming at me!"

"Oh, that's choice. Now you're going to fucking cry, like the retard baby that you are. Wah! Wah!" He was screaming so close to my face, I thought our noses would touch. "You sure you can make time to cry? You're not too busy repeating things or talking with your magic hands?" I cried harder as he mimicked the way I spoke with my hands. "Jesus, you make me sick. Don't run away from me. I had to listen to your whining, so now you're going to listen."

"I'm not talking to you when you speak to me like that," I managed to scream, knowing I'd have been more effective if I'd said it softly. I ran into the bedroom, locked the door, and threw myself onto our bed and cried until it hurt to swallow.

I thought it was a fight, something couples do. I thought it was normal. I trembled as I wrote in my diary:

He makes me feel small when he screams at me like that, yet I stay with him, which makes it so hard for me to look myself in the mirror. Things would be different if he could control his frustration and not be so mean to me. I know I don't deserve it, but I love him. He makes me feel so small and ashamed of who I am. He makes me hate myself.

The second to worst bit of that entry was: *but I love him*. I can't think of a worse phrase. He belittles me in front of his friends, *but I love him*. He screams so close to my face I can feel his spit, *but I love him*. He tells me I'm not pretty, that really, it's only my red curly hair that makes me special, and without it, I'm nothing, *but I love him*. When the fuck did love excuse horrible? Yeah, and that was only the second to worst bit. The absolute worst part of that entry is what followed on the next page of my diary, dated only a month later: *"Gabe and I got married today!"*

I went from "he makes me hate myself" to "wife" in the flip of a journal page, and I know exactly what I was thinking. "Love trumps all." I thought as long as there was love and we were willing to work at it, everything would be okay. But loving someone is easy. That's the part that happens without thought. It takes more than love for a relationship to work. It takes admitting when you're wrong, compromising, swallowing pride. I thought it took tears. I didn't know love shouldn't make you feel bad.

In my mind, it was all very chicken/egg. Had he shared with his parents what he'd told me, how in love he was, how I made his life better, how he wanted children with me, perhaps they'd have supported his decision. Instead, he sensed his parents' disapproval and went mute. Except when he was with me. With me, mute became mean because he was frustrated. That's what I thought it was. That's all I saw. I also knew I was marrying an adolescent, not a man, but I'd invested so much time and love into us. So, I thought, okay, he'll grow up eventually. We'll grow together.

I hate when people ask me if I think I got married too young. Too young always buddies up beside naïve, and I don't think I was either.

When people ask me that question they're really asking one of two things: "Was being married more important than who you were marrying?" or "Were you so young that you didn't really know what love was?" I hate that question because my answer isn't a yes or no. I was in love with Gabe, bathroom floor, middle of the night, unconditional love. But I was also in love with the idea of having a husband, someone to take care of, a home with magnets on the refrigerator with his and her to-do lists. I wanted to become each other's memory. I thought I'd found that in the man I loved. It's why I endured his temper. He'd grow up one day, I assumed. One day, this will fit the way I want it to. In the meanwhile, there might be some tears, but mostly there will be laughs and memories, and that's exactly how it was. Until it wasn't.

So, no, I don't think I married too young. I think I married the wrong person. Yes, there were signs warning me, but I was in love and ready to face our fears together, supporting each other. I was certain if we both wanted it enough, we could make it through anything, even a nightmare of a mother-in-law. You can't, however, want it enough for two people.

I look back now at the pages of my life, and I'm embarrassed. I mean *embarrassed*. I cannot believe I settled for what he gave. I didn't know I deserved a William up there at the altar, a man ecstatic to be marrying me. I'm humiliated that he made me hate myself, that I let myself feel small. My marriage didn't fail—I failed myself. All that talk of facing fears should have been directed my way too. Because on some level, I allowed myself to be in an emotionally abusive relationship because I was frightened I wasn't worth enough without him. I believed I mattered more because he wanted me. I gave that authority away, to another person, which is just flat-out appalling, and far too common.

So many women do it. Smart woman. Stupid choices. I would know as an educated woman who read the books they told me to. I knew from working hard until I succeeded. I thought relationships worked the same way. The more I cried and worked through our fights, the harder I was working to endure. I was fighting *for* something, to keep something I wanted. He'd finally enter the bedroom, rub my back, and say in a small voice, "You're right. I'm sorry. This is my issue, and I will work on my temper. Thank you for being patient with me. We're an us, Stephanie, and we'll work it through. I want that, always." I did too, so I let myself believe that all the fighting and making up was training. It would make us stronger. I thought it was perseverance, not psychosis. I was certain it would work out between us, if only Gabe would pull his weight and learn to either speak up to me or speak up to his parents.

He finally spoke up in January. "We can't get married in January or February because that's when I have my hardest rotation." I feared he was stalling and grew impatient. Great, the first of March! "No." The ides of March. Screw the soothsayer! "No." Someone always had a reason why it couldn't happen. So once we marched into May without a date, I put my patent leather-loafer-wearing foot down. I didn't care anymore about the damn location or which colors best suited me. Instead of sending guests home with fresh strawberries and scones lined in a wooden berry basket to enjoy the morning after our wedding, how about no guests to send home at all? Fuck the goddamn guests. Fuck the flowers that are in season this month. Talk of linens and pin-spot lighting, duties and charts, thank-you notes, and don't forgets made me forget it was ever about marriage.

We agreed to have a small ceremony, with immediate family only, in May, before he took his third-year medical boards in June. We'd honeymoon in Italy after his exam, and then we'd have a wedding reception to celebrate with everyone else. Gabe asked his father to pick a date that worked with his May conference schedule. It was decided. May 28. Gabe booked the rabbi at Temple Sinai, a synagogue in a town near where we'd grown up. It was his way of assuring me this is what he wanted too. Then, we began to tell people to save the date. I would qualify, "Yeah, it's May 28, but I'd write it in pencil if I were you."

I made sure Gabe told his parents first. This time I heard him say it, right there in front of me. I was certain they'd heard it because two hours later, Gabe's older sister Jolene phoned, screaming into our machine. That was the proof. She heard the date from "Mommy and Daddy." It was the evidence, right there in her temper tantrum. "Clearly," she screamed, "you don't care if I can even be there because I can't get off work." Right. As soon as she heard the news, she called us, not her employer. We knew she could attend. She was acting out, as she was prone to do. In August, she'd refused to be part of the wedding party. Her mother Rome confided in Smelly one afternoon while we shopped for bridesmaid gowns, "Ugh, Jolene is just so fat. She'll look horrible in anything. I hope one day when she gets married she only has thin friends, for the pictures." We knew, in the end, Jolene would do whatever her parents told her to do. It ran in the family.

Gabe's aunt, a school teacher with an infectious laugh, phoned a week later to congratulate us on setting the date. At least someone was happy for us. She invited us to her home for a family barbecue with the other cousins. Her home and family were warm and easy to be around. I was relieved Gabe's parents were at their Atherton home that weekend. It meant I could actually eat and enjoy myself. Whenever they were present, I lost my appetite and became anxious. In their absence, I devoured ribs and ate chicken off the bone. Corn on the cob.

His grandmother—an elegant upmarket woman who, upon seeing me, always asked, "So is my grandson treating you well, Stephanie?"— wanted to know what I'd be wearing on our wedding day. Then she squeezed me into a hug and patted my face. I liked spending time with her. Where would we be doing it, and who would marry us? "I'm just so happy for you both," she said hugging us together, a knot of three. It felt good knowing his family was behind our decision, made me think they knew how happy I made Gabe. Finally, everything would be okay.

That night, we arrived home to a blinking answering machine. I hit Play, not realizing the button I'd pressed was actually the vomit trigger.

"Gabe, this is your father. We heard again through the grapevine that you're getting married May 28 at Temple Sinai with a rabbi. Obviously, you can't tell us these things, so we will not be there to participate in the event because obviously I intimidate you, and we wouldn't want to embarrass you. This is the last phone call I will make to you."

I wanted to vomit. On Marvin. I was certain they knew about the 28th. Maybe they didn't think it was finalized, but to pretend it was the first they were hearing of it was absurd. God, I was even finally excited again, looking through wedding magazines, telling my family, booking plane reservations for my mother, and now this.

"I'm just not doing this anymore, Gabe. I can't. There's always some excuse. Your family, your work schedule. I'm just not doing this to myself anymore. Look at these!" I pointed to the stacks of wedding magazines I'd collected over the years of our engagement, the scrapbook I'd started, photos of hairstyles, photos of me from different makeup trial appointments. "I've just fucking had enough!" I screamed, and my voice cracked into a sob. "I just can't do this. I'm sorry."

"I'll do whatever you want, Stephanie. It's ridiculous at this point."

"I just can't take it anymore. They always have an excuse." Snot was hanging from my nose.

"Baby, I agree with you. I'm on your side." He handed me a towel.

"You told them, right? I mean, I heard you."

"Yes, Stephanie."

"Right, so I'm not going crazy here, but they're saying we didn't tell them now. It's an excuse because, in their eyes, I'll never be good enough for you. I will always be—I don't know. Am I that horrible? I mean, don't I love you? Don't I make you happy?"

"Yes, baby. Of course you do." He wiped the tears from my face and hugged me.

"Gabe, I just don't understand. I love you. You love me. Why can't they just be happy for us?" The I love you, you love me bit was a bit Barney of me. I was in despair and couldn't see beyond me.

"Sweetheart, what if we just got married and didn't tell anyone? That way, they can pick whatever the hell date they want, and it won't matter anymore because we'll already be married. So then, we'll have the reception and ceremony all on one day, without any pressure."

"Fine. When?" It was all I could manage at that point. I didn't really believe him.

"The next three weeks are a nightmare for me, but I'm not making excuses. I know that's what you're thinking. I'm free the weekend of May twentieth. That way, we can go to a hotel or something for the weekend, and it gives us time to find a rabbi. Okay, sweetheart?" He gently lifted my head by my chin, bringing my eyes to his. I nodded okay and cried in his arms.

He rubbed my back and whispered that it would all be okay. "You'll see. I promise. I won't ever let anything bad happen to you, sweetheart." To this day, when I hear the word *sweetheart*, I look for the nearest bathroom. Somehow my body communicates bullshit through diarrhea. *Sweetheart* gives me the runs. I only wish that time, I had run away instead of toward him.

"DO YOU PROMISE TO LOVE AND CHERISH HER?" I WAS glad I decided to hit my cousin's wedding solo. I couldn't have sat through a candlelit ceremony with a knock-off date on my arm. I wanted the real thing, the genuine article, with the brand name L. Hearing Electra and William exchange vows, I felt their importance, probably more than someone who'd never been married because I knew their weight. "In sickness and in health, for richer for poorer, for better for worse . . ." It was coming, the onset of sobbing. I felt it rising through me, caught in my throat. I knew if it were to come out, it would be loud and people would turn. I swallowed. I had no one to hold. What if this was my life, attending weddings, sitting in pews, listening to I do's, perpetually wishing for someone to share my life with? Where the fuck was the alcohol?

Instead of a yellow bridesmaid's gown, I should have been wearing green. I was jealous, happy for her, but jealous just the same. It felt like Valentine's Day, when you're single and each time you pass a cluster of cellophane-wrapped roses, you try to sneak a glance at the card, hoping they're for you. They never are. That's how it felt to be me. "And forsaking all others, keep yourself only unto him, for so long as you both shall live?" While I'd never said those exact words, the sentiment was still there, in Hebrew, somewhere, except Gabe and I didn't have our friends and family present to witness our promises.

William and Electra's ceremony ended with family and friends wishing each other peace. "Peace be with you, Steph," Lea said suddenly, throwing her arm around me.

"And with you, my dear."

"I know this sucks balls for ya, but don't worry. We'll be at the reception hall soon. I'll get ya drunk on Redheaded Sluts." Only my sister would know there's a drink called Redheaded Slut. She was the best date I'd ever had. I regretted at that moment, in our embrace, not having her there for my own wedding. I wanted to share it with all of my family, even Yiya and Fay, with whom I'd share a dinner table at Electra's reception soon enough. This would mean inquisitions from the Spaniards in my life. Screw the Redheaded Sluts—this called for tequila.

IF SHE SO MUCH AS ASKED A SINGLES CROWD TO FORM, I'D leave. I had already cried during the father-daughter dance, blowing my nose into Fay's handkerchief, and God only knew where that had been. I survived the cutting of the cake. I couldn't handle the craptacular bouquet toss. Everyone would look to me to step forward. I'm not *single*. I'm *divorced*! Yes, I want to get married again, but I'm not standing in a circle, putting my left foot in, so another wedding guest can hokey pokey his way up my thigh with a four-dollar garter. Leave me the fuck alone!

"I think I'm going to leave now," I said when I noticed the single men forming a cluster near the dance floor.

"Oh stop! The bouquet toss is a delightful tradition." I was surprised my grandmother knew of it. The way she spoke of her upbringing, I had imagined her wedding traditions involved a goat eyeball.

"Then you go out there Yiya. If I leave, I'll be improving your chances."

"Are you kidding us?" Fay interjected, "If we go out there and catch that bouquet, it means we'll have to let go of our walkers."

"Yeah, but Fazie," Yiya responded, "it also means the man who catches the garter will slip it on our leg!" The sisters looked at each other for a silent moment before releasing their siren laughs. "Wooo hoo! Now that's a wedding, Fazie!"

"Well, at least dance with a fella, Stephanie." There really was no fella with whom to dance. Besides, I was tired from being forced to twist and shout with Lea. "You know, in my day we needed chaperones at dances. They measured to make sure he was far enough away, but I'll tell you, I was so naïve back then."

"What do you mean back then, Fazie? Just last week, you still thought it was a cigarette lighter in his pocket."

"Oh, stop it!" Fay laughed as she shooed my grandmother away with a hand. "Stephanie, I'm telling you, I actually believed I was pregnant because I was tongue-kissed by a man. But I tell ya what. I'm happy to tongue kiss any man here tonight!"

"Knock yourself out, Fay."

"I'm telling you, Stephie, life is short. Live it up while you can. Take a lover." Oh God, where was Lea when I needed her? "Though maybe that's not the best idea. Lovers get jealous. I had one once who hunted me down with guns when I left him." On the word *guns*, Fay made guns with her thumbs and pointer fingers, then said, "boom, boom!" "Nah, it's all worth it, so kiss some fellas now, Stephie dear, because the change of life, I don't care what they tell you, makes you crave a whole lot of boom boom."

I craved my bed. I didn't care that I'd be in it alone.

"I think I'm going to go now." I said it, then smiled, hoping they'd pat me on the shoulder and kiss me goodnight.

"At least stay for some cake. Going home alone is one thing, Stephie, but alone without cake is more depressing than your well running dry." No, depressing is when a woman refers to her vagina as "a well." I forced a smile.

I left without trying their wedding cake, and before the bouquet toss. I'd survived my pew tears and their first dance. It was enough. After hearing my grandmother and her sister tell me to "live it up because it goes by so fast," I wanted to throw a bouquet of a fit. I wanted to scream and make a drunken scene, but there were video cameras and a bridegroom to consider. So I left alone, slipping out the door without good-byes or good wishes.

In bed, Linus licked my tears. I hated that Fay said time went by so fast. When I was suffering, time was stagnant. So now that I was single and dating it was supposed to be rushing right by? If these were to be the best times of my life, I was seriously screwed. This couldn't be the good stuff, not yet. The good times came in jumps on a sofa until you laughed, in kisses to each other, in a car singing, rolling your eyes laughing at someone you love. It comes in snorts when you stop caring how you sound or look. You stop caring if you're doing it all wrong because you know. You know in your heart it's amazing and right. You just know. And you love selflessly—the man, the woman, the kids, the dog, the lack of space. You love it all. That is the good stuff.

I thought I had all of that with Gabe. When I realized I didn't, that I was living a knock-off marriage, I questioned all my choices. With old people telling me to hurry up and enjoy my life because it goes by so fast, how was I going to find happiness in the moment?

Of course I wanted to make those memories with someone. I wanted to start that life and to make a past with someone who could remember my embarrassing moments, someone who'd roll his eyes and tell me that's not at all how it happened, then kiss me on the head and love me anyway. We all want that. But maybe it's not where we're looking for it.

I didn't really attend Electra's wedding alone. I was armed with my III, the three I'd found in family that night. My grandmother grew old with her sister, and mine made me snort and stop caring about my flabby arms and lack of date. Maybe that's whom we really grow old with, siblings or old friends who link us to our pasts and remind us of who we are.

I knew one thing for certain: my proclivity to care what people thought had gotten *old*, and had I brought a *new* rent-a-date, surely he'd have outed me to the charming wait staff. It was about time I *borrowed* some esteem and left a wedding feeling something other than *blue*. So yeah, I was alone in bed, but I'd be okay because, really, what would be the point of staging anything, especially for my family? And, when it comes down to it, who was looking anyway? So, I embraced "stag," despite how wretched and dripping with stigma the word is:

n.
1. The adult male of various deer, especially the red deer.
2. An animal, especially a pig, castrated after reaching sexual maturity.
3. A person who attends a social gathering unaccompanied by a partner, especially a man who is unaccompanied by a woman.
4. A social gathering for men only.

adj.
1. Of or for men only: a stag party.
2. Pornographic: stag films.

How can a word meaning "unaccompanied by a partner" also mean "castrated pig" and "pornographic?" No wonder people are frightened into borrowing and, ultimately, "*stag*ing" love. I spent too much time there, caring what other people thought, what Gabe's family thought. I wasn't ready, just yet, to share pew space with a date, despite what anyone would hiccup about time going by so fast. Forget having a date for the wedding. I wasn't sure I should even be dating anyone. 'Cause "anyone," I feared, would turn out like Gabe. The kind of love who wasn't patient or kind, who was easily angered, and kept a record of my wrongs. Stag, by any definition, was better than that.

three

CEREAL MONOGAMY

"I REFUSE TO GO OUT," I DECLARED WITHOUT APOLOGY to Max over the phone the following week.

"What the hell's your problem? I said dinner, not diva."

"I know. I'm sorry. I'm just so sick of this dating. I'm beginning to forget which stories I've told to whom."

"Then stop. You act like one night at home means you're wasting time." That was exactly right. If I found someone who loved me before Gabe found someone, it would mean I won. Yeah, won the psycho award. Max was right, and he was there, usually willing to do whatever I suggested.

When I was having the "I'll never meet anyone"s, I twirled my spice rack and Eeny Meeny Miny Maxed. My neighbor Max was my pantry, as comforting as Darjeeling, yet as strong as espresso. He was a new neighbor now that I'd moved west, but he was also an old friend who predated my marriage to Gabe. It wasn't as though I didn't get my share of deliciously fresh men. I did, but too often, they cropped up in colonies and seceded in stampedes. Max was my when-in-doubt, always there, Macaroni & Cheese in the middle of the night. So why aren't we married already? It's simple.

Some people are close talkers—you're worried they might touch your face with their tongue when using words with "L"s. Then you've got the loud talkers who speak as if they're at a Megadeth concert, even in waiting rooms. Max is neither. He's a small talker. He doesn't do weather, politics, or movie prattle. He does *infantimbre*—a form of baby talk so cloying it deserves italics. Uses words like *seeping* in lieu of *sleeping*. I couldn't date this, never mind vows.

"Oh, and before I forget, when I die, I want to be cremated and encapsulated in a firecracker," he added over the phone.

"What?"

"Yeah, in a firecracker that you'll explode over the ocean. Poof." Not "bang" or "boom" but "poof." This is why he's Gay Max, despite the fact that he's heterosexual, and we once fucked until we broke the bed. No one could quite understand why we weren't together, including us, when we were lonesome.

I wasn't quite ready to invite him to an *I'm-not-dating-him-so-now-you-can* party, where people bring companionable members of the opposite sex to meet other former ill-suited lovers. I knew I didn't want him, but I didn't want anyone else to have him either. My pantry of past men was teeming with faded dill weed, thyme, and, unfortunately, onion powder (he was an unsightly mistake). But Gay Max was the saffron of the bunch, the most auspicious member of my past.

It's hard to leave a history and watch other people date yours. Some people are aces at it—it seems more of their best friends are exes than not. When I first met a man who told me his best friend was an ex of his, I held my breath a little. The "count to ten" carried me past irrational, and I was left to exhale and fake a smile. *It didn't work out for a reason*, I chanted as I gulped espresso and cream. *Hopefully the reason wasn't timing. What if* now *is their timing?* Then I picked the polish off my new manicure and headed back to my own pantry.

"THERE'S NOTHING TO EAT IN THIS GODDAMN HOUSE." Linus was whining at my feet as I stared into my empty cupboard, hoping something new would catch my eye. I scanned the familiar as my free hand weighed on the small knob of the wooden door. My brain eliminated decisions. There was a lone package of dried spaghetti, with no staples to initiate a sauce. I remembered the time I'd made my spaghetti and meatballs recipe for Gabe. We toasted over a bottle of Chianti in our apartment. He made me laugh so hard a piece of spaghetti actually came out of my nose. He wanted to save it.

"Come on, Steph, can't we put it in a case or something?"

"What for?"

"For the next time you say, 'not funny, Gabe. Not funny.' That way I can just point to the spaghetti case." Usually, I reserved "not funny" for his Austin Powers impressions.

"You're sick, you know that?"

"Yeah, but you love me." He was right. I did.

THE ONLY OTHER BITS OF FOOD IN MY CUPBOARD WERE graham crackers, which are a good time when you're six, not when you're hungry. Usually, I found solace behind another door: the refrigerator. I'd have to get past the condiments and salad dressings. Satisfaction was typically tucked away in the dairy drawer. I can't believe refrigerators actually have drawers for dairy. As a child, I always thought it was wrong. Gosh, it's not like the milk fits in there. I didn't think about dairy as a solid, the way steam and ice don't really seem like states of water.

The fridge was barren, save for the baking soda and ketchup. It occurred to me just then: even my refrigerator screamed single. This was more depressing than crow's feet.

"Steph, let's go get food, and you can cook for me," Max suggested. "I mean that's so not going *out* out."

"Okay." I pepped up at this idea.

In a moment, that's our relationship. Right there. Boiled and pared down to that simple happy lick of an exchange. "You can cook for me." "Okay." Max is sensitive in a way only a former lover notices, so his requests for food are never met with my feminist fatal fencing. There's nothing worse than cooking for those who eat to live instead of live to eat. Max is a seasoned counselor at Camp Livetoeat. Our relationship is just as campy: flip-flops on the beach, arms draped on shoulders, and white protective cream on each other's noses.

"Alright, are we going or wha?"

"Okay, I'll meet you at Citarella."

"You're too fancy shmancy, Stephanie."

I wasn't about to argue. Gristedes to the rescue.

I WAS ALWAYS WAITING FOR GAY MAX TO ARRIVE. I MADE myself useful at Gristedes and started us off with a shopping cart—I was, after all, cooking dinner for two. As a rule, I was relegated to the solitary world of handbaskets, which sometimes made me feel like a hook-nosed nursery rhyme—some wirehaired spinster in a rocking chair whirling golden threads into needlepoint, living in a boot. It was new, this idea of shopping just for myself. When I first separated from Gabe, I might have actually looked over my shoulder before gripping a green basket. Back then, I was still living in our two-bedroom, hospital-subsidized, Upper East Side apartment. Alone. God only knew where he was living, so I was constantly paranoid I'd run into him or any of his medical colleagues. Shopping with a basket for one was one of the first moments divorce felt less like an idea and more like my life. Grocery shopping made divorce tangible. I felt it in my negligible handbasket filled with low-fat dairy, two apples, and high-fiber crackers made from seeds. A basket like that says two things: single and miserable. Perhaps I'd add that to my online profile.

At Gristedes, I was half-past dejected and a quarter to liberated. You feel the idea of "mine" right away in a grocery store. These are for me. This makes me happy, and this, right here, this is *mine*. I didn't have to consider what someone else might like. It felt selfish and wonderful. It meant I could eschew the round pods of tuna fish I normally had to obtain for Gabe. Aside from organs, there's nothing I hate more than canned tuna fish. I cannot believe they even make it. Who decided one day to can meats? Canned fish, chicken, and oysters—who, dare I ask, awakes with a craving for canned chicken? It's wrong on too many levels. I'd sidestep the canned gross aisle altogether if Gay Max ever showed up. I was quite certain I'd *never* prepare canned anything, ever again. It's the liberty that comes with divorce—using phrases like "never, ever again."

Just then, it was tuna fish. Later, it would become men who tiptoe around confrontation and kowtow at the pedicured feet of their controlling mothers.

You can always spot a young mother in a grocery store. Her cart is filled with chicken in the shape of stars, boxes of juice, and string cheese. She's got Band-Aids and wipes. I can spot the married ones, too. Despite being just from the gym, in a frizzy bun with leggings, the woman beside me was undoubtedly married, sans wedding band. I saw it in her potpies and Hungry Man drumstick dinners. Even the dude with the canned Hormel, who might privately be into leather facemasks with rubber ball gags, was shopping for someone else, unless he was also into maxi pads and Skintimate shave cream. Publicly, he was in the mistake that is the color orange, with a hint of a moustache that makes you feel for the safety of your wallet. But his fridge wasn't single. Even losers have love.

It had been ten minutes with no sign of Max, and I was frozen. Grocery stores are always cold. I was wearing sweats and a wife beater, looking I-really-don't-care-how-I-look-but-I-look-hot-in-this-don't-I? Fuck that noise. I'd get a basket. I wasn't cart-worthy anymore, and I sure as shit wasn't waiting—Voila! Gay Max to the rescue. Just like that, he stood before me with a shiny silver cart of his own. I was looking for his red cape.

"Nice tits."

"Excuse you?" I looked down covering my nipples with my forearms.

"Hey, don't put 'em away on my account. You look hot in a 'beater. What the hell are you doing with a dinky basket? We're going to cook." Max stretched his arms out wide, as if he were a child telling his father how much he loved him. "You know, *cook!*"

"Well, now you get no say at all in what we're eating, Mister Late."

"Fine, maybe just something I can pronounce this time?" Max swatted me on the tush with a Gristedes flyer as I headed toward produce.

"Something with artichoke." I turned to look at him, one finger on my chin. "I love to eat the hearts."

"I bet you say that to all the boys."

I would put Max to work that night, have him punch out ravioli from the fresh pasta I'd made earlier in the week. "Artichoke heart and brin d'amour ravioli with a wild mushroom sauce, my friend."

"*I said*, something I could pronounce." He crinkled his nose as if I'd just asked him to smell my armpit.

"Say it with me, baby. A. More." I traced my finger along one of his sweet dimples.

"How about this: Oy. Vey. Miss Fancy Pants."

"What the hell is up with that fancy pants shite? Greg said the same thing to me this week."

"Which one's Greg?"

"Hello, nice to forget my life."

"Hello, it's not like there aren't too many of them to keep straight," Max repeated using my snarkerrific tone.

"Greg's the Lower Least Side guy," I replied.

"Ooh, shit. That's right. That was fucked up. I love when you're mean and devilicious, just not to me." I wasn't devilicious. I was discouraged.

IT WAS OUR SECOND DATE, AND IT WAS A TUESDAY. I WAS in jeans with black heels, and in a white tank with an inner bra shelf, so if it got cold, he could admire my nipples and start thinking about sex. Who cares what he was wearing? It wasn't memorable, which is better than remembering some Hawaiian shirt à la Larry from *Three's Company*.

We'd made plans on Monday morning, so he'd had some time for reservations, for linen somewhere, for a place with more than just appetizers. It wasn't about getting fed . . . shit, most women only do tartare, crab cakes, or salad anyway. Not me, but most women. It's about showing interest. A guy asks me to meet him at some inexpensive East Village shitbox, and I'm thinking one of two things: 1) he's cheap, or 2) he's poor. Either way, he's not the guy for me. I supported poor through medical school. I'm not dating the Frugal Gourmet.

The first indication ought to have been when I suggested we meet at Balthazar for our first date drink. "How fancy shmancy," he said over the phone. Oh, fuck—he had to have been in cahoots with Gay Max. Who else says this? Still, I went, despite the suspected cahoots cues. Greg was cute, witty, and I felt we were on the same page, aside from the fact that he was the type to throw a solstice party in lieu of anything religion-oriented. Yes, let's celebrate winter. Feh. Yet, we liked each other enough to commit to bread. Then, an additional glass, and with an additional glass and a half, the hunger kicked in. Before I knew it, there was a seafood tower obstructing my view of Greg. We drank more and ordered fries and a goat cheese tart. More wine. Then, we finished off our shoreline, and suddenly we were kissing on the sidewalk while he tried to hail me a cab.

"Come meet my friends," he suggested. I didn't want to say good-bye yet. I was having fun with my new match.com friend. We cabbed it to McGee's, the bar beside my first apartment with Gabe. I'd have preferred a bar with more wine variety than "white" or "red," something perhaps with a cocktail menu or saketinis. That would've been my choice. Guinness on tap, hockey on TV, and a chalkboard outside announcing two-dollar pitchers was McGee's. The men who frequent Irish pubs have goatees. They own sports jerseys and even wear them in public. They use toothpicks after a meal. Okay, so I might be pushing it, but you get the point. They've played football or hockey at some point in their lives, but now they play softball. I was agreeable, though, and ordered "red" because I was certain their idea of "white" was Chardonnay. I met Greg's friends, who were also agreeable.

After a half glass of in-your-face merlot, Greg began to rub my leg under the table, telling me he wanted to be affectionate so I would know how much he liked me. It was a callow move, but it was nice just the same.

Between conversations, where we sided with each other against the group, he leaned in and whispered, "I can't wait to make out with you." So when the rest of his group took consecutive nicotine and bathroom breaks, that's precisely what we did. Then we left and went to the next place where everyone said we should go because they were going. After an unsuccessful hour there, trying to get a table, we left and had more watered down drinks at the next place. But we kissed well together, and his hands felt really good around my waist, so I broke the rules and agreed to a second date on our first.

Which brings us back to Tuesday night. He IMed saying he didn't quite have a plan. I kind of wanted to kill him because he's the boy, and this is his job. I just wanted to have to look cute and be smart. Despite knowing I live on the Upper West Side, he suggested the Lower East Side, which might as well be Jersey, and when I heard, "The Bowery," I wanted to cancel. "Look, sorry to be a brat, but I'm not trekking down to the Lower East Side." Normally, I would have swallowed it, but come on, he should've known better. He ought to have suggested what was convenient for me. "Well, I know you work midtown, so what do you think of this place or that place." That is ideal. "How about someplace citysearch.com categorizes as 'dive' that's completely out of your way? Sawdust is such a good time . . . keeps you grounded." That was my date.

I pulled out the honesty via e-mail . . . it's so much easier to be brave when you're hiding between well-constructed sentences:

So here's the deal. I'm a big believer that the man should treat the woman as if she's the good china: he's got to use both hands. I believe in chivalry, in "can I pick you up?" vs. "The Bowery." I believe in a man treating me like I'm special, and when that happens, I'm all too willing to spring to "over the top," let me give it back tenfold position. But when I don't get it, I don't stick around to respond to anything tenfold. All I want to do is run.

ABRASIVE BUT HONEST.
I really needed to get the T-shirt made.

We circumvented the hurdle when he responded, "On a weekend, I'd leap at the chance to pick you up. I'm having a tough day." When I heard "tough day," I thought of what my father has said to me, more than once:

"Hey Steph, stop being such a ball-breaker. People have tough days. Take it easy." So Greg hit a soft spot. I could do relaxed.

Greg was one drink in when I arrived at Cibar, which he later said was "too fancy." It was *not* fancy, unless fancy means they serve martinis in actual martini glasses. It was a normal, good, first date place, for our second date. There was no actual food served there . . . which is not such a good second date place. He looked the same, in an unzipped black cardigan sweater and jeans. Cute, actually. I ignored his fancy comment, we had some drinks, and then the real fun began.

"Stephanie, I could never really love a woman unless I lost her. You know, I'm the type of guy who never realizes what I have until it's too late, until it's gone."

In vino veritas?

In vino, heisanass.

Okay, so, that was his way of telling me he's still not over one of several of his exes. It was also his way of telling me he's a big baby boy. I responded, I kid you not, with the following diatribe. . . .

"Well, this is the part where I ask for the check."

"Come on. Are you serious?"

"Quite. You see, I believe people when they tell me who they are. Clearly, you know you, way better than I ever could, so I'm going to take your word for it. And some boy who doesn't know a great thing when he sees it isn't the guy for me. I hate to use the 'I want a man not a boy' line, but that's me telling you who I am."

"Oh, come on, at least go out with me one more time."

"Um, we're on our second date, and we're FIGHTING. Don't you think that tells us something?"

"It tells me you're smart. I mean, we're not fighting—we're having a discussion, and most of the girls I date don't know how to do that." Oh man, I knew what would come next. "You know, 'cause I date a lot of gorgeous, dumb girls." Okay, I said he was cute, but he was in no position to say he dated a lot of anything, never mind with the word gorgeous in it.

"Um, okay. How's that working out for you?" Then I really did ask for the check. He then tried to backpedal out of his statement, but the truth already slipped out when he was playing with the thin red straw in his nothing-but-ice-now glass.

"Please, just go out with me again?"

"The only going out with you again will consist of is going out to the street to get a cab so I can go home. Alone." There'd be a lot of this in my future. Oh, joy to the world and the deep blue me.

ALONE, IN A GRISTEDES AISLE, I HUNTED FOR "NEEDS" INstead of "wants" while Max collected the remaining dinner ingredients. Wee-wee pads for Linus—big time need. The beauty of having a small dog is his turds are rarely bigger than baby organic carrots, so I can encourage him to make on the floor of my apartment. *Make:* I love this word. "Can you please pull over? I have to make." "Make what?" "You know, MAKE!" I also love saying, "Baby, let's go make it." It's so retro. It's like a full-grown bush.

I was clutching rawhide chews and a thick plastic sack of Luvs diapers—because Gristedes doesn't sell puppy training pads—when I ran into a "want."

This is when it happens, when you're in the grocery store! That's what people say, right? You'll meet him when you least expect it, when you're in the Goya aisle. Hot Grocery Store Man catches my eye just as I approach the adobo seasoning. Our eyes lock, and I swear we both stand still, staring, too long for it to be trivialized. I look down quickly. He looks down. I was suddenly fourteen years old, carrying tampons, or worse, some sort of maxi pad box with pastel blue doves and wings. Oh Shit. He's going to think I have a kid. And then it happened, as fast as that. Hot Grocery Store Man sees the Luvs and realizes he can't give me *the luv*. Sigh.

How was this my life? I'd drown my sorrow in snacks. Ben & Jerry's, Pepperidge Farm, Cinnamon Toast Crunch. The cereal aisle hosts my rebellion on its shelves. My mother never permitted sugar cereals in the house, save for Frosted Mini-Wheats, which is so not a sugar cereal by virtue of the word *wheat* in the name. I'm talking marshmallows, purple and green loops, cereal that makes the milk change color.

Along with my rebellion, the shelves hold the key to dating. Managers keep the sugar cereals and variety packs toward the bottom shelves, down near the economy-sized bags. The dancing rabbits and toucans attract kids. They needn't reach, only grab the easiest. The sensible choices are harder to attain and often overlooked. I'm your basic high-fiber top shelfer, but most men can't see past the chick with the nice toucans.

I'm a harder reach. Most things worth effort are, and too many men prefer the variety pack to anything with the word *millet* in it. Why elect only one cereal, no matter how good it is, to have every single day for the rest of your life when there's a variety of other great cereals out there?

"Max, variety packs are for cowards," I said as he stared at the one he was holding in both hands. A toothy smile escaped when he looked up at me.

"I hear it's the spice of life."

"Seriously. Instead of Tony the Tiger on the package, it should be the Cowardly Lion from *The Wizard of Oz*. I'll tell you this: a man terrified of commitment invented the Variety Pak. I'd sell my hair on it. God forbid he wakes up to his favorite cereal until death do they part. No, he's gotta surround himself with flashy empty calories."

"Oh, puhleeeze. You're one to talk. When we were together, you opted for variety instead of me." Then he put on his sad face, the one he makes when he wants something, like affection, food, or a blow job.

I blasted him with a forced smile and offered, "timing," as I batted my eyes.

"Yuh, the timing was bad," he said while rolling his eyes, "and besides, you're not my type." Max put the variety pack back on the shelf and began to stroll down the aisle. Without turning to face me, he continued, "Look, put it this way, why are there like ten flavors of Coke?" He paused even though he wasn't expecting an answer. "People like choices, but sometimes they don't like making them."

"Wait a minute. I'm not your type? What the hell is your type, then?"

"It doesn't matter."

"You really have a type? I mean, really?"

"That's not the point."

"No, come on! You said it, now go there, you whiner."

"Okay, I picture her." He stood still, looking up toward the canned coffee, as if he could see her waving to him from just beyond Juan Valdez's Colombian mountaintop. "She has dark straight hair and dark eyes." Clearly, not me. I kind of wanted to stab him. "She's opinionated, but she babies me. She makes fun of everyone else, so they all think she's a bitch, but she's super nice to me." How can anything with a scrotum say "super nice?" "She has an addiction to giving oral sex and sex in general."

"Well, duh." I began walking ahead of him.

"She's got a great set of bagpipes, is smart, and knows what a vasectomy is. And she doesn't use words that she doesn't know to seem smart—because she *is* smart. She has a real job. Like, she isn't an actress or a bartender." He held up the plastic bag of artichokes, shaking it. "She knows how to cook because I sure as hell don't."

"Who doesn't know what a vasectomy is?"

"Dumb Elspbeth." Girls with names like Elspbeth memorize Grateful Dead sets and head up Amnesty International. They don't know from vasectomies. "She has to be loving, at least when we're alone. Like, she has to be able to cry with me because we miss each other or something like that. She can't be too tough in that sense." Too tough meant me; it had to.

When Max and I were dating, he expressed his need for soft as often as he complained he was hungry. "You come off as so, so abrasive. There has to be a pile of mush in there somewhere. I just wish you'd let me see it, sweetie." I hated this, having to manufacture feelings and invent something to foster tears and closeness. Wanna see mush? Pull up a chair and have a front seat gander at my ass. Okay there, Big Guy?

Just after splitting with Gabe, I wasn't ready to do vulnerable again. All I wanted was affection and really good sex, the kind you could smell on your fingers and taste on your breath hours later. Sadly, Max couldn't do dirty unless I did vulnerable first. How chicken/egg.

"Ew, Stephanie," he had said when I asked him to talk dirty to me while I watched him masturbate. "I can't be that open with you. I need to feel a connection first." He was ingesting too much reality TV for any manly diet. *Connection* is right up there with *spark*, and unless you're an electrician, it shouldn't be uttered, not even in a whisper.

And then, in the frickin' cereal aisle, he was talking about wanting a woman in librarian glasses who'd wear her hair in a bun, then whip him with it in bed when it all fell down. "She has dark straight hair, wears dangly earrings, and she should be a good planner," he added. "I like plans."

"Yes, you mentioned the straight hair before." Jackass. "You're too funny." The funny part was listening to him describe me to me if only I'd get on with the Japanese hair-straightening thing and dye my hair boring.

"Bottom line, she can wear the pants, as long as she lets me get into them from time to time. Oh, and she's a good napper, too."

"What if she snores?"

"That's okay."

"Really? You can sleep through that? I can't date a snorer. Spend the rest of my life with someone who keeps me up all the time? I doubt Linus could deal with it either. He'd crawl on the guy and try to suffocate him with his fur necklace move."

"And then when he'd try to push Linus off, he'd get bitten in the FACE." He enunciates face as if it's mostly *s*'s.

"He doesn't bite when you move him," I reminded him.

"Yes he would, if you push his FACE." I laugh whenever Max talks about Linus, especially when he mentions his face because when he does it, he lifts both hands into the air and pretends he's squeezing Linus's little mouth shut.

"You have to grab him by the belly." Common knowledge for anyone who's sleeping with me.

"Well, it's dangerous when his mouth is next to your EYE." Max shouted the word *eye* and pointed to his.

"She'd have to put up with the fact that I'm a big wimp sometimes," I mocked in a whine.

"Think what you want, but I'm not a wimp sometimes."

"Fine, all the time?"

"Am not."

"Are too."

"What-ever," he said smiling, making it seem like they were two words. "When I meet her, I'm going to call her Bunny."

"You can't pick a nickname. It just has to happen."

"Nah, I'm going to work it in, 'cause it's cute."

"Alexandra calls me Cookie. Sometimes Cooks. Today she called me Cookie Monster Face, but mostly she sticks with Cookie or Cookie Face." Alexandra was a new instant best friend who called all her girls "Cookie." She probably heard someone else say it once, decided she liked it, and made it her own.

"I like Bunny."

"Well, I guess I can understand Bunny for a lover, 'cause you can fuck like rabbits. But you can't choose a nickname—it just has to happen. Like I call Linus Noodle, Bear, or Roast Beef Sandwich Head depending on my mood. I'm never called anything but Sweetie. How lame."

"Or Red." He pulled on a lock of my hair.

"Nah, you'd think people would call me Red, but they don't. And I always wanted Gabe to call me Red because of *The Philadelphia Story*, with Cary Grant and Katharine Hepburn. Grant calls her Red, and when he does it, it's powerful and submissive all at once. Yum. I've never been a nickname, ever. Oh, except for Moose in high school, but we won't talk about that. 'Cause I'll start to cry."

Max kissed me on my forehead. "Okay, Red, we won't talk about that." And with that, he skipped down the aisle, working up speed, so he could hop onto the back of the shopping cart and coast. Skipped, for the love of God and all things girly.

At that moment, seeing him ride the back of the shopping cart, I stopped walking and shook my head. How was this the same guy I'd undressed in candlelight and associated with Norah Jones songs? I wish I associated him with something less mainstream, something harder or punk. Norah Jones and baby talk. Nothing really changed from when I'd first met Max years ago; he was the same kid. Only then, it wasn't the back of a shopping cart—he rode a skateboard around our office. He was a final-semester computer science major from Princeton interning for the summer. I was dating Gabe, but I noticed Max, the way you notice anyone who's that good-looking. Max was a Diet Coke commercial. Dimples, bronzed arms, tough guy strut. He's a stack of flaxen hair, indigo eyes, aquiline nose, and probably the greatest smile I've ever seen. He wore a thin leather rope around his neck, and sometimes I fantasized about pulling him to me by it. What I didn't know then was he was also a cheerleader who highlighted his hair and enjoyed knitting and gardening as "favorite pastimes." "What-ever. Cheerleading was normal where I grew up." He grew up near Amish country, Pennsylvania. Horse-drawn vehicles, suspenders, and prayer bonnets are normal there. Candlelight, fieldwork, sewing. Cheerleading? Notsomuch. "And it's not gardening. It's a green thumb. Sheesh." Yeah, and to this day, if he gets a zit on his face, he'll tent it with a Band-Aid, cancel plans, and tell people he fell out of bed and hit his head.

Still, my gaydar equipment farkled then because he is, in fact, straight. And he heterosexualed his way through every day and night with his live-in girlfriend Gabby. The duo continued to date for the next five years, and in that time, I'd switched jobs and performed a triple jump through engagement, marriage, and divorce.

I lost touch with Max when I began working at an advertising agency, but two years later, two months after discovering Gabe's betrayal, I longed for what I knew. I longed for pantry. Max met me for an adult beverage at Ocean Grill on the Upper West. I wanted oysters despite December.

I waited bare-shouldered in my Wathne scarf, wrapped as a top, pressing my lips together. It wasn't summer, but shoulders were in order. I'm not good at waiting without a glass of wine or napkin to finger, so I looked out the window and tried to spot him. The streets were filled with peculiar couples, and upon a glance, I struggled to understand what united them. I spotted the foreigners. I could see it in their teeth and hemmed Levi's. Children in colorful tights walked hunched under the weight of violin cases and backpacks. A patron extended a folded dollar bill to purchase a dirty water dog and pretzel across the street. Taxicabs. Glittering twinkle lights on small tree branches. The city was busy, and I was lonesome.

I watched Max approach the restaurant through the window. He looked beautiful under the soft fall of lamp-lit snow, and when he came inside and hugged me with "hello," it lasted too long for "just friends." Over burgundy and blue points, we both shared our sad stories, his blue eyes staring into mine even when we laughed. If I believed in love at second sight, this was it.

"Yeah, I'm happier now that I'm single," he said with a face that conveyed he smelled something rancid. " 'Cause dealing with all her issues was worse than alone could ever be." I didn't believe him. "Actually, the worst was when my therapist sat me down, and kept saying the word *fuck*." When Max said *fuck* he lowered his voice but exhaled the "ck" as if he were trying to blow out an Amish kerosene lantern. "He kept saying, 'why do you want to be with her? She had some other guy's dick in her. She was busy fuCKing other guys and lying to your FACE.' I didn't want to hear it, or believe any of it. Hearing *fuck* like that, though, it was what I needed." Max looked up from the table and smiled apologetically. "I'm sorry," he said sheepishly.

He was adorable. Seeing Max's vulnerability convinced me I could tell him anything. He would understand my fears because he was on my side, knew what it felt like to be betrayed. Since we were already friends, there wasn't any of the "When should I call?" anxiety. Everything was natural. Over the next two months, we became best friends who couldn't keep our hands off each other. Just like you'd see written in a personal ad under the header, Ideal Relationship. There was just one problem: I wasn't allowed to date him.

Okay, well, I could date him, but I couldn't date *only* him. Phone Therapist reminded me of this often. "I know you want full throttle, 24/7, 365." I knew when she whined "24/7," she felt hip. "Stephanie, right now, any relationship you enter, you're going to want to pick up where you and Gabe left off because it's what you know. You need to move beyond this comfort level, push yourself to grow. Jumping into something again is unhealthy because it's too soon. You won't know what you're jumping into. Healthy is slow-paced." Slow-paced. It was as wretched to me as canned tuna fish packed in oil.

So, I forced myself to continue to see others without really mentioning it to Max. Okay, it was lying by omission. But, unless there's some exclusivity clause mentioned in a talk somewhere, you're technically not breaking any dating rules. Max might have assumed exclusivity, but it was never discussed. Maybe he knew, deep down. Maybe it's why he continually wanted to talk about feelings.

By seeing others, I avoided the deadly dating sin of "diving," "jumping," and "shooting." Headfirst, shallow waters, and something to do with asking questions once it's too late. I was guilty. All I wanted to do was find a bathing cap and go running off a cliff headfirst into a new relationship.

"And if you jump into the wrong relationship, it will only leave you rocking on the bathroom floor in pain again." Ouch, lady. It was her way of saying "fuck." "What scares you about being single? You need to figure out why you want a relationship so desperately." Why was I paying her again? Wasn't that *her* job? Holy shit, all I wanted to do was cry and eat hamburgers.

As for variety, I had it all wrong. The real cowards aren't the ones who enjoy the variety pack. Cowards pogo jump from one relationship to the next out of a fear of being alone. Cereal monogamists. They eat out of their safe pantries because they're too terrified of walking beyond the perimeter of what they already know, exposing themselves to new "styles."

That's what Phone Therapist called them, "styles." She argued in addition to coaxing me out from behind my preferred comfort zone of "serious relationship," an assortment of men would expose me to new ways of thinking. "New styles," she advised, as if they were overcoats. "There's more to life than Jewish doctors who believe the planets orbit around their pants. You need to realize there are men out there who don't even like golf. Sure, go ahead and date Max, but you can't stop there."

So, I didn't. I dated a variety of men hoping to find "attentive," "thoughtful," and "selfless." I didn't know, at least not from experience, if they existed in men other than my father.

But of course, it all came down one day to a postcoital talk when Max questioned, "You're not seeing anyone else, are you?" I didn't need to answer. We stopped talking.

Days later, I tried to rescind it all. "I only want you. I don't care what Phone Therapist says." I felt needy and hungry for what I knew. I wasn't that different from Lower Least Side Greg, unaware of just what I had until it was too late, until it was "better off as friends."

"No, sweetie," Max said. "I knew something wasn't right. You're too fancy for me, anyway." *Fancy* meant I didn't own my own dartboard and preferred bars without sawdust.

"Can we still," I wondered how I'd redeem this, how I'd not have to lose him completely, "be friends?"

"Of course we can. But some time needs to go by. Let's give it a few months."

So, just three months out of my marriage, anxious as a fly trapped in a jar, I needed to move beyond the Max and, at a minimum, pluck a few other fresh fish out of the water and do some examining. Leave my apartment and check out their colorful scales and slick gills. I had to see what all these fish in this enormous sea everyone kept mentioning were like. I just wasn't permitted to engage in any deep-sea fishing yet. Well, thank God for argyle-print waders. Now all I needed were some fishing buddies. "Ew, do I have to touch his worm?" Oh, for the love of God.

four

PACK
ANIMALS

IT WAS TIME TO GO OUTSIDE AND REALIZE LIFE DOES AC-tually go on beyond the walls of my very small, so this is what it's like to live alone apartment. Linus crawled onto my chest and pawed at my forehead. Okay, so I wasn't *alone* alone. It was worse. I was one of those women who thought she wasn't alone because she picked up shit and fed something. "Wanna go for a walk?" I needn't ask twice. The runt was ready to go.

It was the Thursday before Fourth of July weekend, which meant I had to air out Linus. On Mondays and Wednesdays, he attended Camp Canine, a doggie day-care facility—resembling my father's basement—which enables New Yorkers' guilt to dissolve like the sugar in their A.M. lattes. For the rest of the week, though, he sulked alone all day—curled into himself like a small black-eyed pea. So I exercised him at the Seventy-second Street dog run where he chased a ball, sniffed some ass, and basically drooled like an adolescent boy upon his first glimpse of bush.

My overprotective soccer-mom instincts extended beyond wanting to make Linus wear shin guards and a helmet. Linus on the streets of Manhattan, even while I was gripping his leash, was a lawsuit waiting to happen. As we walked to the run, strangers leaned toward him and made nice nice. His tail curled between his legs like an apostrophe. "Aw, he's so cute." Yeah, lady? Wait until he devours two of your knuckles. "Look at that face!" His head lowered, ears pinned back. "His eyes are so intelligent. What is he, a Jack Russell? I used to have a Jack, too." They tried to pet his head. "They're the best—" GRORWRERESRRR.

I yanked the furkid off with a breathy apology. "I'm so sorry! I told you—he really doesn't like people." Or dogs, or pigeons, or anyone but me. So listen to me when I say it, and stop molesting my Notorious D.O.G. No one asked these ugly Tevas-with-socks strangers to handle my toy fox terrier dog (thank you very much). Maybe I'd humiliate him soon with a T-shirt: CAN'T TOUCH THIS. M.C. Hammer would be proud.

"Linus, baby, I don't blame you. I wouldn't let her touch me either," I whispered into his rose petal ears. "Now let's go chase some tail."

At the playground, it's not like I strapped him into a swing or anything. I mean, I wanted to, but that's as degrading as forcing him to wear a glamour gem collar with a jailhouse rock doggie tee. Oh, I've seen it. Way too many women in New York treat their dogs like surrogate children, right down to the wipes, bottled water, and booties come winter. They bring a blue bouncing baby ball and try to entice their canine to fetch it as though they're encouraging first steps. The problem, of course, with balls at dog runs is everything is up for grabs. Any dog can swipe the ball from Linus's jowls, leaving him flustered and vicious, picking fights with dogs that consider him nothing more than an amuse bouche. On occasion, though, miracles happen. Miracles like BooBoo.

BooBoo the Boston terrier suddenly pounced off her owner's lap and sadistically raced Linus for the ball. "My God, BooBoo never chased a ball before!" Her owner, a tattered woman with a voice like Tevye's from *Fiddler on the Roof,* exclaimed, suddenly on her feet, clapping, with the excitement of a new mother. "It's a miracle, I tell you." Clearly, she also smoked unfiltered cigarettes for a living. "A modern-day miracle." Was she talking about BooBoo or Botox? Just as easily, I could have heard, "Bobby never went down the big slide on his own before."

I smiled at her, one of those sympathetic, you poor sad sack smiles usually reserved for those who choose the wrong impressive vocabulary word at the right dinner parties. This is the best she'll ever have, right here, in this moment. She was sadder than air guitar. I was suddenly terrified. What if this were me? What if this was it, a life revolving around dog accessories instead of making play dates and helping with home-work? Living my life from the bench beside Burberry dog carriers and Swarovski-studded leads.

Linus was back, unexpectedly with a pack of other dogs, panting at my feet. "What? What is it, baby? You want me to throw the ball again?" Upon hearing me address him, he scampered off, clearly embarrassed by my baby talk now that he was runnin' with the cool kids. It's as if he for-gets for those forty-five minutes that he likes to sleep under the covers with me and that his favorite toy is a stuffed frog. Instead his instincts kick in, and he's suddenly one of the pack, asking me to drop him off around the corner from the movie theater. At that moment I understood why parents sob at weddings.

Just then my cell phone buzzed with a new e-mail message from Alexandra Geddes, a post-divorce girlfriend I'd met through Dulce, my pre-divorce friend. It's amazing how significant events in life divide everything into "before" and "after." Sure, doctors get a rap for having a God complex. Gabe was more like Christ. Everything was reduced to BG and AG.

"We're going out tonight, cookieface! Markt: reseys at 9 P.M. sharp. None of your fifteen minutes of fashionable lateness crap." We'd be go-ing to Markt, a new restaurant in the meatpacking district. I stood from the bench and danced a jig.

> To Markt, to Markt, I am a fat pig.
> Home alone again, home alone again,
> Will it always be my gig?

At least for most of the evening, I'd be out with a pack. The New York single scene wasn't all that disparate from the Upper West Side dog run. Like wild dogs traveling through twilight in nonstop strides, con-stantly in jeopardy of ambush, with a need for securing their own prey, my pack of chicklet friends announced their presence, not with howls, but silently, through scent, communicating their territory to neighbors.

You could nearly see Creed's Fleur de The Rose Bulgarie, as if it left tracks indicating where we'd been, who we'd conquered, and who we'd left for dead. If a dog strays from the group, he's less likely to eat, so his chances of survival increase when he stays, not strays. When a woman strays, deciding to abstain from a night out with friends, she's less likely to meet anyone, and more likely to sit on her fat ass watching Lifetime TV, increasing her chances of doing just that for the rest of her sad-sack life. It's precisely why women move through the night in groups, right down to their lengthy bathroom visits. It was going to be a great night. I could smell it.

REMARKABLY, I WAS FIFTEEN MINUTES EARLY TO DINNER. Nevertheless, there was no chance we'd be seated anything short of a half hour after our actual reservation at Markt. The dinner was in honor of Dulce's twenty-fifth birthday bash. Girls like Dulce were always having "bashes," yet this was only the second time I'd celebrated her birth since meeting her on a double date with Gabe, two years prior.

Her beauty intimidated me at the onset. There I was, married to Gabe, wearing matronly capri pants, a cashmere cable knit complete with pearls, and a ribbon headband—always the "tell" of a married woman, dressing the proper preppy part to complete the proper married picture—when along comes girlfriend d'force, in heels and hoochiewear, complete with perfectly threaded brows and overly glossed lips. She wore a minute of a jean skirt with a pink baby tee clearly made for a Chihuahua. Dulce looked like a soft porn DVD cover featuring young dirty college girls on spring break. I remember touching Gabe's arm to make sure he was still there.

I imagined she'd be aloof and only warm when prompted to speak of her childhood abroad, where I was certain she partied on the bronzed shoulders of men while wearing little more than a belly chain. Gabe had mentioned something about Chile, but I imagined Brazil. He couldn't have birthed a more erroneous story if he'd actually closed his eyes and pushed. Apparently, Dulce was really Allyson Reese of Austin, Texas. She acquired the pet name *Dulce* from her sorority sisters when she'd returned from her Chilean semester abroad, not speaking Spanish, but "a speaking a English with a Spanisha accent" to replace her sometimes southern one. If Dulce were a scratch and sniff sticker, she'd smell like birthday cake.

The guy from the double date broke up with Dulce two weeks later, claiming, "I need to focus more at work, and you're a distraction." I didn't really believe girls who looked like Dulce could ever be abandoned. She was *Austintatious*: big jewelry, big breasts, big heart. She'd just moved to Manhattan from Baltimore, where she'd gone to college, to live with him, so this didn't just make Dulce dumped; it made her homeless. Gabe relayed that, really, his friend believed she was just too immature.

"Immature how?" I wanted to know. Gabe just shrugged. How infuriating men can be with their lack of probing questions. "So you're a real stickler for details, huh?" I crossed my arms waiting for a reaction. "You mean, you didn't even ask?" Gabe shrugged again, then diverted his attention to his medical flashcards. "Where's she going to live?" Another shrug. Clearly I was speaking to a mime who'd cut out of "shoulder shrug" class to vault imaginary walls and pick make-believe flowers.

"Well, is it okay if she stays with us for a while?" I was surprised it came out of my mouth. From where was my new concern for her coming? I only knew her and her skirt for a minute. Shouldn't my loyalties have rested with Gabe's friend, who was by extension my friend, or at least our friend? When breakups happen, sides are taken. Loyalty becomes black and white. I was playing the part of the sensible driving shoe wife. My mothering instincts kicked in, and I wanted to protect this young blonde Manhattan transfer.

"Yeah, she can stay."

SO, DULCE LIVED WITH US FOR A SHORT TIME WHILE SHE hunted for a job, an apartment, and a new life. I know. Was I crazy to invite this leggy Texas cheerleader, with her itty-bitty pink terrycloth running shorts, to lounge on our sofa cross-legged without the slightest hint of a thigh dimple? Really, just let her ample bosom heave just a room away from us in the dark of night? Truth is, Gabe's fidelity never even came into question. Instead I wondered if this woman would ever be the kind to put her oar in married waters. And the answer was always, No. Not because she'd be afraid someone would discover the indiscretion, but it was the kind of thing *she'd* never be okay with, in her own buffed skin. Now why couldn't I have married someone like Dulce instead of Gabe? That's the only question I should have been asking.

Though Dulce appears to be nothing more than a sugary soufflé of blond hair, with bonbon breasts and skin as soft as confectioners' sugar, she's as real as the Bible. Sadly, I only began to appreciate her once I discovered Gabe was on the cheat. Only when the shit comes down do you learn who your real friends are. When shit landed on my welcome mat, Ms. Dulce was there to help me scrape it all off, phoning me every single morning to ensure I got out of bed. She wouldn't hang up until she heard the shower water. And in the middle of the night when I had to talk but was afraid of the hour, she always answered, "I'm glad you called." Dulce became family, never sugarcoating the facts. "He is a liar; he specializes in it. Don't let this be your life." She is my strongest friend.

We became each other's pack in the face of ambush. Now, we're two little bitches, strutting side by side off into the sunset, leaving our piles of dog shit by the curb where they belong.

DULCE BELONGED AT HER OWN DAMN BASH HALF AN HOUR ago. While I waited for the birthday girl to arrive, I did what I do best: drink and eavesdrop. Before even asking her name, the part-time Fifth Avenue man beside me spoke of the part of time he spent beyond the city.

"See, I love the warmth, but South Beach is insipid these days. The crowd is so pedestrian." He sounded like a black man impersonating a white news anchor.

This man, who ought to have been in his late forties, was probably only thirty-three and referred to his parents' summer home on The Vineyard as his home. Schooled at all the "right places," places with crests and "the" in the title, Mr. Madras Pants carried a degree in poplin with a minor in seersucker. He wore his conceit neatly behind the gold button of his navy blazer, and I could tell by the way he inspected the rim of his Cape Codder tumbler that he was the type of man who was at complete ease when sending his order back to the kitchen. I imagined his way of "ending things" was not returning phone calls.

"I prefer Nevis these days," he continued. I'm sorry, since when is Nevis in the same realm as South Beach, and who says insipid? The guy was *awkwords*.

I looked around watching new couples write big ideas on small cocktail napkins, communicating in squares. She's got her heart on her sleeve, he's got his monogram. It's rare to find real in a city where the wine is sixteen dollars a glass, the lighting is scarce, and all the boys are necked out in Ferragamo . . . and occasionally Zegna. But only if he's in a suit because Zegna neckties are all about the suit. But you knew that. Okay, you didn't.

When a man who is clearly the boyfriend of the woman Mr. Madras Pants is trying to impress approaches, touching the small of her back and accepting a kiss from her on his lips, Pants rose to the occasion.

"May I offer you *both* a drink?" He looked into the boyfriend's eyes as if he'd just walked away with a golden regatta trophy for his fifth consecutive summer.

"No, thank you," Boyfriend responded in a tone that said, "and it's a yacht, not a boat, you dinghy."

So, she had a boyfriend. Please, every attractive woman in this city is attached. Boyfriends are not deterrents—they're accessories. I wondered if they made one in my size.

"Oh my God, this is too funny!" It was Dulce with Alexandra approaching me from behind. Dulce's hands were touching both my shoulder and the shoulder of Pants. "Two of my most favorite people." An actual squeal escaped her fuchsia lips, followed by introductions and double-cheek kisses. Apparently Pants was Paul Williams, a trader at Merrill Lynch with a fiancée of his own . . . though on drunken occasions, he left this item off his social CV.

Just after he'd broken up with his "very serious girlfriend," Dulce had set Pants up with Alexandra. The two dated casually but fucked formally for months, and he continued to bed down Alexandra, even after he made it clear that he'd reconciled with his ex. "It was one thing, screwing around with him when she was his girlfriend, but now they're engaged. That's where I draw the line." Evidently, Alexandra used pencil to draw her lines.

After Alexandra and Pants exchanged wanton smiles and gazes laced with future promises of very naughty things, she greeted me in a whisper. "I cannot be-lieve he is here. Hilar! He looks so good for him. Oh, sorry we're late, Monster. I tried to talk her out of it."

"It" was Dulce's mistake of an outfit, constituting black leather hotpants, so short they looked like training underpants. The knee-high boots were the black icing on her devil's food cake. I knew she had added the pink long-sleeved turtleneck as an attempt at conservative.

"You couldn't talk her out of that leather wedgie?"

"Stephanie, believe me, everything here represents a compromise." She swept her hand through air, like a magician's assistant revealing an ordinary object. "You should have seen the lace stockings she had on."

"Where is everyone else?" I asked the planner of all planners, Alexandra, an events planner at *The New Yorker* who numbered her arguments, always thought before speaking, and wouldn't dream of living life without her Bluetooth and a series of digital to-do lists.

"It's just us tonight. The real party is on Sats." Alexandra spoke in abbreviations to save time.

"What? What's on Saturday?"

"Angel, we told you." Alexandra petted my arm with her manicured hand as if she were petting a sable coat. "It's all about the Hamps. We depart at 8 A.M. . . . destination: Whore It Up All Weekend Long." We regularly referred to ourselves, lovingly, as sluts, despite the fact that the only breathing thing I'd shared any horizontal space with lately was my dog.

"I thought we left on Saturday to avoid Fourth traffic." Dulce and Alexandra stared first at each other, and then back at me, cracking into a harmony of laughter.

"Sweetie, please. This is the best frickin' weekend all sum. Wake up early, pack your ass, and sleep on our drive out." I needed to see if they made Cliff Notes for being fabulous. I would devour its pages and commit full paragraphs to memory. I didn't want to be the matronly one, the divorcée in the pearls. I wanted to be part of Alex's spectacular world. She was my VIP card into single life.

I wasn't really sure why we were even out just then. No one was going to eat a proper meal knowing we'd be wearing bathing suits poolside tomorrow. It was a "what are you doing on your actual birthday" dinner without dinner. The three of us drank two bottles of sixty percent marked-up Riesling, snacked on Reblochon, and let retired men buy us pink, sugar-rimmed champagnes.

Then my stomach plummeted upon sight of Brad, one of Gabe's old camp friends, walking straight toward our table. His face stopped and smiled, hovering over our chairs as if lit from beneath with a flashlight. It was surreal, like seeing my doorman in a different neighborhood. Fuckity fuck. I held my breath.

Okay, I'm just going to come out and say it. Gabe and I attended the same sleepaway camp. There. But don't go jumping to the, "Oh, they were childhood sweethearts, no wonder the marriage failed" conclusion. Back then Gabe and I were never friends, and we were certainly not sweethearts. We didn't date until my senior year of college, when we were reacquainted through mutual friends.

"Hi there, Stephanie. Nice to see you." Liar, you couldn't care less. I smiled and blinked, extending a limp handshake. Kisses, intros, forced smiles, and then the unexpected, "So how's Gabe doing? I heard about your divorce. Sorry. But he's a urologist now, right?"

I knew the question had to be answered gingerly, with finesse, and a sense of understanding. Delicately. Kid gloves.

"Yes, he's a doctor and an asshole, just not in that order. Thanks for asking." I stared into the pupils of his eyes and put my elbows on the table. Brad cleared his throat, raised his brows, and scurried off like a scolded dog.

"Steph-an-eeeee!" Alexandra shrieked. "It's one thing to think it, but saying it makes people uncomfortable." This was a major difference between us. Alex grew up in a formal southern home where "Ladies don't do that" was stirred into big pitchers of sweet Georgia tea and then sipped medicinally after praying to the Lord. When Alexandra was soused to the gills, she became the alpha dog, aggressively attacking what she wanted with complete disregard or forethought. When she became drunk, she became me.

"Saying it makes people uncomfortable? Mentioning *Dr. Cock & Balls* to my face makes me uncomfortable. Don't ask the fucking question if you're not ready for the answer."

"I just hate when you sound defensive, that's all." Alex's tone was softer now.

Dulce was scraping the last bits of Reblochon onto a piece of crusty bread.

"You bet your ass I'm defensive. I'm going to defend my life. Damn, screw Bradford and his uglyass loafers."

Dulce touched my hand. "Actually, Stephanie, I applaud you. He has real nerve to walk over here and ask you about Gabe, especially after admitting he'd heard about your split. Good for you for saying what's on your mind. I say we make a toast while we've got the champagne."

I wanted to finish the meal in silence and respect the dead of my relationship. I hated how my past could walk through a door like that, through someone else's body, like a successful night with a Ouija board. I hated that no matter how over it I ever felt, or how rational I was, something as small as an acquaintance from our past could make me feel vastly ashamed. "Yeah, we're divorced now" seems as embarrassing as admitting you've just been released from rehab. It's admitting you had a problem, that your life hasn't been perfect. Well, whose has? Enough with the silence. I raised my glass. "To champagne-in-the-asses." We all smiled, raised our flutes, and clicked.

When we finally presented our waiter with a fan of nearly maxed-out credit cards, he assured us the meal was already taken care of. Had Brad suddenly come down with a severe case of remorse? Could it be? I turned, looking to find his chipmunk face in the crowded restaurant. Our waiter stopped me by resting his hand on my shoulder then nodding toward Pants, who smiled the smile of a middle school boy who just learned the meaning of the verb *teabagging*. Alexandra lit up, straightening her posture and pressing her hand against her stomach, as if to keep her excitement contained in her body. She wanted to get Pants off, and let him get into hers. When drunk she believed the technical term for fiancé was "not married yet." Dulce and I looked at each other, and in unison, grabbed Alexandra by both arms, escorting her out of Markt in minutes, saving our fellow pack member from being ambushed. She could be her own worst enemy. We all shared a taxi uptown. Next stop Sagaponack.

I HATED THE IDEA OF HAVING TO STRESS FOR A RELAXING weekend away. Unpacking from a weekend in the Hamptons is one thing. Despite only ever wearing a third of what I actually packed, I turned my bag upside down into my laundry hamper, emptying it all: shoes, toiletries, everything. A few days later, I'd need the toothpaste.

Okay, that's gross. True, but gross. Packing for the Hamptons is stressful. It takes prudence, patience, and Pucci. You have to consider the weather, bring the right walking shoe that won't give you blisters. Is dinner espadrilles in the garden or stilettos at Sunset Beach? I don't care what my mother said about horizontal stripes, this still looks good on me. Right? Find room now for loungewear, bedding, tennis racket, and don't get me started with the hair products.

The Hamptons are like sleepaway camp with heels. You leave packed with all of the above, then realize you forgot a pillow and towels. You grab some bottled water and fem mags, and then your real life stops counting. It's left behind with your doorman and your privacy. Work, worries, and "will he call"s genuinely fly out the window when you crank up the car radio, roll down windows, and inhale the smell of summer. We knew we'd have a terrific weekend, the way we knew it was time for farmstand corn, Wolffer's rosé, and flip-flops. We turned the radio up with our arrival song: "Lay a whisper on my pillow . . . leave the winter on the ground . . ."

It was a house that looked like a child's drawing: connected triangles, a two-car garage, windows that looked like wrapped presents. It sat on four acres of green land, complete with a pond and a lone tire swing hanging from an ancient oak. The house was modern but not in a mirrored walls and raised Formica platform bed bachelor kind of way. Rooms were imbued with natural materials—stone, wood, and sisal— suggesting a connection to nature right down to the seashell-loaded glass hurricanes on the screened-in wraparound porch. The fireplace was left unadorned by art, save for the American flag, fixed along a wooden ceiling beam. With its cushy, oversized, white denim seating and whitewashed wooden floors, the house always made me feel clean, as if I were moisturized and freshly French-manicured. The bedrooms and bathrooms were strewn with the contemporary and the timeworn: glass lamps, leaning orchid stalks, log magazine racks, and primitive sailboats. So, the designer was a little heavy-handed with the lighthouse and anchor art. I could almost hear the National Anthem.

I felt like a grown up living there, even if it did mean sharing the space with strangers who played Quarters and high-five'd at the dinner table using words like *boyz*, *homey*, and *playa*. It was a home where, upon arrival, it was as if the beds were forever made and the bathrooms always smelled of lemons. Upon leaving, the house looked like a picnic ground and smelled of coffee filters, rain, and vomit. And I shared it all with my girls, bunking up in one basement of a room, which we soon referred to as the Diva Dungeon of Dare. Forget sharing a room with two other women or sharing a bathroom with nine other people. Roughing it is a weekend in the Hamptons without a pedicure.

That first night, I phoned my father from the backseat of our rental car, as Alexandra circled East Hampton looking for "the scene."

"Is my little monster behaving himself?"

"That's no way to refer to your father, Miss Stephanie."

"Har har, Dad." I grew up on a diet of his corny jokes and learned early on to starve him of encouragement.

"Linus was fine in the car ride out here, but he's been stealing the toilet paper and dirty items from the bathroom trashcan ever since." "Here" was his Manhasset home with his new wife, Carol.

"Dirty items, Dad?"

"Carol's feminine products." Ew. I never should have asked. Now all I could picture was Linus with a maxi pad stuck to his mouth. "And when we try to get it away from him, he growls." My father laughed while telling the story. I actually bit down.

"So, he's good then. Glad to hear it."

"And you, my dear? Are you having fun with the girls out there?"

"Yeah. But the real fun is tomorrow when I go shopping at Calypso for a snag-a-man outfit. Everyone is so put together out here."

"Linus Paddington Klein, you get back here. Stephanie, that's ridiculous. Aren't you in the Hamptons?" He said "the Hamptons" as if it were Fire Island. My father didn't realize the Hamptons aren't about tranquility and self-service—they're about bottle service. "Do you know how ridiculous you sound? If a woman is as beautiful as you are, she can wear nothing but a garbage bag, and she'll still be beautiful. Guys aren't exactly looking at your shoes, you know."

"Yes, Father Knows Best, I know. Give the pooch a peck for me. I'm out the door." Click. It occurred to me just then that I wasn't out the door. I was in a moving car, and I hadn't felt this particular feeling since I was in high school. I worried I was regressing. No longer married, cruising the streets for the "it" spot made me fearful I'd never find what I was looking for. We might as well have been driving in reverse.

"I'M SICK OF DRIVING. THAT DRAGON ROOM WAS ASS-AND-a-half. At this point, I'd even hit The Almond, where everyone's in their forties." Alexandra preferred young boys she could boss around.

"I love men in their forties," I responded after some thought. "They know what they want, already paid their career dues, and can't claim they haven't sowed their oats." What a wretched phrase, sowing oats; it's so Wilford Brimley. "Except, there's always the forty-year-old bachelor who should come with a Beware sign that barks self-centered."

"Yeah, but with older men," Dulce added while lowering the radio, "there's that whole limp dick Viagra problem."

"Pulling taffy," I said simply. "There's nothing worse, and then you have to pretend you don't notice. Please, everyone involved knows it's not working. I hate having to pretend I'm compassionate."

"Yeah," Dulce added, "but look at Jean Claude. He's young and never fully gets hard."

"Really?"

"Yeah, even when I dress like the kitten that Pepé Le Pew chased around."

"Dulce, I told you, that's because he's so big." Alexandra submitted this as if it were exhibit A in the case against the flaccid penis.

"What?" I yelled.

"Yeah, Stephanie, it's because he's so big. Some dicks never fully get hard. It's like porno dick. It's because they're so big and heavy, there's not enough blood in their body or something."

"Believe me, the fact that it's big has nothing to do with his gummy-bear dick problem. If I had a name like Jean Claude, I wouldn't be able to get hard either. Is he uncircumcised?"

Dulce took a moment and looked up as if she were trying to remember where she'd last left her pearl earrings. "Yes."

"So when you pipe him, what do you do with the extra skin?" I was sure she was doing it wrong.

"Pipe him?" Alex asked.

"Yeah, go down on him." I know I sounded like a guy. I'd heard it in a bar once and always wanted to say it.

"I . . ." Dulce moved her hands into position, as though she couldn't remember, but her body would. "I take it along for the ride."

"Girl, it's not a carpool. That's your problem." I shook my head knowingly, like a doctor sure of her new diagnosis. "You've got to smack that shit down, and pull it taut before you go down on him. I'm telling you, the uncircumcised penis has a whole separate owner's manual."

"Ew. Girls, enough," Alex added sternly.

"Does this feel like high school to anyone else?" Alexandra was too busy playing radio president, executing veto power over Dulce's Dashboard Confessional selections, wheeling her way toward a static-free alternative she knew all the words to.

"How'd ya mean?" Dulce turned to look at me.

"This whole thing, being in the backseat of a car for starters. I mean, the last time I was in a car that wasn't yellow and smelling of incense and BO was in high school. And back then, the music we blasted was Led Zeppelin. I remember when Hillary Cohen lowered the volume on me. She turned to me saying, 'Steph, it's one thing to blast some top-forty song, but it's just not cool to blare Zeppelin or The Dead. You just don't do that.' I was such a dork. How do you two deal with me?"

"It's not like we a have a choice. You invite yourself everywhere, bi-atch." Alex flirted with me, looking for my reaction in the rearview mirror.

"Ooh, leave this." Kelly Clarkson was midsong, singing "Miss Independent." Of course she was. How very Fourth. "We keep circling, like we're missing out on something. Stop here. Forget this place. The crowd is too decrepit or too hoochy island, so we're onto the next, hoping. It's so Jan Brady, looking for the cool party." I knew this would make Alexandra laugh, and when she did, I felt myself light up. I loved delighting her.

"Ladies, we are here now," Alexandra roared as she put the car into park. "And we're going to have fun because this is our fabs summer. Now, get the fuck out, and let's go enjoy Jet." I saluted her with a stiff cut into the air, then blew her a kiss.

WHERE ARE UGLY FRIENDS WHEN YOU NEED 'EM? MY RE-
splendent pack of friends looked liked grown-up versions of Sweet Valley
High girls. Beneath the poetic featherweight whites of summer, their
bronzed shoulders twisted, above their stacked wedge heels and tanned
calves. It was that time again—for sunglasses, outdoor seating, and oysters; for shell jewelry, pulsing white on tanned skin; for main course salads, beach sarongs, and pots of crème brûlée, beneath green awnings,
above white linen, beside a half-full bottle of Pellegrino. Everything
looks beautiful at the beginning of a season. My friends aren't seasonal.
They're exceptional year-round. Their beauty is arresting, and I'm not
saying that like Joe Soccer Coach, readily spitting out "you're all win-
ners" after the team has just been pulverized. I'm also not talking "inner
beauty," while dangling a purple crystal and burning sticks of incense.

Alexandra has a face you notice from across a room: dimples, vexing
eyes, and a plume of straight hair that shines like onyx. If she were a su-
perhero, she'd be Wonder Woman. If a man preferred vanilla, there was
always Dulce with her model figure and striking Texan beauty. Alexandra
cornered the market on chocolate. What need would any man have for
me, strawberry? No one ever chose strawberry over either of the classics.
As long as I rolled with the pretty pack, I'd be packing it in alone every
single night. Still, didn't the fact that I willingly joined them in public at-
test to my security?

It occurs to me just now, quite seriously, that I don't have an ugly
friend. Okay, I do, but she lives in Connecticut, so she doesn't really
count. Do we see our friends as a reflection of ourselves, as accessories,
like our choice of dog breed?

Had I velvet-roped it to Jet East with a pack of chicklets, each more
recherché than the next, would men find me more exquisite than if I were
in the same situation, flanked with homely fems, each more coarse and
boorish than the next? Before you answer, consider Loehmann's.

Bargain shopping certainly breeds a rush of excitement when you reveal a gem. You almost have to check yourself, looking behind you, to see if anyone else is on to you. But bargain shopping takes work, digging through piles of mismatched clothes, whipping through wheels of hangers by sizes. Even when you reveal something you think you might like, you figure, how good can it be? It's at frickin' Daffy's! Maybe you take the periwinkle sweater home but never really love it the way you love an expensive Neiman's purchase. You don't bother to fold it with scented tissue paper in your armoire. Instead, it gets tossed on a shelf atop the closet. It's something to throw on.

Now consider a boutique store, along one of the historic streets of Southampton, with a trained staff and pools of natural light. You're surrounded by neat order. You can almost smell the verbena soap. You want to buy it all, hoping your life will become the store, fresh, clean, and airy. It's hard to decide, but once you do, you walk home swinging the bag with your periwinkle gem tucked neatly in a sleeve of wrapped paper. You rearrange your shelves to accommodate it. You're in love.

It's the same item, er, same woman, but the scene certainly reinforces the sale. If you find her packed in a bargain basement bar, you might not appreciate her as much if she were surrounded by more comely surroundings. Still, it was taxing on my ego always being the ugly chick the martyr wingman had to entertain so his buddy could hit on my friend. But that's New York. It would've been easier had I assumed that centerfold-caliber women were vapid, deplete of soul, passion, or wit. I mean, would God really make women that perfect just to spite me? From Manhattan to Montauk, I realized, I just had to get over it. Anywhere I turned, I was likely to find someone wealthier, smarter, and much more beautiful than I'd ever be. I could hate 'em or join 'em. I just wished joining 'em didn't mean Jet East.

The only respectable boys at Jet East were too short to date and equated their self-esteem with their Prada loafers. Mostly, the place was peppered with short, spiked-hair boys with tall spiked attitudes who called it "Jet" because they were trendy and on vay-K, too tired to add "East." I waited twenty minutes for my overpriced dirty martini. The waiter was certain I'd asked for the flirty martini. How fucking annoying. While I waited, I overheard the name-dropping and witnessed the lifting of velvet ropes just beyond the window. This one was hemming and hawing about the Sony party and the Hiltons' new record label to Dulce. That one had his hand on Alexandra's knee as he mentioned Lizzy Grubman's reality show, "filming at Cyril's tomorrow. Care to join me?" I wanted to vomit, and I would've if vomiting weren't such a cliché. No one wanted to talk to me.

But then I heard Prince and his reassuring words about not needing someone rich, or cool, for them to rule his world. And suddenly, I was encouraged. I sang aloud and kissed the air, feeling like my very own *Pretty Woman*. My calves were smooth and about to be tanned, and my hair fell in uniform ringlets that bounced when I pulled them. I was part of the pretty pack, in a pretty house with pretty things. I should've been smiling and, just like that, knowing I was supposed to be happy made me sad.

I listened to the words as they belted free from my lungs. The song was bullshit. It should've been outlawed anywhere south of the North Fork of Long Island, where even the streets are named after money. It is money and looks from the gray gravel driveways flanked with hydrangeas to the French tulips for her dinner party and the orange Birkin. Southampton is old money, East Hampton is new money, and Westhampton ignores money and surfs instead. Don't tell me men don't care about manicures, watches, and "it" bags. I assure you, the men who pay top dollar for their iced hooch, who hang in the Hamps wearing black, do care if it's a garbage bag or Gucci. Been there, married that. It was clear my summer would be wretched if it meant places like Jet East. I ought to have been west with the low-maintenance WASPs and their greased-up boards, sitting outside in cutoffs listening to a steel drum band sing "No Woman No Cry".

I couldn't ask to go home because both the girls were heavy into light conversations with new men. This called for a solo bathroom break. Usually, women hit the bathroom in a gaggle, even if they don't have to pee. Most of what women do in bathrooms is barter complaints for compliments.

They stand in front of a mirror and put themselves down. "Ugh, I'm exhausted. Look at these bags." She pulled the skin taught around her eyes.

"That's nothing. I'd rather have those bags than these." An atrociously thin woman used her pointer fingers to poke what I can only assume she believed were her saddlebags. "I have to stop donating to the gym and actually go."

"Oh, shut up both of you. My skin is breaking out, and my period is bloating me. I look pregnant."

"I know a great cream for that."

It was reason enough to pee in the street or cut the men's line, claiming desperation and ovary pain. Bathrooms are just bad for the head. As I glossed my lips, it occurred to me that the *crème fraiche* of the Hamptons passed the same bouncer test I had, and here they were beside me looking in the mirror and picking themselves apart. I wasn't any different than these thin self-deprecating models after all. If a guy were going to choose a different breed of woman over me, he'd always choose that. What's the use in comparisons when I can't change who I am? And why in God's overused name would I want to? Why would I ever want the "it" bag everyone else wanted? It becomes common and expected, like Hamptons traffic. Well, fuck that noise. I'm pretty damn spectacular: me, my cellulite, and my anxious-as-all-get-out dog.

"Barkeep, another martini—make it filthy, not flirty!"

"Now, that's a woman who knows who she is." Damn. Usually a man who'd say this type of thing was a retired Long Island cop who wore more gold jewelry than a pawnshop, but this guy was cute. Very cute, and he'd just called me a woman.

"And that's a man who knows how to use a line." We were flirting already. His eyes were warm, and his shirt was perfect. I'm such a sucker for preppy. I swear, if I could, I'd marry preppy and make grosgrain babies.

"Hey, that wasn't a line." He feigned offended and looked good with his hands on his hips. From the boyish look of him, I could tell he was the kind of guy whose favorite movie was *The Princess Bride*, but he'd never admit to it unless someone else did first.

"Here you go, Kenny." The bartender passed Prep Star a brown drink.

"Not a line? *Right*. You can tell I'm a woman who knows who I am just by my drink choice?" I peered up at him, my chin tucked to my chest.

"No." He came closer and pushed his shoulder into mine. "Anyone who uses the word *barkeep* is a person with little regard of what others think." Shoulder to shoulder, now, both of us leaning our forearms on the bar, I gave him a head nod and shoved him right back. "And you've got a killer smile."

"Well, shit. Now you've gone ahead and captured my attention. How ever will you keep it?" I was drunk. Don't hate me.

He didn't even pause. "I can teach you the military alphabet."

"How do you know I wasn't a ROTC cadet in college?"

"Damn, you went to college?" Suddenly, he was speaking like a trucker with a toothpick in his mouth. "Woowee, girl, your folks must be proud!" I loved him. I smiled, biting into one of my olives.

His camp counselor voice returned, asking, "So, was I wrong to assume you're a woman who knows what she wants?"

"You didn't say that. You said a woman who knows who she is."

"It's the same thing, isn't it?" Before I had a chance to figure out if I wanted to argue, he barked, "G."

"G?"

"Yeah, what's the military word for G?" I had no idea.

"Golf."

He slammed his drink on the bar without spilling. "I was betting everything you had no idea."

"I'm right?" If I weren't in heels, I would have hopped.

"You guessed?" He slapped me five, and we began laughing as if we'd known each other since crapping your pants and wearing emergency OshKosh was the thing to do. "Okay, it's your turn. Ask me something."

"Okay, where'd you grow up?" I stopped smiling and began to look at him as though I wanted to lick him somewhere.

"Oh, come on. I know that one! It's too easy. Give me something tougher. I promise not to cry."

"Vanilla, chocolate, or strawberry?"

He stared into my eyes. "Strawberry blonde." A smile escaped his sunburned lips as he slid a finger into a coil of my hair. "Strawberry. Every day. It's more interesting."

I matched his smile and raised my glass to toast "Kenny, was it?" who, as I found out much later that night, had a half share in my Hamptons house. Normally, it's don't shit where you eat, but share houses are weekends only. They're not elevator doorman buildings with uncomfortable someone-should-say-something mailrooms. Surely I could make an exception. Besides, strawberry!

"Yes, it's Kenny, but you can call me whatever you want." I wanted to verb his noun.

"Okay, see, now that was a line, my friend."

"What are you looking for in a man?" I stared at him blankly. Whenever a man asks this of you, he's hoping you'll describe him, right down to the favorite sport he likes to participate in but not watch. "See, now that's a line." He said it as if it were the punch line. "But now you have to answer."

"Have to, like I have to pay taxes, and have to be home by midnight?"

"I have news for you, little girl. I'm keeping you out past midnight." He smelled like flannel. "Now come on, tell me."

I stirred the remaining two olives in my glass, drank more than I'd expected to, and answered plainly. "I'm looking for a man with balls, Ken. Some serious stones. A man who can tell me the truth even when he knows I won't like what he has to say."

"Well, then you've come to the right barstool. I'm all balls, baby."

I returned my almost finished martini to its napkin on the bar, looked my new neighbor in the eyes and placed my hand firmly on his crotch. "Kenny Boy, no girl wants *all* balls." I let my hand linger on his groin, then slipped it back around the stem of my martini.

"Damn, girl, you just had your hand on my cock. That was awesome. Do it again." I loved that he said cock instead of dick. It meant he'd be good in bed.

"I'm trying really hard this summer not to repeat any of my old mistakes." And with a wink and a smile, I pivoted and found refuge in the arms of my beautiful friends. I knew, despite my flabby arms and the slight bump of my nose, I belonged with them. I was a member of the pack. After all, I had potential: I just pulled a *Pretty Woman* of my very own. And why not make the boy sweat it out a bit? It was summer, and there was always tomorrow night. Yum.

five

RED WINE
WITH FISH

HOW ABOUT THIS FOR A NOD TO INDEPENDENCE? I'M NOT fucking going. I hate Cabana and its Page Six customers, cloned out in couldn't-be-couture-but-I'll-pretend-it-is, consuming cosmopolitans, and speaking of "the left coast." It was Saturday night when my friends revealed their agenda for the eve, fanning out tickets to HBO's private kick-off party for *Entourage*. We'd begin our evening at Star Room, then hop to Cabana in Southampton, a motel made must-go meat market that crams in more boldfaced names than a tabloid paragraph. We'd mouth the words to all the exact same songs we'd been hearing all summer. I'd have sooner eaten a fistful of rancid chopped meat than join them. "Sweetie, are you sure you don't want to come? What will you do?"

"I'll do just fine. Have fun." This wasn't passive-aggressive—I genuinely wanted them to enjoy themselves, and doing so meant I couldn't participate in their night. If I had to abide more chair dancing on a velvet banquette, screaming to make Mickey Mouse conversation with girls who tried to figure out if I was more Longchamp than YSL, I'd have cast myself into the middle of the road and thrown myself in front of the Jitney. There had to be more to "the Hamps" than all the have-beens doing their should-be things. Besides, my breasts were too sunburned for a push-up bra.

After they'd gone, I braved the diva dungeon alone, ready to settle in with a book and the obligatory curl. I needed to stray from the pack, at least for a night. Otherwise, I'd have become that girl, the one who stands there with her arms folded, tapping a foot. I'd rest up so I could throw a barbecue birthday dinner for Dulce the next night.

Midcurl in the curling up with a good book process, there was a voice saying, "Knock, knock," by the dungeon door.

"Who's there?"

"Ken."

"Ken who?"

"Ken I come in?"

I was freshly showered and moisturized wearing an overpriced tank top sans bra and black Juicy capri velour pants. Damn straight he was coming in. But when I opened the door he was dressed in a conservative button-down, car keys in hand.

"Steph, what are you doing in here all by yourself? Aren't you coming out?"

"If coming out means Star Room or Jet, then no. I'm not."

"Well, what if it means Stephen Talkhouse and me?" Stephen Talkhouse was the one place in the Hamptons I knew was never a scene. Pine walls, pool table, paltry stage. It was perfect.

"It means I need five minutes." I took ten.

A COVER BAND WAS STRUMMING UB40'S "RED RED WINE" when we arrived at the Talkhouse with a few other people from our house. Good idea. I'd have some. On our struggle to approach the long narrow bar, Ken reached for my hand without looking back. I love when they do this. It's a move that throws any idea of platonic intention to the winds. He grabbed it and took his time, rubbing his thumb across my fingers like a blind person touching a face for the first time. "Oh man, I love this song." He shouted it casually, as if he hadn't had my pulse in his hand.

Once we made it to the bar, he pulled me into his hips. "So how long are we going to do this, Steph?" "This" meant not attack each other like African animals in heat.

"Aren't you supposed to ask me what I'd like to drink first?"

"I only ask questions I don't already know the answer to." There was a trace of laughter in his voice, and I somehow wanted to touch it.

"Someone met his minimum daily requirement of Vitamin S today."

"Vitaman S?"

"You've got a little too much Smug in your diet there, Sparky."

He smiled and bit his lower lip before adding, "I thought I told you, Steph, Ken is the funny one in this relationship." Then he tapped the tip of my nose with his finger. "You, my dear, are the pretty one. Don't go confusing things this early on in our relationship." *Our relationship?* I loved that he said it. Of course, I knew what he meant, that we didn't have a relationship, but it was a good sign that he wasn't afraid to say it. If that slipped from my mouth, I would have quickly apologized, fearing I'd scare him off. He then kissed the tip of my nose. "So like I said, how long are we going to do this? All you have to do is just . . ." he kissed my cheek. "Say." Then the other. "When." Then his lips brushed mine, softly at first. His hand pulled me in closer, and he kissed me like he meant it.

Once we came up for air, I glanced at him with a smile for a moment before mouthing the word, "When."

He tilted his head and stared at me, as if he were trying to observe the negative space of an important sculpture. It's the face my father makes when he's proud of me. It's the look I associate with love. Then he said, "Can we try that again, but this time can you tilt your head the other way?" I felt my eyebrows pinch together. "I'm a lefty," he added, as if it explained something. Since when is there a "right" and "left" way of kissing? I know there's a right way to kiss. It involves trying not to suffocate the person with your tongue, slobber on their chin, or make 'em worry you didn't eat enough dinner and want to consume their face in one big gulp without even a napkin. But a lefty kiss? Who makes this stuff up?

After our follow-up kiss, he drew his knuckle across my jaw, lifting a stray curl off my face and tucking it behind my ear. It was his power move. See, there's opening her side of the car first, the half-stand at the table, walking closer to the curb with her by your side. Those aren't power moves, they're manners. Ken had practiced moving misplaced hair mid-sentence everywhere. I wouldn't fall for him. Oh, please, it was too late.

We danced—okay, let's face it—we grinded to the stylings of one mister Johnny Cash and then some song about redheaded chicks. I almost got on stage but decided his hands felt better than any other attention could. With anyone else, I might have apologized for my sweat as I tried to wipe it off from under my tent of curls, but with Ken, I grabbed him by his wrist and led his hand beneath my shirt, to my slippery lower back. When he felt how wet I was, he drew me in closer, his breath warm on my neck. He kissed me hard; I tasted his want.

When it got too hot, he led me outside, where we drank from plastic cups to cool off. He told me about his family, his nephew. "Yeah, he's my sister's son from her first marriage." When I heard "first marriage," I knew there was a second. It made me feel better. It meant he wouldn't be judgmental.

"Yeah, I'm divorced too," I said before taking a long sip of my mint julep.

"Oh, I'm sorry." I hate when people say this. No one died.

"It's okay, it was a long time ago." It was less than a year ago.

"Yeah, break-ups suck," he said. We both looked down at his shoes. He was kicking his feet. "So what happened? Why didn't it work?"

I'm never sure how to answer this one, unsure of how much detail to reveal. It's like an employer asking you why you want to leave your current job. Because it sucks the big fat hairy moose cock, that's why! "Oh, I'm just ready for a change. I've reached my potential there."

"Honestly, it didn't work because I was too ambitious." Ah, the perfect answer. Right up there with, "Um, yeah, I would have to say my biggest flaw is that I'm a perfectionist." Riiiiiight.

"Too ambitious? Come on."

"No, really, women of my generation were told all our lives we could be or do anything we set our minds to: a doctor, lawyer, molested White House intern. So growing up, 'I will get whatever I want if I work hard enough' became my morning mantra, stirred that shit into my day with the honey in my farina." Ken began to lean in closer. "And guess what? It worked. I got everything I wanted. The grades, the school, the jobs. But no one ever told me it didn't apply when dealing with relationships. Kinda fucked myself there."

"I don't understand."

"I was so used to getting what I wanted, as long as I worked at it. So, naturally, when it came to relationships, if I decided I wanted it enough, I assumed it would work out. Look, I was married to a charming Jewish docta! Okay? I was married to the perfect piece of paper, and having that made me feel . . ." I hesitated. "Made me feel worthy. Important. I don't know. It just felt like it was one more thing on life's to-do list I could cross off." Shut it, Klein. "But, it wasn't. You just can't work hard enough for two people."

"And he didn't want to work?" I was startled by the green in his eyes I'd never seen before.

"He was lazy. The guy sat down to pee. I should've known."

"Uh-oh. Remind me never to pee in your presence." He laughed at his joke, then pinched my waist. I wiggled to break free from his embrace. "You're not getting rid of me that fast, Steph." Then he kissed me. "So, does this mean you've sworn off weddings?"

"Given that I never had a wedding, I certainly can't swear off them. But if you're asking if I've sworn off marriage, well, I'll let you know if you're ever on bended knee."

"You never had a wedding? Come on." And this is how it goes, every single time.

No one believes me when I say it: "We eloped." They bounce back with, "Come on!" They smell my hair products and eye my pedicure, thinking I'm high maintenance. No one can believe, at the end of the day, I didn't care about a stupid wedding. I was never *that* girl, the one who dreamt of her wedding day. I dreamt of being a singer or a writer but never a bride. I always skipped that step in the dreams and went straight to the wife and mom part, imagining myself in driving loafers planning a Make Your Own Taco night. But I did care about missing the dance with my father.

WHILE I NEVER IMAGINED IT, IT'S NOW SOMETHING I'LL never forget. May 20, 2000. The day Gabe and I eloped. Actually, eloped isn't the right word. It implies romance and a sandy island somewhere, me with a bikini bottom embroidered, "Just Married." Ours was a secretive marriage, and it felt shameful. I was nervous it wouldn't happen. I told Gabe I wanted to know it was what he wanted, not something he was doing for me, not something to be pressured into. He responded with love, saying, "While I'm not happy with the situation, I still know this is something I want. I know I want to marry you, Stephanie." It was overcast. Gray and spitting, as if God just sneezed. Gabe began to cry in the cab ride downtown. I kept looking out the window, praying. Praying for God to give me strength no matter what the outcome, and I didn't even know if I believed in God. Some force, anything, just give me strength. Once we arrived at the synagogue, we walked inside holding hands. I pushed the elevator button. Once it arrived, he asked if we could take the next one. "Steph, I don't know if I can do this." He was white.

"Are you going to faint?"

"I might." He trembled.

"Let's go, they're waiting for us." I whispered.

We got off the elevator and arrived on the second floor.

"I can't go in there," he said. "I'm not ready. Maybe if I was given the chance to get here in my own time I'd be able to, but—"

"Don't give me that. Here we go. Let me say this, Gabe. This is it. This is what it comes down to. If you can't do this, fine. But you might as well leave here alone because I will never see or speak to you again. This is what it all comes down to."

"I need fresh air and time to think."

I went in alone to speak with the rabbi and cantor. I went in ALONE. It's our goddamn wedding day, and he doesn't know—I don't know— what's going to happen next. The rabbi, with his gold chain and blue necktie, looked like a shriveled up Rocky Balboa, except his eyes were gentle and inviting. The cantor, Romina of all names, had a soothing, soft voice. She smelled like wet wool and dry cleaner steam. I sat and explained to them how nervous Gabe was, how controlling his parents were, how torn he was feeling. "My God, what if he doesn't come back? What if I'm some girl sitting in a synagogue in all white and he doesn't—"

Romina rubbed my shoulder and said, "Well, this is the true test. This is the moment. Now is the moment of truth, and you'll know forever. Have courage and faith." It was as if I were sitting with God.

I went outside to check for Gabe, and he said he couldn't do it, that he thought he'd be more ready. I told him to "go inside and tell them so." I wanted him to say the words to someone else. I needed to hear them again, with a witness beside me. I should have handed him my heels and run full speed in the other direction. Shit, I hate myself for how much I wanted him.

Upstairs, he cleared his throat and apologized to the rabbi for keeping him waiting. The rabbi motioned for us to sit beside him. Gabe told the rabbi he loved me, and before he could say much more, the rabbi responded, "That is all I needed to hear from you. Do it then, we shall?" The man was Yoda before Lucas went mechanical. I felt safe, like the rabbi was on my side, the good side.

Gabe asked if he could speak with me outside the room again. That's when he spilled it.

"It's just that I'm afraid if it doesn't work out, I'll have to pay you a quarter of my earnings for the rest of my life if we get divorced, and fifty percent of marriages end in divorce. It's worse for doctors, and I don't want to get punished for something I'm worried about. So I want you to sign a prenuptial agreement." I heard his father's voice. "My father gave me a lot of money for me to start a practice one day, and . . ."

"Please. Holy fuck, I would never want any of that money." And I didn't. When we were going through our divorce, I wanted no part of any money he had before we married. I didn't want anything that belonged to that family, including their son. Gabe's waiting until the minute before we married to bring up a prenup was as unexpected as being served red wine with fish. He wanted an out because he was afraid. I was afraid, too, but I wasn't about to sign over my security. I was supporting him, keeping our home, paying his credit card debts, and I'd be

sacrificing and tolerating his long hours, too. I told him "fine" after argu-
ing for a while because I wanted to marry him and thought he was just
scared. When he heard me agree, he turned around completely, grabbing
my hand and walking me to the rabbi.

"We're ready now," he said without wavering.

The rabbi prayed, we signed our names, Gabe began to cry, but this
time, it was joy. He couldn't stop smiling, and looked at me the way I
always wanted him to, the way my father looks at me when he's proud.
I knew he loved me like family, and I didn't have to earn it. I could just
be me.

Gabe was elated, and I was confused. He went from terror-stricken,
trembling, ready to faint, to ecstatic. He kept asking the rabbi if he could
kiss me yet. I cried the entire time, the one day neither of us brought tissues. When I later brought up the prenuptial agreement, he said, "I agree,
we're above that. I was just nervous. I am so happy you're my wife. I'll
never leave you." I believed him.

WHEN KEN AND I WERE READY TO LEAVE, WE SURVEYED
the bar looking for anyone from the share house. Specifically, we were
searching for his friend Sherman, who looked like a bull mastiff but had
the voice of a dachshund. Privately, I called him Meathead all summer.
There's always one Meathead. It's like every state having a Springfield.
"Do you think Meathead and Ken will be at the house this weekend?"
"Do you think Meathead does that on purpose?" Halfway through the
summer, I stopped trying to conceal it and called Sherman Meathead to
his face.

"Hey, Meathead, she asked you three times. Can you please get off
the hood of her car?" It was like breaking wind for the first time in a new
romance.

He didn't seem to mind. Instead he offered up a goofy smile, flashed
a dimple, and said, "Cool. I finally have a nickname." Then he climbed
down from the roof of Salila's car (whom I nicknamed Saliva) and
quickly joined the other boys by the grill, looking hapless, circling, in

need of a task. Meathead looked like he always had to go to the bathroom.

"A-D-D," someone whispered.

"There's no need to whisper. Meathead has no shame." I felt like his mother. He needed more chew toys.

Meathead must have hitched a ride home with Saliva. Perhaps they'd hit it off and exchange some. Ken and I headed toward the car holding hands. The salt-swept street was surprisingly tranquil and pink. He pressed me against the passenger side door of his car before unlocking it for me, sliding his hands around my waist. He kissed me, then said, "I'm so glad this happened." "This" was "us," the couple we were becoming. I wanted to shriek and tell him I felt like the luckiest girl, that we were so perfect together. Instead I kissed him back and smiled, knowing full well that voicing any of this would cause his hands to move from caressing my waist to a protective stance involving hands cupped over balls.

My phone began to vibrate. "It's three in the morning. Who the hell is calling me?" After looking at the caller ID, I smiled. "It's the girls. Hello ladies?"

"Oh my God, Stephanie, you're awake. Can you please pick us up? We're on the side of the road in front of Star Room." It was Dulce, and she sounded like she had to pee.

"Well, I'm not exactly home." I covered the mouthpiece and asked Ken, "Can we pick up Alex and Dulce at Star Room?"

He smiled, nodded his head affirmatively, and opened my door with a grand bowing gesture. "Your chariot awaits, and so do your drunken friends. Ken to the rescue."

"I'm with Ken leaving Talkhouse. We'll be there soon."

ONCE WE PULLED INTO THE DRIVEWAY OF OUR HOUSE, each of us stepping out from the car, Ken didn't offer to hold my hand. I worried he was embarrassed to show his want for me to the others. It felt like camp, and I suddenly felt twelve.

"I wonder if Sherman made it home," Ken finally said, walking up to the house, two steps at a time. He then searched the house while I poured myself a goblet of red wine. What the hell. I slipped out back and found refuge in a hammock. I wanted to hide. After some time, Ken poked his head out from the sliding door on the porch. "Hey Steph, I've been looking all over for you." He walked toward me looking less confident, almost like a kid up at bat after his second strike. "Care for some company?"

"Sure, but I'm not sharing my wine, so get your own," I half mocked.

He joined me in the hammock, and then for no reason at all offered up, "Steph, I really like you." I knew a "but" was coming. Anything after "but" is what really matters. Here we go. I couldn't brace anything. "But I just got out of a relationship. Actually, she broke up with me, and it's kinda why I'm here. I'm trying to get over it." I hated that I let him touch my sweat, that he knew how I kissed. I wanted to collect my things from him, but the things were only moments. "But I really like you. Look, I could've been an ass and just used you, but I respect you."

"You don't even know me. How can you respect me?" Now I was pissed. I let my shoe dangle from the tip of my foot as I drank more wine and thought of what to not say next.

"You remind me of Howard Roark." What the hell? "Have you read *The Fountainhead*?"

"No."

"Well, now you have to." Of course I had to. I needed to see who he thought I was. "You are so much like the protagonist. You just don't give a shit what people say—you do your own thing, and you see the world differently." He then pointed to one of the trees from which the hammock was suspended. "See this tree? I see an oak tree, but when someone like you sees it, you envision a pile of wood to make fire and light. You see the potential in things."

"No, that would make me destructive." I didn't know if "Thank you" would work.

"Well, you get what I'm saying, though. You see potential in ordinary things. I see it in the photographs you took this weekend. You notice things I would have otherwise never seen."

I didn't understand where all of this was coming from. It was flattering that he thought he knew me after such a short time. He saw in me what I did, and that made him all the more desirable—unavailable, but desirable. What a cliché.

"Look, Steph, I'm not telling you I just got out of a relationship because I don't think we can work. I'm telling you so you know where I'm coming from. I just want to take things slowly because I still love her." *Love her.* I could see the words, but I still wasn't sure he actually said them aloud.

"Okay, you've told me. Now I know." I felt doctor-naked, the kind when, at twelve, you're just beginning to sprout hair and bud things, and they make you do a naked duck walk on the cold tile floor so they can check for scoliosis. He'd only moments ago said, "I'm so glad this happened." And now, what? Forget this. I pushed my legs forward and tried to get up. In my rush to leave, though, my red wine spilled all over the center of his checkered button-down shirt.

He didn't even flinch. He just lay there, defeated. "You missed," he said flatly, as if I were aiming for the dramatic drink-in-the-face maneuver.

"Baby, no. It's you who has missed." Dear Lord. Me and my ABC daytime TV mouth. It almost makes me want to vomit in its telling.

Dulce was passed out, still dressed in something she ought to have apologized to someone for, on a sofa in the common area. When I opened the door to our room, I heard a female gasp. It was Sherman, peeking his shaggy blond head out from beneath Alexandra's comforter. It was musical beds. I needed *my*Pod. "Sorry, sorry, I'm not looking. And I'll crank up my iPod so you two can do your thing."

Alex began to laugh. "Please, Stephanie, we're not doing anything. Sherman was busy telling me about the mating rituals of hippos."

"Rhinos," he corrected her.

"Anyway, sweetie, why aren't you in Ken's room?" Alex sat upright and began to swig gulps of her Poland Spring water as I spoke.

"Oh, forget Ken. He's not over his ex. It's too unnerving."

"Quit sounding all Les Miz about it and tell me what you mean." Alexandra is amazingly patient and interested in all of my dramatics.

"I mean, we have this great night, we kiss, and I like him so much."

"And the problem happens when?"

"When I open my mouth usually. Ugh, Alex, I just can't take it. I really like him—"

"What do you like about him?" I knew this was a test. I had to think. What did I like about him? I liked how much he liked me, that I was attracted to him, that . . . I had no idea.

"I like how witty he is, and the way he touches me and makes me laugh."

"Okay, and the problem?"

"Ugh, he tells me he's so glad this all happened, blah blah, and then we come back here, and he's all, you know my ex just dumped me, right? What the fuck? I am not getting involved with someone unavailable." I was becoming animated, my hands slicing through the air. "Not going to do it."

"Angel, you have to give him a chance. You're being silly."

"Yeah, besides, she was Asian," Meathead added.

"So."

"So she's Asian," he said again as if it explained everything. I blinked at him waiting for more. "Ken's not going to marry some Asian chick. He'll fuck her, yeah. Get that whole fetish thing over with, and then he'll marry someone who's good at hiding his matzo." Meathead needed a plug. "Just go back in there and tell him you're better than she is. Ask him to show you his matzo balls."

"Sherman, are you four? Alex, shut him up."

"Sherman, quiet!" Alex scolded him with a pointed finger, then broke into a smile only I could see.

"No really, I mean, getting dumped sucks, but when she's Asian, it really sucks," Meathead continued, but I tuned out the rest.

"Cookie, you have to stop preemptively ending things before they even start. I know you're afraid of making yourself vulnerable, but if you keep impeding things before they even begin, just out of fear, you'll never know." I'd never know joy. Shit damn. I worried she was right.

What if I was snapping into "screw you, your loss" mode too fast? How do you take back, "No, you're the one who missed"? Me and my drama trap doors.

"KNOCK. KNOCK." IT WAS MY TURN.

"Who's there?"

"Steph."

"Steph who?"

"Steph up and answer the door before I change my mind."

It was how I did sorry.

The rest was kinetic. Like riding a bike or learning rhythm, you learn by doing it. Your body has a memory, remembering what you've forced out—trauma, pain, a kiss. My head does what it can to force out pain, to keep things in check, hush vulnerability to a scant whisper. But my body makes up for it. It accepts affection, and it gives.

After some kissing, he began to trace a pattern on my stomach with his thumb, occasionally slipping it beneath my underwear. That's when I decided to fake *not* having my period. Read that again. I know your immediate instinct might involve pregnancy, a woman tricking a man into thinking she might be pregnant. Let him feel heavy with guilt and the like. Well, I don't do that, and that's not what this is about.

I didn't fake having my period, pulling the Advil equivalent of "not tonight honey, I have a headache." I *had* my period but didn't want him to know it. I just knew; I felt it, suddenly. How exactly do you fake not having your period when you do indeed have it? You get rid of the evidence.

"I'll be right back," I whispered before quietly stealing away to the bathroom. My suspicion was correct. I discovered the spot in my underwear, so I ripped them off, tucked them in a balled fist, and buried them in a travel bag I had stored beneath the bathroom sink. I flushed the tampon applicator and wrapper. I tucked in the string. What evidence? Had

I been a cat, I might have choked up a feather, but if I had, he wouldn't have noticed. He wasn't exactly looking at my mouth.

I climbed back into bed, wearing only my sweat shorts, so the last thing he'd suspect was "period." Why all this effort? I easily could have just told him I had my period, but then I wouldn't have earned good girl points. See, he had to think I was being "good." Had I not had my period, I probably wouldn't have pushed his hand away, but men need to think you're tough and valuable. They enjoy working for it and don't want it from a woman who gives it up too easily. So, I omitted the truth and let him believe I was, indeed, a good girl, with a little curl. "Goodnight, Mr. Ken."

I tried to fall asleep in his bed as we listened to The Rolling Stones' "Wild Horses," an iPod earbud in each of our ears. In the dark of his room, I flipped onto my stomach and silently rehashed, parsing through the moments of my day, like cards laid flat on a coffee table. How would I ever meet someone if I always killed it before it began? And that's all it was, a beginning. Why did I have to make every guy I met into "could he be the one"? I hardly knew him. I was in like with an idea.

Declaring "I hate games" was my way of excusing impatience. If games aren't played, things move along quickly without anxiety. People cannonball off the cliff, plunging into relationship waters without forethought, before knowing the first thing about the other person, save for how much they're liked back. Then they're left hanging onto driftwood, hoping to stay afloat. Damn, I should've known better. It can't be "he's A-MAZE-ING" before I learn how he handles anger, stress, or his mother. He couldn't be "sweetheart" before I knew what kind of drunk he was, how he handled deadlines, phone messages, or me when I've gone and chicked out in the middle of the night. At least I could cross that last one off the list.

As for independence, I was glad I'd decided to leave the pack for the night and, despite it all, I was still looking up, anticipating some fireworks. Even if I was the one who had to conjure my own noise and light. I've always been wicked good at that.

FAR FROM MONTAUK, ONCE MY FEET WERE FIRMLY planted back on Manhattan concrete, I did some math. Turns out two e-mails and an IM do not equal a phone call. Ken hadn't called all week, and his e-mails were noncommittal where plans were concerned. He was working things out with his ex. I didn't need a theorem or proof. Perhaps I could've had Alex call Meathead to get the scoop. No. Bad. Okay, new mantra. "I'll work hard enough for the both of us" would be replaced with a deep breath, followed by, "Let. It. Go." Letitgo.

I couldn't let it go. Instead I hit the refresh button of my e-mail. "Come to Momma." Oh yes. Then the e-mail that turned it all around bubbled to the top of my inbox:

Yo dude, pencil in Aug 2nd to be my date (if you want) for the premiere to "Open Water," the "scariest shark movie since Jaws," aka the "Blair Fish Project." Not confirmed yet that I am going, but I'll know soon. Peace out.

—K

That sealed it for me. Let it go, indeed. Normally, girls are excited when he talks of the future, committing to things in advance, showing his faith in the relationship. This was not one of those times. This was a Skipper e-mail. You know, Skipper, of Ken and Barbie. Okay, fine, let me explain.

Some girls collected floppy bunnies with pink noses and whiskers, fluffy white kittens with rhinestone collars, or stuffed bears with X-stitched eyes. Their otherwise flat rooms had hills of mushy companions along their dresser tops, with puffs of soft cotton, hovering like mountain caps. Stuffed dolls were strewn in the valleys between throw pillows on floral bedding, there for hugs and to sponge childhood tears. I was not one of these girls.

Bunnies, kitty cats, and bears don't have breasts. There was nothing sexual about any of them, so they never, not one, ever appealed to me, but there was always Barbie. My Barbies always made it on the first date.

Barbie had fragrant sweet-smelling plastic hair, shiny, flowing like a river, while Skipper, her kid sis, was unscented and forced to wear overalls and bangs. Barbie got insane proportions, a 1950s waist and slim, sculpted calves leading to her always-pointed toes. Always. Clearly Barbie was always midorgasm, her ass cheeks clenched in pleasure, her arms slightly hovering as if she were unsure where they belonged, and there, hiding beneath her petticoat, a square, wide vagina. Ken was behind the orgasms. Skipper stayed home and masturbated.

Skipper, in contrast to the orgasmic Barbie, was more board than babe. Flat, uniform, solid, like a square digital clock. You couldn't find an hourglass anywhere near her. She counted the minutes until she'd see Ken again, scheming away during those long pent-up nights while Ken and Barbie relaxed in Malibu tossing a beach ball. How wretched. Ken would never see Skipper as a Barbie. She'd always be that pal, the one who got relegated to the backseat of the Barbie Jeep. And when he dropped her off at home, he shouted, "Peace out," rather than planning their next encounter.

I am not Skipper. I'm not a buddy or a pal. I don't want pats on the head or to be called DUDE by men. I do not have a penis. I have a vagina that works, that's anatomically correct, and I'd like to be treated as such. And that's how Skipper felt, but Skipper didn't have a book with chapters about oral sex.

If I responded to Ken's e-mail with a "sure, sounds fun" e-mail, I would be reinforcing the behavior. It would be like introducing myself as Skipper in place of Stephanie. Instead, I phoned him.

"Look, I don't want to be your buddy. Clearly, you're working things out with your ex." I knew it wouldn't work. Usually, "going back" to an ex is just "going backward." They do it because they're lazy, lonesome, and lustful. One of them claims "love." So they reconcile and begin to order in dinner and watch their shows again, too lethargic to autopsy what went wrong in the first place. Then the wrong creeps back in again, leaving you sad, missing the times you ordered in and watched your shows.

Ugh, there was no point in trying to convince him he was making a mistake. Forget words, even. It wouldn't have mattered if I'd just applied a fresh coat of Want lipstick, kissed my skin with his favorite scent, and paid seventy-five dollars for a Bumble and Bumble blowout and spoken with him in person. He wouldn't want me more. The boy needed to figure it out on his own. Let it go!

"So, I'm just calling to wish you the best. I'm not closing a door here. I'm just letting you know how I'd like mine to be opened."

"Fair enough, Steph. Fair enough." Christ, what a Malibu line.

The only skipping I'd be doing was right past Malibu Ken. I might have been a little more Skipper than I would have liked to be in my past, but now I'm more Barbie. More Veronica than Betty, more Ginger than Mary Ann, more Laverne than Shirley, and don't even bring up Thelma or whatshername 'cause they were just crazy. I'm more Puss than Boots, more arsenic than old lace, more seek than hide, and yes, more Lady than Tramp . . . despite the penis grabbing. And, now, hells yeah, I was letting it go.

NEXT.

six

THE ORAL SEX SOUTH BEACH DIET

THE AFTERNOON DATE IS A BIT OF A QUANDARY. SOME BE-
lieve it's his true attempt at getting to know you. He cares less about the
hook-up and more about something substantial. He wants to get to know
you without the alcohol, makeup, and heels. Yes, he's just that into you.
And if you adore each other, afternoon parlays into evening.

There's, of course, another school of thought, majoring in noncom-
mitment. According to Dulce, "If he really liked you, he'd book you for a
Saturday night. Period." He's hedging his bets, so if your time together is
intolerable, he still has an out and alternate plans for dinner.

I subscribe to the latter, except I actually prefer afternoon dates.
They feel like courting. Poodle skirts, malteds, and the beginning of
something. Afternoons typically mean walks through some park on the
way to something, something more, you hope. You smell it in the grass,
see it in the dog leashes, and children with balloons tied to their wrists.
Weekend afternoons remind me of family, so the date feels like a beginning, like a chance, laden with promise and friendship, more real in the
daylight where you can't counterfeit chemistry with two glasses of Veuve
Clicquot.

I was certain Christian said, "Proper date," so I anticipated his showing up for one. You know, at my door. Maybe along with a woefully romantic gesture of a lone red rose wrapped in plastic from the bodega
beside my apartment. I'd even say, "How nice," and pretend it had a
scent. I should have known he'd disappoint me. He was Gabe with an accent.

Midweek at the outdoor garden of the Hudson Hotel, I'd met Christian, a thirty-three-year-old Eurosexual sponging off someone in Manhattan. It was worse than metrosexualism. Tack on an arresting British accent, chaotic hair I knew he'd molded with designer "mud," and discourtesy often favorably confused for detachment, and you've landed yourself one of your very own Eurosexuals. This wasn't the plan, of course, to meet another creampuff of a man who preferred tanning beds and vintage over *my* bed and vagina. But I decided to put my reservations on hold and entertain his "proper afternoon date" invitation. Maybe it was time I took "holiday" from judgmental.

Though it's a tall order not to judge the urban dater who believes he's clever for suggesting the zoo. It's just so milk and water. The zoo has been done, I mean really *done*, and it's never as exciting or original as it sounds. I'm left feigning interest in the behavior of western lowland gorillas and, in turn, of the "clever" date who's obsessed with the reptile wing. Far worse than the zoo, though, is when a date suggests we "check out *the* new art exhibit." As if by saying "the" I'm supposed to already know he means the much-awaited Guggenheim display. It's not like I'm anti-art, but I prefer to visit museums alone, to stroll at my own pace and discover something just for me. I enjoy it quietly, inside myself. Typically, though, I got roped into these anesthetizing dates out of old-fashioned pity. I'd choke up a "sounds fun" at the mention of art, otherwise my taupe date would read me actual reviews of an exhibit. Yes, that's right. Plural. *Reviews*. I won't so much as glance in the general direction of a movie review, fearing it'll influence my thinking.

Because Christian was an art dealer, I was expecting the worst of it, certain he'd suggest we hit the galleries, the ones with reviews I assumed he'd dog-eared from varied sources. I was sure I was screwed. I'd sooner have plucked my entire pubic area than spend my Sunday afternoon proving I could discern Kandinsky from Chagall. But twenty minutes after our date was scheduled to begin, when I still hadn't heard from the cunning Eurosexual, the museum didn't sound so bad. It was certainly better than being stood up.

I deserved it. Why was I even considering going out with this man?

He was all flash, right down to his bleached Invisalign smile. Clearly, I was only interested in him because of those dimples, the nose, and his man scent. He smelled like Sicilian citrus, rosemary, and shaving cream. I was sure his cologne came in an orange leather box.

Okay, so he did have some redeeming qualities. As an art dealer and European, he came across as cultured and world-traveled, educated, and poised. He reminded me of my grammar school librarian, Mrs. Charles, who read us fables on rainy afternoons beside her twirling lantern that cast shapes on the walls around us. Christian, and his velvety British accent, was a whirlpool of mesmerizing, and when near him, I couldn't help but stare at his shapes. It's exactly why I deserved to be stood up, favoring little more about him than his looks. I warranted a life of knit one, purl two, cats, and old maid clichés. But since I was terrified I'd be lonely for the rest of my life, I allowed my happiness to rest in the manicured hands of an Englishman in New York. I was worse than a Sting song.

Despite what I deserved, on the half-hour, I received a too-loud phone call from my too-late date. "Yeah, come to 'Felix,' dahling." I was both relieved and insulted. Relieved he hadn't stood me up completely, reassured he wasn't suggesting a day of art, but irritated that my walking pocket square was hardly an old-school gentleman. I sort of hated him. The kind of hate I couldn't sit home with. I'd need to yell at him properly. Besides, I looked too good to sit home alone.

Restaurant Felix, on a Sunday afternoon, was a Eurotrash nightclub hiding in skin-tight bistro clothing. It was the epicenter of Eurosexuals, teeming with dark-haired men who stood in the middle of the restaurant, hovering above their cassoulets, nicoises, and croque monsieurs. They hawked their prey by extending a new glass of their old French wines to a gallery of deserving talent. "Deserving" meant she summered in Monaco, owned a leather corset or four, or screwed one of his friends who subsequently touted her as "the bouncing bird." When I first saw Christian, his French-cuffed arm was draped 'round the narrow shoulders of one of these very men. He was wearing narrow faded Diesel jeans, two sizes too small for even me to ever wear. I felt like the man immediately. This was his Sunday afternoon station. I was not "deserving."

Upon seeing me, he whispered, "Don'tworrylove, we'llbedininga-lone." If calligraphy had a sound, it came from Christian's mouth, in one winding strip. I was unsure of where one word ended and the next began, but I didn't mind. His breath in my ear felt like want. He introduced me to the Jean-Lucs, Edgars, and Pieros of his crowd. In a phrase: SPF anti-wrinkle moisturizer. That pretty much summed the crew up; thirty-somethings who took the year off to party, absorbing time at safari-themed nightclubs, spending their days fakin' bakin' it after waxing everything from their brows and backs to their sacks and cracks. I could almost smell the melanin.

At a small wooden table toward the back of the restaurant, Christian offered me the girl seat, the one against the wall with the view. "Fabulous top," he commented as he draped a napkin on his lap. This made me smile. Scarves are my signature. I use them for everything: belts, beach sarongs, headbands, and yes, as tops.

If there were a soundtrack to this next part, you'd hear Carly Simon's "You're So Vain," and you'd turn up the volume. You'd start to really sing along for the chorus, but you'd picture Gabe's face when you heard, "You had one eye in the mirror as you watched yourself gavotte." Routinely The *Was*band complained I dressed too matronly, without ever using the word matronly. He'd regularly survey my closet. "What the fuck, Stephanie, you act like you're fifty. No one our age wears scarves." As he held up my Anya Hindmarch snakeskin bag, he'd command, "Go buy some Gucci, and get with it." Gabe would stand shaking his head, in a saw-horse stance, and judge the contents of my closet as if it were a Rothko. "Here, take my gift certificate and buy something. You need it more than I do." Clearly, when I agreed to marry him, I gave him the wrong finger.

When the waiter approached to recite the specials, Christian interrupted him without apology. "Yes, we'd like sparkling water for the table and a bottle of your Châteauneuf-du-Pape." I wasn't in the mood for either. I arrive at a bistro mid-July and I'm thinking two things. Mussels and mussels. And where I come from, that means vin blanc. Maybe it was his way of taking control, proving to me he could be the man in the relationship, despite his waxed brows?

Open mind. Open. Mind. Good girl.

He ordered his burger well done, which meant he was terrified of death. Why else would you char a perfectly good piece of cow? After submerging the patty in a swamp of Dijon mustard, he removed the bun, placing it on his pristine bread plate. Would he butter it first? I'm afraid not. His bread plate was his discard station, housing all the unwanted food objects from his main dinner plate. This made me think of a child. "Mommy, eww. Take it." A child would whine, unable to eat his dinner if a pickle touched his burger. Christian had pickle issues and then some.

"What are you doing?" I asked in a voice that definitely conveyed disgust.

"Dahling, carbs are the enemy." *No*, I thought, *you, my friend, are the enemy, your own worst enemy*. He was a thin man with a thin frame, and he wouldn't touch a carb. I imagined a life with him where he'd eventually refuse to dine out and insist on eating chicken from a can. He then began to cut his burger into manageable bites, all at once, like a mother cutting her child's lamb. He was such a Mary.

This is where I need to stop. If you're a man watching your weight, counting those carbs, do it off peak, please. While dining with a lady, if you happen to eat your burger without the bun, anticipate "visions." The visions flashing before your date's eyes are not of pectorals or biceps. Here's what she sees: you double-knotting laces, you racing to the bathroom after sex to clean, you holding surprise inspections of your children's sock drawers. All that from a missing bun? Oh yes, because chances are a man who kiboshes the carbs is also quite inept in the bedroom. He might as well just order the fruit plate for dessert. Nothing says "lights-off-only sex" like a dish of berries in lieu of the chocolate soufflé. If he's that picky about what he'll eat at the table, I promise he'll be just as finicky about what he eats in the bedroom. Eurosexuals are so concerned with following decorum, having the "it" cell phone and designer body, that they never really let go. When they hear *unbridled* instead of *passion*, they conjure images of an Hermès Oxer Buffalo Saddle and riding breeches. But hey, I could've been wrong.

So one black bowl of mussels and fries later, I was determined to find out. I needed to give Mr. Eurosexual the benefit of the doubt. It wouldn't be fair to categorize him as a Gabe too quickly. I needed more data to plot along the axis of "ex" and "why?" That meant giving him a chance. It made sense at the time.

"I need to get this out of the way now," he said as he leaned across our table, "because I've wanted to do this all day." A glint of tongue, a shimmer of wet tooth, his lips full and ready. He kissed me softly. It felt like he was opening a present, pulling the bow apart in one smooth sweep and pull. I felt myself open to him, wanting to become easier, less judgmental, and as fast as that, in a single kiss, I caught power. His coveting me made me feel worthy and important, beautiful. He was proud to be seen with me, introduced me to his friends, in front of whom he now just kissed me. He wasn't afraid to wear his want, which meant something because Gabe rarely did, worried someone might sneeze up a "pussy-whipped" and smack an "L" on his forehead. Gabe was more "L" than libido.

"I really want to get to know you. So far, I think you're just fahntastic, but I want to learn so much more."

"Well, that was nice of you to say, Christian." His wanting me made me want him back.

"No really, I do." He held my hand with both of his. "Dahling, let me see your card." This is why afternoon dates rival evenings. The proof: he wanted to see where I worked, my title, my address so he could send me flowers at the office. I began to fish for my maroon business card. Once I extended it with a smile, he corrected me in a whisper, "No, dahling, your AmEx."

Holy motherfucker.

He actually whispered it to me, as if he were telling me something mortifying, as if he'd noticed I'd just had my period in my new white pants. I knew Felix had sautéed skate fish with capers on the menu. I just had no idea I'd already had *Cheap*skate staring at me from across the bistro table. Here he was dressed to the nines, sporting Paul Smith every-thing, and the boy spent more on his cufflinks than my half of the bill. Who does this? And then he actually exhaled with a smile and the word *Dutch*. It wasn't about the money. It's about being a woman and feeling taken care of. If it's raining out, and we're circling for a parking spot, I would hope he'd be chivalrous enough to suggest dropping me off first while he looked for a spot. Opening doors, standing to greet people, and looking people in the eye are basic points of entry. Of course, I believe it all comes out in the wash, that a woman should offer to pay, eventually, let him know she's with him for him, not for what he buys her, or where he takes her. But when your date mentions the word *Dutch*, it better be about the clogs he thinks you'll look cute in. Going Dutch is nastier than giving head after anal sex. I'd sooner pay for the entire thing. So, I handed him the AmEx prepared to do just that.

Christian instructed the waiter to split the bill between our cards. I wasn't about to argue. I became annoyed and tried to breathe through it. On my count to ten, I reminded myself to be open-minded. I mean, enough with nixing men too prematurely. I had to give him a chance. He was, after all, trying to establish a business with his brother, whom he'd repeatedly referred to as his "nagging wife." Instead of pigeonholing him as cheap, perhaps fiscally responsible made more sense? Oh please, I wasn't buying any of it.

The boy had class, all of it low. He was cheap, but at least I knew what I was dealing with. He was pretty, very pretty, and smelled like packaged goods. I knew we didn't have longevity, but for the night, at least, he was a cute guy who'd fill a need. It had been a few months. He was there, and he had dimples to die for. Okay, so the boy was nothing more than a Hostess Twinkie. Twinkies are easy, simple, and self-contained, but they're concoctions, always leaving you unsatisfied. Oh God, I married a Twinkie, and now I was on a date with another one. Forget South Beach or Fatkins, I needed Sugar-Busters, stat.

HERE'S HOW IT WENT DOWN AT MY PLACE: HE DIDN'T. That's the point. Maybe it was my fault. Maybe I'd sent him the wrong message by changing into navy sweats in my bathroom. It was tricky, figuring out what to slip on before he slipped it all off. It was already implied that he'd be spending the night, but since we weren't going at it yet, I wasn't sure how to get from A (standing around) to B (messing around). We were mildly soused and about to *not* watch a movie. Let me be clear, this was a casual first time sleep-over, not a let-me-at-you-now grab fest. So, I didn't know what to wear to bed or where to change into my oh-so-(in)appropriate outfit. My armoire heaved with sexy underthings: garters, thigh-highs, and silk. But those are boyfriend goods, for when you're keeping things racy. It's not for beginnings. So I seized an itty bitty wife-beater, lacy boyshorts, and sweatpants.

I didn't realize, by wearing sweats to bed, I was issuing a "don't think of touching me" missive. I was so not stripping down to a t-back thong to not watch *Hope Floats*. Since I didn't own anything with the name Orchid or Weeks in it, I could have gone as obvious as *Secretary* or *Unfaithful*. But really, make-out movies with erotic scenes are the equivalent of a high school date, where he's cued up Eric Clapton's "Wonderful Tonight" on his car tape cassette player after our "let's go ice-skating" date. I might as well have piped in some Morcheeba music and shrouded myself in black mesh. It's been done. I wanted to be undone.

If I'd been to the gym or skipped a few meals, if my stomach felt flat, I would've disrobed casually as if I were alone. But I wouldn't let him behold my behind because of the cellulite. If I were slightly more stewed, I might have made him watch me undress. I know there's nothing sexier than confidence, that he wouldn't notice the five pounds, but sometimes I'm overcome with shy. So in the meanwhile, I'd be an "I'll just be a minute" girl toting sleepwear to the john. Yick. The john. I mean the loo. I thought it was all about the lace boyshorts. You know, as long as I was the one wearing them. Clearly it wasn't.

Christian was wearing a black mesh pouch for underwear. No, not underwear, a thong, a full-on man thong. I can't believe any man who isn't in the porn industry would own this. He spent money on this garish display and wouldn't buy me mussels. I needed to get my head examined.

"Kiss me here," he said as he pointed to his pouch.

"I'm sorry, what? Can you have a beer?"

"No, come touch my junk. It wants you."

"Your what?"

"You know, my stuff," he said as he cradled his balls.

Okay, I gotta stop you here for a second.

I've heard of naming your penis. I don't really get it. It's not a car, but I know it's done. What I don't get is referring to it in the third person, as if it has a personality and sense of style. "Willy wants to come out and play." Ew. That's just wrong. Don't do that.

Women don't want to think of your penis or balls as stuff or junk. For starters, "stuff" evokes thoughts of the middle of Oreos, of a grandfather with his grandson drinking whole milk on a porch listening to the sound of a twisted cookie. And "junk" evokes thoughts of The Trash Heap from *Fraggle Rock* or Oscar from *Sesame Street.* Guess what? You can't win with either. Oreos bring us back to roller rinks and Members Only jackets, and Oscar regresses us to the whole Big Bird Snuffleupagus conundrum. And there's nothing sexy about an eight-foot-tall bird that wears a propeller beanie hat, whose legs look like ribbed condoms, and who drinks birdseed milkshakes from Mr. Hooper's store. Now, Snuffleupagus, on the other hand, had quite a trunk, if memory serves. Still, ixnay on the unk-jay. There has to be a better word. I prefer "area," which evokes a modern clean television show. I could at least work with that.

Okay. Play. Balls back in.

Christian smiled and pulled me to him for a kiss. He tasted like cologne and kissed like a whack-a-mole, poking his tongue in and out of my mouth to presumably give me a preview of his lingual lapping style. Men do this sometimes. However, I've been privy to one exceptional encounter. A man once instructed me to kiss him exactly the way I wanted him to go down on me. "That's it," he prompted, "long laps on the lips. Now show me what you'd do with the clit. My tongue is your clit. Show me." Holy shit. Now that's hot. In contrast, whack-a-mole kissing should remain at the amusement park with the clowns and carney.

Unfortunately, metrosexuals and their Eurosexual cousins can't kiss worth their weight in manscaping supplies. They devour articles about technique, margin to margin in GQ, and call it a day. With so much focus on skill and style, they sidestep the passion it takes to receive an invitation back. When a man is all about technique it begins to mimic clinical and feels as cold as stirrups. Let me be clear on this, though, plunging in and becoming a sloppy moaning mess does not pass for passionate. It passes for proletarian.

I wanted a man who knew how to live without *Men's Health Magazine*, who took what he wanted. Christian was not that man. I was certain he'd practiced his "I'm in control and going to have my way with you" stare in his oversized mirror; it wasn't genuine. Then he'd probably spent another twenty minutes seeing how his sunglasses looked when pushed onto his head.

Perhaps he'd be skilled at other things. He struck me as the type of guy who, while performing oral sex, relied on the alphabet technique. I wouldn't know. The closest he got to my "como se llama" was maneuvering my lacy boyshorts off my hips and declaring his grooming preferences. "I like a full-grown bush."

Yes. I swear to God, he said that shit aloud.

Truth: that was as hot as it got. How animalistic, his wanting a nineteen-seventies bush. It seemed promising. "Now, let me slip off these saturated panties of yours and taste your nectar." That would have been hot. Instead, it was, "Dahling, this runway bit is so nineties." I wondered where he was hiding his Sharpee marker and which part of my body he'd criticize next.

I *had* wanted to drag him across my body and grip him in handfuls. Shoulders. Hip flexors. Skinning it. Pushing and pulling him over me with force, I was drenched in want. But, I'd stopped at the first mention of Terax Conditioning Crème. "It's so important to condition the scene of the crime, dearest." The scene of the fucking crime? I hate you. I felt like I was supposed to apologize. Jesus, if I wanted to feel like shit I would have gone shopping at Scoop and let anorexic saleswomen apologize that they didn't carry anything larger than size twenty-eight jeans.

A man knowing and taking what he wants without apology is arresting and gets me going every single time. Mentioning products sold at Sephora is not my idea of foreplay and had me wincing with thoughts of Helga the Waxing Nazi. This was wretched. I refused to play through.

"Sorry, but I can't do this." I said it as if I were emotionally wrecked, not annoyed.

He stopped slurping in my ear and sat erect, his head tilted in question before asking, "Which bit?"

"All of it. I'm sorry, but I, I just can't." I deserved an Emmy. My bra was still fastened. I yanked my shirt down to cover the rest of me. I was surprised he was still incredibly handsome. Dimples, commas of hair, luminous cat eyes. None of it mattered.

"Dahling, I was only getting started."

"I wish you wouldn't," I whispered, hoping he'd think I was somehow scorned and deep in miss of a past he hadn't learned yet. He didn't buy it.

"Come on, I can learn. I swear." He must have garnered this grievance before.

I wasn't about to have any kind of sex with a man who was more waxed than I was. "No, I think it's just best if you leave." He looked like a wet seal.

"Please, seriously, I need to know how you Americans like it." We like it circumcised for starters.

"You think it's an American thing?"

"Yeah, my British birds don't give a flick. I want you to teach me." Coo Coo Ca Choo. I could take this shit on. Make it my mission. Martyr on up. That's right, ask not what your country can do for you, but who you can do for your country. So, for the love of the USA, and under the influence of the French Châteauneuf-du-Pape, I would take the Brit between my legs and give him a proper afternoon lesson in the subtleties of linguistics. Just call me Paul Revere.

The British are cumming!

The British are cumming!

"I'M NOT GOING TO LIE TO YOU—THE BOY PULLED A DIANE Keaton." I can't believe I was discussing this with the Phone Therapist. It's what I paid her for, to get a complete picture so she could tell me just how fucked up I was.

"What do you mean, a Diane Keaton?"

"Every frickin' time I watch the Oscars or Golden Globes, the woman shows up a la *Annie Hall*, in an uglyass vest with a wide tie, or a damn bowling hat, forcing us all to reassess femininity and traditional gender roles. Please. That's not her job anymore. Someone has to get the men to wear menswear, not the women. I mean, really, would it kill the woman to wear a dress?"

"So you have views on the topic, then."

"My point is this. Every year, she thinks her fashion sense is improving. She'll say things to Joan and Ugly Rivers. Something like, 'See, see how cute I look? No more worst-dressed this year, right Joan?' Then Joan changes the subject by making a joke about how she just stepped on her sagging boob."

"I don't understand, Stephanie."

"I don't either. I mean, can't she hire a stylist? Clearly her friends and family are of no use. Sure, they give her support when she gets bad reviews, but are they there when it counts? Are they there for her in her time of fashion seppuku? I think not."

"No, I meant I don't understand what this has to do with Christian."

"He asked me to teach him stuff in bed. So I tried, communicated with him about what I liked. Schooled him on placement, pressure, and the precision of timing, and then he emerged from the sauna that happens when you're pleasuring someone under the covers with this arrogant face. He looked like Gabe. I didn't even stiffen. I could have been doing my nails. He really thought he'd improved, pulled a frickin' Diane Keaton. I'm telling you, he must have thought he was signing up for fashion lessons, not passion lessons." She wasn't amused.

"It's interesting. Did you hear what you just said?" Of course, I love listening to myself talk. "You said he looked like Gabe. Did he remind you of Gabe in any other ways?" I sat thinking, twirling the phone cord with my finger. "Let me ask you a different question, Stephanie, why did you decide to become intimate with him to begin with?" Ugh. It was going to be one of those sessions, the Catholic kind.

"Because he was handsome, and it has been a while." It had been four months.

"Why else?"

"Because he wanted me. He was handsome, fashionable, and educated."

"I see." I hated when she did the "I see." It meant something big was coming, and she'd make it come out of my mouth. "So this Christian is a handsome man who has told you he likes you, yet he didn't pick you up for your first date and asked you to pay for half of it, right?" I didn't need to answer her. "Would you say he put your needs ahead of his own at all?" Fuck. "I wonder, does he remind you of anyone else?"

"What is wrong with me? Haven't I already learned this lesson with Gabe? Haven't I suffered enough? Why did I even start dating this foreign clone?"

"Because it's familiar. It's what you know, and nostalgia feels good." This is why I paid her. "You've become so used to emotionally unavailable men, Stephanie. Men who put their needs before yours every single time, and whenever you asked for anything for yourself, do you remember what happened?"

"He'd tell me he didn't want drama."

"Which really meant he didn't want to discuss anything emotional." I picked Confrontation Houdinis every time. If there were a problem, he'd sooner escape it via the trap door labeled Passive-Aggressive than face anything as emotionally strapping as a discussion with the word *need* in it.

"And this is the type of man who feels familiar to you. It's what you know, but it's not what is best for you. I caution you to recall what we discussed in our last session, remember?" In our last session, Phone Therapist lectured me on milk. Told me an infant fed on a diet of sour milk, who is subsequently nursed with fresh milk, will spit out the good in favor of the turned. "We are programmed to find comfort in what we know, even when it's not in our best interest. Fighting that programming takes work, but if you don't do it, you'll keep repeating your mistakes." I hated that I had to fight my natural inclination, had to be aware, assess things, unearth patterns. Clearly, a relationship isn't all that takes work. Being single should come with pay stubs.

"I feel so broken, like I can't do anything right."

"Stephanie, this has been your programming all your life. You can't expect to change overnight." Fine, I wasn't broken; I was under construction. And that Christian boy would not be touching my golden globes again.

"Stephanie, Christian isn't the only one who pulled a Diane Keaton, you know."

"What?"

"Didn't you say she must have friends who tell her what's right, and she still makes the same mistakes?" Touché. "Eventually, if you want to change badly enough, you'll make it happen." A tear slid down my face and slipped into my smile.

"Yeah, well, at least I can dress."

seven

CELERY AND FUNNEL CAKE

OLIVER DURÁN INSISTED HE HAD IT, THE TAB FOR MY bowl of coffee at Columbus Avenue Bakery. "Really, it's my pleasure," he insisted as he extended a bill to the cashier. Chivalry wasn't dead. It was five-foot-eleven, Cuban, and wearing faded Levi's with Jesus sandals. "May I join you?" he questioned before I'd chosen my seat. Instead of answering, I thanked him, then walked to an empty table, set my coffee down, and bowed my hand toward the empty wicker chair beside mine. I couldn't decide if he was cute.

He joined me at the table with a wedge of quiche, iced tea, and five sugar packets.

"Someone has cavities."

"Yes," he said, "sugar is my one joy in life."

"God, that's sad."

He snickerwheezed as if Dastardly were beside him, then stirred the contents of four packets into a brown iced-tea cloud with his straw. "Yeah, work sucks the life out of me." He licked his finger and dipped it into the remaining packet of sugar. "So I suck my share of it right back." That's when he licked his fun-dip of a finger and allowed a full smile to escape.

His mouth was something you witnessed. All I saw were fangs. I looked over my shoulder to see if anyone else had seen them. I'm not talking slightly long incisors here; we're talking Stephen King's *Cujo*. I held my breath.

He detected my newfound panic and served up a warm, "Don't worry. I don't bite unless you want me to." I rolled my eyes and began to twirl my hair.

After twenty minutes, I learned he was a pediatrician. Something in me fell when I heard it. What if this was the familiar Phone Therapist warned against? I mean, was it asking too much, meeting a man without a pager and call schedule? He invited me to dinner, and I panicked. "It's just a date, Stephanie. Not espionage." I thought he might have been quoting a movie, so I laughed and decided to accept despite his MD. After a while, I felt comforted by him. I didn't have to work hard or sell myself. For once I just listened and thought, "me too." When Oliver mentioned fondue and live music at Joe's Pub, I spoke up.

"A man who eats cheese? I might just love you."

"Who doesn't like cheese?"

"My ex-husband wouldn't even look at it." I was glad I'd said it. Oliver struck me as someone who might be mildly uptight. I needed to get the *Oncewife* thing out of the way now.

"You were married?" I nodded. "But you look so young. When did you wed, at like twelve?"

"No, I was too busy wetting the bed back then to wed." Good girl, pile on the embarrassments. Underwhelm the guy.

Actually, it would take quite a bit to underwhelm Oliver. He was as safe as celery (more on that later) and "in like" with me from the start, especially after learning of my adolescent proclivity to wet the bed. Turns out, he was kind of hoping I hadn't outgrown the habit, but that's a whole 'nother book.

"WOULD YA TAKE A TWENTY-MINUTE TIME-OUT FROM your damn dating schedule and make time for your friend? I need to talk with you." It was Smelly, phoning me from her office phone, and she was whining. "I'm having a panic attack over here, Steph." She used *panic attack* as liberally as I did, attaching it to everything from cooking dilemmas to erroneous "reply to all" work e-mails.

"All right, shoot." I turned my instant message status to "away" and gave her my full attention.

"He still hasn't called me back." "He" was Alan Ryan, a twenty-four-year-old Abercrombie replica she'd met on a flight from Oregon to New York. They had been *casudating* for months. He'd e-mail often, paragraphs about how he was spending his day, the bitch-grinding he had to do as a sales associate for Henri Bendel's, how his younger sister would be in town, did Smelly have any "typical New Yorky things" his sister should do? But when it came to making plans, he never asked my intellectual property attorney friend out. Instead, Alan and Smell called each other late at night when one of them was drunk or bored. They'd meet up at a bar and lose a bottle of wine between their chance sentences and deliberate gestures. He'd declare how pretty she was and hoop his arm over her shoulders, resting it on her, heavy. They were hardly friends with benefits. They'd have to be actual friends for the term to apply.

"Have you tried e-mailing or IMing with him yet today?"

"Please, he says he can't IM with me and get his work done."

"Oh, that's bad."

"What?" Smelly panicked.

"If he can't IM and still get his work done, he's a wretched multitasker. You'll never achieve simultaneous orgasms."

"Will you be serious, please?"

Serious meant the straight-up truth. It meant I'd have to be sensitive to her feelings, understand, empathize with where she's been. Think of her entire life's journey and respond in a deeply feeling way.

"You huss, you slept with him, didn't you?" There was an urgent silence, as if the words "slept with him" were a blade, splitting her tongue and leaving her mute.

I imagined she closed her office door before answering, "Is that bad?"

"Well, you two aren't exactly exclusive, so maybe he's bored now that he's bedded you down. And from the alarm in your voice, you're giving me the feeling you want more with this guy. Smell, you gotta go on an actual date first, don't ya think?"

"He doesn't date, though. That's what he said." I am not sure how to respond to this.

"What do you mean he doesn't date?"

Smelly laughs in response. It's her nervous laugh, the one that happens when combative saleswomen affront her, when someone steals her taxicab in the rain, when she's insulted. "Well, what the fuck is that, Smell? He meets you out and lets you buy him wine? You *hang out*, and that's that?" Silence. "Okay, listen. You know how my sister refuses to date? Well, she resists it because she's not ready to deal. It's not that she doesn't want to meet someone. She just doesn't want the anxiety that comes with 'does he like me?' and 'will he call?' On occasion she'll meet a guy who tries to persuade her into the nondate. You know, let's just happen to meet at the bookstore and read magazines together. But at the end of the day, even if he thinks it's a date, she doesn't. She doesn't want to because she's just not ready."

"Please, I'd settle for that. He doesn't even ask me to the bookstore."

"Smell, you're not supposed to relate to Lea in that scenario. The boy is telling you he's not ready to date, and you're not listening to him. And listen to what you just said. I'd settle for that?! What the fuck, Smell?" I took a breath and continued in a docile tone. "Okay, explain this to me like I'm a four-year-old. Why do you want to be with this guy?"

"Well . . ." she hesitated. "Steph, you haven't seen him. He's so damn cute."

"Yeah, that's another thing, lady, why haven't I seen him yet? Why would you want any type of a relationship with a guy whose friends you haven't met and who hasn't met yours? I mean, part of knowing someone is knowing what they're like in a group setting."

"Ugh, I know. Why do I want him so much? What's wrong with me?"

"Good question, love. Answer it. Not what's wrong with you, but why do you want him so much? Do you have similar interests? Oh, wait. You wouldn't know, now would you? Because you two haven't actually done anything together. I'll rephrase, Counselor. Do you have similar taste in wine?" I was being harsh. It's what I did with Smelly because she let me, because I've known, since we were roommates in college, that it was the only way to get through to her. Smelly was the type who would yes me to death and agree, "You're totally right," but then she wouldn't do anything about it—except complain again a few days later about the exact goddamn thing.

"I don't know why I want him so much."

"Fine. I'm going to tell you. It's because you love being anxious."

"No I don't! Are you insane? I hate feeling like this! I can't get any work done."

"Okay, let me ask you this. Do any of those other boys who keep calling and asking you out make you feel anxious?"

"No, but I don't want any of them. They're boring."

"But Alan excites you, right? Like, you get butterflies and all keyed up when you think you might get to see him, right?"

"Yeah . . ."

"Yeah, well. Welcome to my world, honey. And you know what I've learned? Boring is better than Bastard, okay? Whenever I explored the relationships that began with that ignition and spark, I was usually left sobbing into my pillow wondering how I ended up so sad again. Smell, sparks can lead to fires, and then to fire escapes, where all you'll want to do is flee the damn scene of your crimes."

"So what do I do?"

"You learn to be friends with someone, get to really know them before you get all excited about the guy. You have to keep it tempered and figure out if you even like him, for who he is, not how he feels about you. I know it's not easy. Believe me, I know. But this thrill you feel for Alan is probably only there because things are new and uncertain. It's not about him. It's you, caught up in you. Your mind craves anxiety, the good exciting kind and the bad I-can't-function-at-work kind. You need to deprive your body and recognize that your propensity to chase codependency is leading you toward a fat, greasy life of miserable."

"Oh, wait. That was good. Say it again, so I can write it down and reread it later."

"Oh, shut up. You should be glad I'm not charging you for this shit." I should have been taping myself, so I could play it all back later when I needed to hear it.

"Okay, I know you're right, Steph. I mean, let's face it. Even if he were into me, realistically it would never work out." I heard her say the words, but I knew she didn't believe them. She wanted him to call. She was tapping the refresh button on her e-mail to see if anything new had arrived from him. "He wants to move back to Wyoming and live on a ranch, which is a shade away from a farm. And I can't live on a farm. I need to be near water and good restaurants."

"I could definitely live on a farm!" I thought of the movie *Baby Boom*. Of peacoats, hot caramel apple cider, mittens, and firewood. "Well, I think." I imagined I was sure.

"Nice, Steph."

"No seriously, if I were married and had a baby to raise, I could occupy my time with writing and cooking. I could decorate and organize, make my life into some Martha Stewart catalogue with wreaths and holly. I'd have time to stack my linens and tie them with ribbon. I'd have a frickin' guest room with guest bathrobes and slippers, an enormous kitchen, and I could buy in bulk, so I wouldn't need to go to the inconvenience store for formula or diapers. But once the kids were grown, I think I'd lose it on a farm. The novelty of brown eggs and red roosters can only get you so far."

"Well, I just wish he were into me." Poor Smell.

"No you don't. You really don't."

"Of course I do."

"No, Smell, you don't. Look at Jonathan and Brian. They'd both gladly give you a testicle Tuesday for a date today. And you want no part of either of them. You think they're wimpy. You only want Alan because he doesn't want you back. If he actually did like you, you'd complain you couldn't handle anything serious now with a man who wanted to be a dude on a ranch. Smell, you don't even like ranch dressing."

"Yeah, I think that's why I like unavailable men. Deep down, I'm not ready for anything serious." Lovely. At least I got her to say it aloud. Perhaps Smell was on the same side of the scrimmage line as her dude after all. Neither of them was ready for more than the casual pass.

"It also makes you feel more worthy. It's like the line outside the hot new nightclub. People stand on it because it's there. If they can get in, they feel more important, more worthy. It's the same thing with relationships. But once you make it inside, you're often left wondering, 'all that waiting and working with the doorman just for this?' You need someone who's your friend first." Almighty Christ, I sounded like the fable about the tortoise and hare. "Just trust me on this one, babe. Look, you're not the only one who chases damn funnel cake, but you need to stop."

She'd heard my theory on funnel cake and celery stalker men before. Most men were either like funnel cake: delicious and interesting, but who at the end of the day just aren't good for the heart or complexion. Or they were celery: a sensible, healthy choice that didn't really bring much to the table but an occasional crunch. If you OD on celery, you end up bingeing on cake behind closed doors.

Funnel cake, while warm and delicious, is difficult to make. But you go there because you long for it like the double-twist stomach-dropping roller coaster as soon as you arrive at the amusement park. Wet ribbons of batter crackle and pop until golden and crisp, yielding in the center. The steamy swirls of tender yellow dough absorb confectioners' sugar like pores. When the luxurious fat melts on your tongue, you exhale. You've got sticky batter, dribbling down spouts, leaving rings on your clean countertops, splattering oil growing darker and beginning to smoke. Layers of paper towels and oil-draining weapons clutter your space. With funnel cake, you've got steps to follow. Procedures. Rules.

No one makes rules about celery. It's always around for the snacking. You choose it when you're dieting or trying not to consume too many wings over football. Come to think of it, you don't even bother eating it while you diet. Instead it's a conduit for blue cheese. You use it to make stocks and stuffing. It becomes filler, pantry almost.

"Alan is your funnel cake. You keep thinking if you spend more time with him, he'll come around and suddenly open up to you and make you a priority. It's as if you want to convince him of something. You're keeping Alan in the picture thinking he'll grow up and suddenly become caring. You'll be the one. Suddenly he'll be sensitive."

"Yes, that's it. That's exactly it. I want to know why he isn't crazy about me. I mean, he says he doesn't like dating, but come on."

"Alan knows Alan a lot better than you do, so listen to the boy. And Smell, you shouldn't need him to tell you how great you are. You should know that without him." Oh, this was so my problem too.

"Yeah. I hear ya. It's just so frustrating. I hate all this crap. I just want to meet someone, get married, and put all this other crap behind me."

"Hey, when I was going through my divorce, do you remember what my mother told me? I know I've told you this before. 'What we wait around a lifetime for with one person, we can find in a moment with someone else.' It's out there for you, hon, but you won't see it until you quit funneling."

"I know," she said, sounding defeated. "I just don't know how to force myself to like celery."

"You've never had my celeriac puree, darlin'. I whip that shit with butter and serve it warm under a potato-wrapped sea bass. Good times, lady. Good frickin' times."

Yes, usually the celery stalkers go out of their way to please us, rarely bringing anything extraordinary to the table because they're too wrapped up in the girl, spending their energy on trying to make her happy in lieu of investing in their own interests.

"Okay," Smelly said, "I'll try. But I'm still allowed to bitch to you about it if I get frustrated again."

"I know, babe; you always do," I said lovingly. "Smell, at least now there's the idea of someone out there. It's not like being dispirited in a fruitless marriage wishing for single. I'd rather be frustrated with hope than stuck in a sexless marriage second-guessing myself. And I should know, hon. I've been on both sides of the grass."

WHEN I WAS MARRIED, I TRIPLE-GUESSED MYSELF, AND "frustrated" didn't even begin to cover it. I'd heard sex ebbs once you're married. Okay, so I did more than hear it—I rolled around in the sheets alone with it. Hallmark anniversary cards depicted the end of an active sex life with illustrations of bathrobes and fuzzy slippers, cushy sofas, and remote controls. Talk shows devoted segments to helping men deal with their "you try wiping the kids' snot all day then giving a blow job" wives.

Yeah, *so* not the case in my house.

Gabe preferred baseball to body language, soccer to sucking, and then the obvious: football to fucking. From lace garters imported from a specialty shop in Cannes to Mary Janes and a plaid skirt, Gabe only offered, "later, I promise" as he lunged for the volume setting on the television. I was married to that Hallmark card.

Did you just yawn? Oh believe me, I'm sidled up right beside ya. We've all heard this sad-sack story before. I'm certainly not the first to sumbitch about it, but here's what I didn't realize then: the antidote to barren bedroom banter isn't about lipstick, lingerie, or lipo. It's not something *you* can fix. It's something you both have to work on together. And lean in close for this one: it usually has nothing to do with sex.

"Sex is the barometer of the relationship; it's a tool to indicate what's really happening in your relationship." It was Phone Therapist's way of saying something else was really going on beneath the surface.

"Yeah, well, it wasn't me," I was quick to defend. "I was always ready for sex with Gabe. Worked out, felt good, and I'm passionate about everything else, so sex was certainly no different. He just never really wanted it."

"Perhaps you made yourself too available to him," Phone Therapist said. "Sometimes you can't let them peek at all your cards." This is exactly what I'd said to Smelly. But I didn't think it still applied once you were married. "Oh, it's the same when you're married," Phone Therapist continued. "I do it to this day with my husband. In the afternoon, he might begin to feel amorous and ask if we can have sex later that night, and even though I know we're going to, I'll reply, 'well, maybe.' Let him work for it a little." She didn't actually use the word *amorous*. She said *horny*. But even thinking of her saying it now makes me cringe, as if I were watching Cinemax (aka Skin-e-max) with my parents in the room.

"Listen, it's really hard for me to now start playing hard to get after treading a lifetime in Lake Hardtogetsome." I was saying it in response to her lecturing me about having taken Christian home to bed with me the week prior. Now our conversation suddenly took a turn toward the past, as therapy is apt to do. I suspected she'd correlate my current behavior to my childhood. Instead we spent the session discussing Gabe. Again.

Here's the thing: yes, I could have pretended more often that I had no interest in sex. I could have smiled wildly when I realized Gabe preferred fantasy baseball to exploring any of his own fantasies with me. I could have, indeed. But I got married so I could stop playing games. Playful is one thing. Games are another. And don't get me started on The Rules. My begging for sex wasn't the real problem.

"Stephanie, like I said, something outside the bedroom had to be going on. A problem between the two of you that perhaps was never discussed?"

"No. I really think we just weren't sexually compatible. Even before we got married, he expressed his fear that I was more sexual than he was. He said he was worried he would be denying me a part of myself. He was scared he couldn't satisfy me. I thought it was just his coming up with an excuse for us to postpone the marriage."

"How did you respond to him?"

"I just shrugged and told him we had the rest of our lives to have sex, that it wasn't that big of a deal to me. I didn't think it mattered then. I just thought, please, it's sex. What's important is that we love each other. I found my best friend. Who the hell cares about sex?"

"And now?"

"I'll never do that again. Sexual appetite can't just be shooed away. And it is a big deal because when he didn't want sex, I felt ugly and rejected. I didn't feel adored. I felt like I was in a one-sided relationship, like I loved him more. And when I felt that way, weak and sorry for myself, I became confused because my self-image had been as a strong, confident woman. Yet I wrestled with this discordance between what I felt and what I knew, which left me feeling like shit, crying all the time, wondering which way was up. I'd cry tears of frustration that I couldn't even articulate. So then I'd act out and pick fights with him, just to hear him apologize for something he probably didn't even do. Just to hear and feel how much he loved me. All because he didn't show me enough, physically." Screw that. He didn't show me emotionally either.

Every relationship takes work and compromise, but some take less than others. With someone else, there would be less bending. It would take fewer steps to get on the same side of the lines we drew. Bottom line, our libidos were askew, which left me feeling rejected and envious of my single friends. Grass greener? At least their grass was getting mowed.

When I was married, I combed the self-help section for a respectable book on the lack of sack act. Searched for something geared toward a woman whose ailment wasn't menopause but dealing with a *manonpause*. I couldn't find a one. However, the magazine racks had no dearth of advice. The covers were littered with promises of improving your sex-capades with a list or a quiz, offering readers one hundred tips to turn him on, secrets to his hidden erogenous zones. Technique articles explaining what to do with his perineum and prostate promised you'd send him into orbit. Dear Lord. I wouldn't be sending him anywhere if he had no interest in being there in the first place.

I flipped through the pages and was assured of only one thing. Had I reached out for help to one of their "carnal counselors," their solution would involve a new pheromone perfume scent, nail polish shade, or attitude. "Suggest doing it with the lights on in front of a mirror." Guess what? It's all bullshit. Because while men are visual creatures, if they habitually prefer playing with their Xbox over your box, something is wrong, and it's not your thighs.

I couldn't tolerate one more fashion show featuring a bearded husband complaining that his dumpy housewife, who always somehow had cake batter in her hair, used to be HOT and now let herself go. It usually preceded another show about how Wifey can't get Hubby to leave the garage for her. "I even tried replacing the batteries in some of his tools with a note reading, 'turn me on instead.'" Everything was solved once they slapped some dye on her and gave her a blowout. Heels. A skirt. Close up on flannel man's mouth agape. It was all a sham.

I took matters into my own hand, and when my orgasm came to a close, I'd cry softly. Staring at the ceiling, I envisioned shapes in the texture of it as the tears blurred. How did I get here? I knew, in those moments, I was more alone than I ever was when I was single. Because now there were shoulds.

I should have had more sex when I was single. Once I was married, I was stuck. Even when I begged and literally got on my knees for it, he was too tired or not in the mood. Then I was selfish because I didn't understand how Hard. He. Worked. or how Tired. He. Was. When you're single, you're salacious. Then you're married, and you're suddenly selfish, selfish for wanting sex with your husband.

It was tragic. I became the wife they show in porno films. Hubby goes to the garage to play with his car, or tools, or something masculine, and I go sulk in the barn, left to stare lustfully at the horses. Then Wifey gets her Mc'Fixins. Brutes arrive and take over, brutes who smell like sports and taste like salt. Gabe and I lived on the Upper East Side of Manhattan, far from the stables. And my diet prohibited anything with "Mc" in it.

I begrudged my single friends' freedom to ring Pavlovian bells and have their men salivate. Over warm sake and charashi boxes, they shared their one-night-stand details, and between salty bites, I wanted to lick up their slutty lives, dig my stacked heels into their limbs, and navigate their walks of shame. I hankered to feel sore and hungover from too much sex. I coveted the tramps their doormen thought they were. I wanted my face to sting from his stubble from a night full of kissing and grinding and hands up skirts. I missed the dirty, missed everything I never had, and I wished for their lives full of funnel cake and celery. I missed the future I was about to have. Be careful what you wish for.

eight

MOVING THE FURNITURE

LITTLE BLACK DRESSES ONLY TAKE YOU SO FAR. I DON'T care what Audrey got away with.

I'd been dating Oliver, the Cuban from the café, for several weeks, even if he was a bit more celery than I would've liked. Since no one is perfect, I tried to enjoy our now together, less concerned about where it was going. He had procured an impossible reservation at Il-something-or-other, and I'd exhausted every hem of cloth in my closet-full-of-nothing-to-wear on my prior dates with him. I required something boobalicious. According to Gay Max, aside from my snark and hair, my breasts are my best assets. I corrected him over the phone, "It's not my breasts. Victoria's 'secret' is the padding, my friend."

"What. Ever. Men like busty. We don't care if they're smacked behind shoulder pad bras of armor as long as we can stare at cleavage. Cleavage is hot." Like balding men in baseball caps, padded bras are false advertising. I'm all about the fine print. Bring on the plunging black necklines and padded bras. All is fair in dating and décolleté.

"Max, do you know what happened to me last time I brought on the cleavage?"

"No."

"Does 'chicken cutlets' ring a bell?"

He began to giggle, which signaled he did indeed remember my chicken tragedy. And I'm not talking about the fact that I was a vegetarian for nine years until Gabe tempted me to eat a chicken nugget. The chicken cutlets I'm now in love with cannot be consumed. They're add-on breasts, silicone cups you slide into your bra; there's even some nipple mimicking going on.

Most men don't know that women tape their tits together. Some bras just don't cut it, and if you're backless, well, it's all about the surgical tape. Back to the cutlets. Do I need them? No. But are they fun? Hells, yeah. Turn my c's into d's—delightfuls. I bring them out on special occasions. Like, okay, you're on a date with a new boy and you know he's not going home with you; it's safe to wear the cutlets. Certain dresses, tops, occasions where you want to be boobalicious call for the cutlets.

A word of warning on the cutlets: don't get caught running late, in a sweat and whirl to get downtown. 'Cause running late means sweat. Running late means slippery when wet. It's exactly what had happened to me the last time I'd braved boobalicious. I was out. Someone dropped an earring. I leaned down to help the girl out, and my cutlet slid out, raw. Tripping to clutch her earring, I actually stepped on my tit-for-the-night. Oh dear God, had anyone noticed? Oh yes. What's a girl to do? It wasn't exactly a Lee Press-On Nail. I pulled a fucking Julia Child. Picked up the chicken, patted it off, and slipped that sucker back into place with a smile. Then I drank a bottle of wine.

"Max, my liver can't handle another bottle of wine tonight."

"Fine, just wear your coat-of-armor bra and a dangly necklace that kind of falls into your boobs. That's almost as hot as those stripper shoes you have."

"I have stripper shoes?"

"Yuh, those ones with the clear heels. Strippers wear them."

"They do?" I felt my eyebrows pinching together.

"Oh yeah, hot. *Hot.*" Ew. When we got off the phone, I put the shoes beside the garbage chute in my apartment hallway. No army would find salvation in those heels. Maybe a neighbor would.

When I suggested Bloomingdale's to Smelly, she revised Operation Outfit for Oliver Durán. "I have two words for you, Klein: Berg. Dorf's." Smelly never had a sister, and I consider myself on loan to her at all hours of the night, indefinitely, despite the fact that she runs actual errands at Bergdorf Goodman's department store. My to-do lists involve milk, color negative film transparencies, and dog toys. Duane Reade and tampons. Smelly's tasks include wardrobe preselection, "trunk shows," and "the most insane stilettos." The only thing keeping me from punting Smelly across the waxed Bergdorf floors is that she's as sweet as Häagen-Dazs French Vanilla, and she lets me borrow anything I want from her wardrobe of "hip without making you look hippy."

Mary, an oversized woman with a higher-pitched voice than expected, greeted us on the fourth floor, near the fur salon. Her scent was more "Kimmi with an i" than "Mary," a plume of cake batter and sparkly Urban Decay products. She probably sat on all the boys' laps in junior high. In true JV fashion, she led us toward a dressing room, looping her arms through ours as if she'd known us since passing notes was the thing to do. Despite her warmth, I was terrified of Bergdorf's. It's not the twirl of floors or The Elevator, toe-to-top looks I abide from the canary-yellow-bejeweled saleswomen. It has everything to do with Rome.

ROME WAS A WALKING AMPERSAND. SHE IMBUED ROOMS with Colefax & Fowler, Brunschwig & Fils, and Cowtan & Tout fabrics. Aside from her estate in Long Island and her five-bedroom home in Atherton, California, she lived at Bergdorf's. She frequented the store in lieu of eating—it's the Bergdorf Binge Diet. I was terrified I'd run into her.

As a size sixteen who insisted she was a twelve, Gabe's mother never felt deterred to shop at Bergdorf's. Cashmere wraps, Judith Lieber handbags, and Manolo's always fit, despite how much she shoveled in for dinner. "Well, I've always had very narrow feet." Besides her mind, nothing about Romina Rosen was narrow, and I always marveled how those tiny kitten heels didn't buckle under the heft of *The Bulldog*. It was her perpetual scowl and way of walking that coined my private nickname for her.

Insisting Gabe and I register at Bergdorf's, Rome took me there when she thought we were only engaged; our marriage was still a secret. I'd already registered at Bloomingdale's with my mother, but this was my attempt at making Rome feel included. I didn't want to be doing this. Any of it. And I didn't want to spend any more time with her than was absolutely necessary, but I did it for Gabe. Acting 101.

As Rome and I approached the escalators, she whispered, "You have to see this woman's engagement ring. Out-rage-ous." Rome wore a sixteen-stone, platinum-set, Tiffany & Co. diamond wedding band from the Schlumberger collection on her right ring finger because her nine-carat, center-cut, oval engagement ring took up a quarter of her left hand. I was curious to see what Rome thought was "out-rage-ous."

"The woman gives me attitude," Rome continued. "Who is she to give *me* attitude? She's the one on her feet all day. I mean, I'm not the one who has to work." Note to faint-hearted self: working is bad. When we passed the fake redhead with the real rock, Rome poked me. "Have you eva?" I didn't notice the ring, only Rome's fierce obsession with the thin woman whose hair probably never frizzed, even in the rain. Rome looked as if she wanted to eat her, and I wasn't sure if my nightmare-in-law hated or envied the saleswoman behind the glass case.

I knew exactly how that felt.

At the end of the day, I was horrified by how similar I was to Rome, how we had the same exact taste in everything from our disdain of fennel to our love of ribbons. We both adored peonies, monkeys, and rerun episodes of Martha Stewart. Each of us saved the Thanksgiving issues of all the cooking magazines and made the same face when we liked something we were eating, closing one eye a little more than the other. Relaxing involved knitting and creative "projects." We had all this in common, yet she made hating me a sport.

I really don't know why she hated me, but I have my suspicions. When little boys are in love with their mothers, sometimes they climb onto their laps—"Mommy, I want to marry you."

That's when mommies laugh and tell their little boys, "No, sweetie, I'm already married, but one day you're going to meet a woman you love, and you'll marry her. And, it won't mean you love me any less." I'm guessing Rome never had that little chat with her dimple-faced son, or with herself for that matter. "It won't mean you love me any less" was a hat Rome would never try on. "Gawd, there's nothing worse than hat-hair." See, sharing Gabe with his previous girlfriends was one thing. Girlfriends come and go. Mommy will be here for you through all the breakups. But like a first-born child who's suddenly forced to cope with a new arrival in the family, she was jealous of the attention he was giving me. "Gabe, are you sure Stephanie is the one for you? I mean, really, how can you be getting married?" It was her equivalent of "send the baby back to the hospital."

To allay her fears, I had sent a card on Mother's Day, thanking her for raising such a wonderful son, to which she responded, "I'm not some creative writing exercise." Although she tried to be dismissive, it was clear she was *infatuhated* with me, the way Nellie Oleson was with Laura Ingalls. What she didn't know was that she was my "have you eva" saleswoman. I envied the life she had: her adoring family, beautifully decorated houses, and car seats heated for winter. The only real difference being, when I scratched her polished surface, I revealed fool's gold. She was saccharine to the faces of her closest friends, but was nothing but salty when she spoke behind their backs. "Audrey really should have those teeth fixed. The woman is all gums, and she thinks they're her best feature. Have you eva?" While I agree there's nothing worse than little teeth, I would never continually lob accolades at someone for her smile while we were together. Rome was faux, false advertising at its worst, way worse than my padded bras with silicone inserts.

I might have had many things in common with Rome, but I had courage. See, Rome was the type of woman who took Nielsen surveys before doing anything, and if her husband asked, "Is that what you're planning to wear out?" she'd run upstairs to change, two steps at a time. "What will people think?" would have been tattooed on her wrist had "people" not turned up their noses at tattoos. I never gave a shit what people thought until Gabe's family entered the mix. I wanted so much for them to like me because I saw how important they were to him. His being at the hospital all the time was hard enough. I didn't want to place any more orange cones on our path to relationship nirvana. Their hating me became an obstacle because I let it, and I hate that my love for him changed my ability to disregard the opinions of others. I was becoming Mrs. Rosen in more ways than a legal name change. I was jumping through her circus hoops, and soon enough, when I took a good look in the mirror, all I saw was a clown.

I NEVER UNDERSTOOD WHY PEOPLE REGISTER FOR FOR-mal china just to have it sit in a cabinet for enough years that your taste changes. All-Clad pots, Wüstoff knives, and a French mandolin . . . that I understand. I can use them. A $3,300 Buccellati jam jar? Are you kidding? Georg Jensen silverware, Baccarat stemware, and Lalique vases are for people with occasional tables and curios, not for a couple living in a two-bedroom apartment too small for a dining room table. Still, Rome suggested we register for these items. "People will want to buy you nice things for your wedding. You can't register at Bloomingdale's." She whispered "Bloomingdale's" as if it were cancer. What the hell? Since when did it become Wal-Mart? Clearly, I missed the double gate-fold mailer. "Oh Stephanie, look at this Herend place setting. It's just like the one I have. You really can't go wrong with Herend." I wanted HER to END.

"Very nice, Rome." It really was nice, but who was going to buy us all of these things? We'd already been engaged for a while, and I didn't have many friends to invite to the wedding. I was concerned she'd equate my lack of friends with a lack of worth. Numbers were proof, like the size of the engagement ring was a sign of his love. I was insecure and worried she'd highlight my lack of friends to Gabe. "How can you marry her? What kind of social network does she bring to the relationship?" I imagined her saying. Today, of course, I wish I could've bitch-slapped myself into reality. You were his wife, not a goddamn country club. Let them think what they want. Stop putting yourself into that woman's head. It's a sick place to be.

Rome often asked, "Oh, what gifts have your parents' friends sent?"

Aside from the stemware my father's closest friends had shipped, we hadn't received many engagement gifts from my parents' friends. They were waiting for the engagement party Gabe's parents had said they would throw for us.

"Oh, you know, some wine glasses. Things off the registry." She didn't actually care what we received, only who sent it.

When I'd arrive home, the doorman would stir. "Oh, some boxes arrived . . ." My shoulders fell under the oppressive weight of dejection. I became enervated with each box I opened. The embarrassment seemed heavier with the unraveling of each slippery white bow. The gifts were a constant reminder of what I wasn't, of what I lacked. She'd parlay any call into, "Oh, and what else did you get? You know, anything from your side?" Thank God for caller ID. I couldn't take it anymore. It was always Rome calling for an update. And her husband Marvin called only when he needed Gabe to be a fourth for a weekend round of golf.

When Gabe's father spoke, he touched strangers on the arm more than once, even while giving directions. As long as his stationary bike worked and his refrigerator was stocked with Diet Coke, he was a happy, easygoing man. Very likeable. And while he doled out "Yes, dear" with frequency and aplomb, Marvin was no stranger to the occasional "Not on your life" when it came to things that mattered to him . . . you know, like his wife's appearance.

"Rome, do us both a favor and put on something that fits. And you might consider ordering the fish tonight."

Despite their battles, Marvin and Rome were a unified, and coordinated, front with a vanguard position against the outside world. I'm afraid I was their WAR. So when Rome was a-ragin', Marvin raised his voice to Gabe on her behalf. "Listen, Kiddo, I'm not messing around. Smooth things over with your mother because as long as she's upset, I have to hear about it. And I'll tell ya one thing: I'm sick of hearing it. Fix it." Then he'd go back to watching the muted New York Jets game on TV as he raised the volume of the radio announcer's play by play.

Half his year was spent traveling, taking legal depositions. He brought *The Bulldog* with him on trips where the shopping and eating were good. Otherwise, she'd attend to their Atherton home, nipping and tucking the house into pastel order. With her expensive sable brushes, Rome painted masterpieces using broad, deliberate strokes. "Marvin, that Stephanie is such a liar." I imagined him rubbing his scalp and exhaling a "What now?" under his breath. The woman could survive on gossip and body fat.

Gabe heard his mother call me a liar when he'd phoned his parents to ask about another wedding date. When I came into our bedroom with his French toast to get a read on how the conversation was going, he was already off the phone shaking his head.

"I have something to ask you," he huffed as my diaphragm puffed all the air out of my lungs at once. Here we go again. It already hurt to breathe. "Did you ever tell anyone you pay for our rent by yourself?"

"No. What the fuck?"

Okay, so here's the deal. As far as they were concerned, we were still engaged, living in medical school housing. It was my understanding that his parents gave a lump-sum check to the school for his tuition and housing. Once we were married, though, they warned, they'd continue to pay for his tuition, "to honor that responsibility, but we'll take no part in supporting your decision to be married." They also wouldn't contribute one cent to the actual wedding, despite having more money than God. "It's the family of the bride's responsibility. We'll throw the engagement party." That was as likely to happen as Rome ever taking a shit in a public bathroom.

I knew an entire day would be spent thinning out her masterful paintings with turpentine fumes. She had tied up the canvas neatly, using pinking shears and magic tape, wrapping her version of the truth nicely behind wheels of polka dot ribbon. It was packaged just as she liked it, and that was the way it would be.

"What does it matter who said it, Gabe? She's very reliable, and I would take her word over Stephanie's any day of the week," Rome had said to him over the phone earlier.

After some coaxing, she admitted it was Debbie Sheraton. My mind

reeled, clicking through a View-Master of hospital dinners, baby nam-
ings, mah-jongg moments, and then finally . . . I spoke with Debbie at
Rome's fiftieth birthday party. She asked how my job was and if I was
planning on going to graduate school. "Yes, I want to go eventually, but
I'll wait until Gabe finishes medical school because someone's got to pay
the rent." It's a fucking figure of speech.

"Uh, I don't want to hear any excuses," Rome said. "Gabe, you always have an answer for everything." That's when she hung up on him,
and I walked in with the French toast triangles.

After hearing it all, I cried at the edge of the bed with my head in my
hands, thinking, my God, they must really hate me—they don't even
want to hear my side. I'd like to say any normal person would have taken
a step back and seen what she was getting herself into. She would have
known she'd have to deal with these people for the rest of her life. Instead, with each word of caution from Gabe's parents' mouths, my re-
solve in my decision to marry him only strengthened. Tell me I can't do
something, and I'll do it.

Gabe sat silently with the receiver in his hand, pressed close to his
pursed lips. He was afraid to speak, as if his voice would sever one of the
marionette purse strings his family controlled. I cannot believe I didn't
have second thoughts. I wanted what I wanted, and that was that. I was
so Rome with red hair.

Fuck this shit. "Gabe, let's just tell them. They're always going to
have an excuse, and I don't want to live like this, walking around wishing
I could wear my ring in public. It just feels wrong."

"We're not telling them now, Stephanie." He said it as if he were
reading facts from a newspaper, with no room for opinions.

"But I hate this. I hate not being able to be honest with my family. I
hate not being able to let everyone know."

"Don't start. I don't need this now. You know I have to study for this
test. Maybe you don't realize how important this is. It will determine
where I do my residency. Don't you understand, it all comes down to this
test?" I felt selfish. I also felt unmarried.

"I feel like that tree in the woods."

"Jesus, fuck. Are you deaf? Did I just not tell you I'm not doing this with you? They'll pick a date, eventually. Don't let this get to you." Asshole, it's your job to not let your mother get to me. Try saying something. Try defending me.

I'd be the bigger person and swallow it. I picked up the phone, sobbing, and called Rome. She acted happy when she heard my voice. "Oh. Hi! How are you?" It was her Stepford voice, and I could almost smell her plastic wires.

I laid into her. "Rome, you know exactly how I am, and I can't imagine you're very happy either. There have been a string of misunderstandings in the past, and I'm very sorry if I have upset you in any way. I love your son, and we are going to be a family. We need to wipe the slate clean and make some changes to try to work things out." Then I stopped, and breathed, and listened, wiping the snot off my mouth with the back of my hand.

"Well, Stephanie, I've just about had it with you." I could now see her scowling through the phone, those vertical lines around her mouth tightening together, like a band of frosted pink soldiers. "Every time we ask you for dinner, you have an excuse. The last straw was when you were at our house and I asked you to stay for dinner, and you said you weren't dressed appropriately, and when I suggested someplace casual where you'd feel comfortable, you said you weren't very hungry." I looked up from the bed to see how Gabe was taking this. Did he want to hear what was going on? He'd left the room, probably to find refuge in front of a muted football game.

"Gabe overpromised and told you I would be there when he didn't consult me. The time you're talking about, Gabe told me he wanted us to be alone that night and have a romantic dinner, and I yelled at him on the car ride home because he didn't say anything to you about it. He made me look like the bad guy." I caught my breath and waited for something like, "Oh. I had no idea." Instead:

Silence.

"Still, what are Marvin and I to think, Stephanie? We used to be so close to Gabe, and now we feel like he's an orphan. I think you see us as the enemy because our family is so close and your family is in pieces." By "pieces" she meant divorced. She meant a supportive mother living in Florida who was overjoyed for Gabe and me, and a father in New York who's my best friend. No, check that. She meant divorced. If she were in front of me, I would have kicked her in the vagina. She continued, "And, don't you dare repeat this, but what are we to think when your mother is in town and she doesn't even bother to pick up the phone and say hello? It's not normal. When two people are getting married, there are supposed to be phone calls."

Last time I checked, the phone worked both ways. "I totally understand how you must feel, but Rome, my mother has things on her mind besides this wedding. You shouldn't take it personally." You know, she has an actual life in Florida. She doesn't twist her moustache counting the ways I've wronged her. "She doesn't know about these things. My family isn't as formal as yours." It's not always about you, you motherfucking, self-absorbed, neurotic, hyphenated twit. "Really, Rome, she just doesn't know any better." Let it go. He's twenty-six years old. Say it with me, lady . . . LET. IT. GO.

And later, when my mother did actually phone Rome asking for her guest list for the bridal shower, Rome insisted she and Gabe's sister Jolene were already planning one. "You know, at our country club." Rome was terrified, because my mother is Puerto Rican, that the shower would be a punch bowl, crepe paper with bunting and streamers type of affair. Perhaps she imagined a piñata. When my mother assured her that she, too, had a subscription to *Martha Stewart Living*, and it would be a classy tea-sandwich luncheon at my aunt's home, Rome said only five people would be attending from her side, "because, well, I don't think Gabe and Stephanie are letting us invite many people to the wedding, that is, when they finally pick a date for it." Oh yes, poor you. Poor sad Rome— everything happens to you.

It went on for two hours, until I realized we were traveling in circles. "Look, I didn't call you to argue. I just want things to improve. All I can suggest is, if you have a problem with me, or if you hear something from someone again that upsets you, talk to me about it, not Gabe." Clearly Gabe was useless in making anyone feel better about anything. He could've reassured Rome: his love for me would never diminish his love for her. He also ought to have set the limit. "Stephanie is going to be a part of this family whether you like it or not, Mother." Instead, he avoided the entire thing, playing the mime, and few things are more frightening than juggling clowns or mimes. Strengths: juggling, creating imaginary walls to hurdle, and always looking sad without communicating. Welcome to my marriage—Rome was the ringleader, and I was suddenly "the other woman."

Rome hung up the phone with a "fine." Of course, no one ever means they're fine when they say it. Fine. Yeah, okay, right. Fine. See if I care. Then the guilt slips in like tax. She didn't want to believe Gabe had a lot to do with the way things were. I knew the only way to improve familial ties was to make her feel less like she was losing a son and more like she was gaining a daughter. Maybe if she felt more involved, she'd feel less threatened.

Hello Seventh Floor, Bergdorf's Gift Registry.

"SO, WHAT DO YOU THINK?" SMELLY WAS EYEING ME through the mirror as she smoothed the twill fabric over her ass. "Stephanie, come on. Does this suit make my ass look fat?" For the love of God, clothing can't make your ass look fat. Your ass makes your ass look fat. Smelly is *Town & Country* hot. It's as if she were born on a balance beam, with a blue satin ribbon strung through her yellow hair. She's too WASPy to be fat.

"No, Smell, you couldn't look fat in a funhouse mirror. Do you even eat anything beside red apples and skim milk? Please don't do this to me today. I need to feel confident on my date tonight, and if we're comparing you fat to me fat, I'm going to cancel my date and run home to watch Ab Roller commercials."

"Oh, please. The boy loves you. LOVES." She was right. I knew Oliver Durán would love me no matter what I weighed. I spent my whole life trying to be thin, so I could attract a man who'd love me even if I got fat. I found him, and he was taking me out to eat carbs and courses. At a size six, I knew he'd love me just as much if I were a size sixteen. It's the fat litmus test. To reward the boy, I'd flash a little heaving breast. Bring on the deep plunge necklines. I swear, there's an outfit for everything. The boy was about to get his and then some.

"Mary, this top is perfect. Now, what do you have in the way of skirts?" I'm asking Mary to aid and abet the dirty. Welcome to personal shopper land, where the irony always fits.

THERE'S NOTHING QUITE LIKE THE FEELING OF ARRIVING home with an entire outfit folded behind tissue paper, tucked into Bergdorf's bags. My apartment was clean, smelling of wood polish, and Linus was asleep in a wan shaft of sunlight. I was excited about my date until I listened to my messages. The reservation had fallen through. "Baby, I thought we'd cook." This meant I'd cook, and he'd clean. If we were staying in, I'd need to create something to be excited about beyond candles and a good Sauvignon Blanc. I was feeling spicy. Lobster Fra Diavolo.

"Babylove, how can I help?" Oliver's clean hands slipped along my arms and tightened around my wrists before slipping beneath my white shirt to rest on the small of my back. It wasn't a deep plunge skirt of a night. The Bergdorf goodies would have to wait.

"Hug me like you mean it, and not like you're trying to feel what kind of thong I'm wearing." After he held me, I kissed Oliver on his sweet nose.

"Okay, put me to work. I know my role around here." He dipped his head in a deep gesture of servitude. "What needs chopping?" All I wanted was sex. "Linus, do you need chopping?" He laughed at his joke with a short wicked laugh. "Think Linus would mind if I chopped him up tonight?" I don't know why Oliver always made "let's kill Linus" jokes. I ignored Oliver's attempts at humor. I wasn't with him for his funny.

Oliver was everything Gabe wasn't. They always are, the rebounds. He was nurturing and gentle. He'd take Linus for runs so I could have alone time, and when we were in bed, he rubbed my belly, telling me he couldn't wait to one day see me pregnant with his baby. He adored me and showed me exactly how a woman should be treated.

Maybe it was the drape of his navy shirt, resting on his shoulders, as he stood in my kitchen, cracking lobster claws, feeding Linus the cartilage part that grosses me out, but I believed in that moment that I wanted to spend the rest of my life with this nurturing man. As I watched him so quietly from the pantry, he kept looking over his shoulder from the kitchen asking me what was wrong. Everything was so right.

There he was, in his socks, hovering near my sink, draining whole peeled tomatoes, breaking them in the palms of his hands, letting the jelly and seeds seep through his fingers, pulling the pulp into strips. Viscous and lovely. I wanted good dirty sex with the man who knew how to get dirty. I'd be wary of anyone who can cook and keep their hands clean. When they do have "intercourse," it's probably clean and orderly, like boxes of soap.

"Can we cook a little later, Oliver?" It's playtime. "Please?" I was purring.

"Oh, I see. Stephanie is frisky, huh?" he asked without disengaging our stare as he washed his hands. His pale eyes were like bits of green sea glass. "Baby, we need to talk first." Oh God, the dreaded four letter word, *talk*.

"Talk is cheap. Let's be lewd instead," I teased as I yanked on his polo shirt, summoning him to the bed, just beyond my hallway of a kitchen.

His face went grim. "If we're going to do this, and God knows I want to, I need to know you're not going to be doing it with anyone else. I need to know you're my girlfriend." He looked twelve years old when he said it. After being married, the word *girlfriend* is just so pom-poms and letter jackets.

"Your girlfriend? Oliver, that's so *Bye Bye Birdie*. You've got to pin me to pin me?" I was certain I wanted Oliver over all the others, but boyfriend?

"Yes, babylove, it's a start, and I'm not pressuring you, or giving you some ultimatum. I'm just saying, after these past few weeks together, I don't think I can see you anymore if I know you're seeing other people." This is the part where, if this were a movie, I'd break character and stare at the camera.

"Ahem, sweet, sweet, sweet man, that is so an ultimatum. It's not even funny." A sinister smile spread across his lips, but before I let him defend his position, I threw him onto the bed and kissed him hard. "You win, now shut up and fuck me like a boyfriend."

After really good, I'm going to be on top and put my legs together sex, Oliver started laughing. "Stephanie, you moved the furniture." My white bed had moved across the room while we were having sex.

I sprung to the kitchen and began to boil water for the pasta, then loaded up the CD player with some classic rock. "Yeah, baby, that's how it's done around here. I'm a mover's daughter. It comes with the gig."

"Does that mean you've got enough baggage to put in a warehouse?"

"No, thank you very much. Wiseass." I flipped my hair and rocked out to Joplin.

We eventually ate in bed. He fed me strings of pink spaghetti, twirled into mountains in my mouth. "God, I'm good," I boasted between bites.

"Yes, you are, Stephanie Tara Klein, and modest to boot. Do you want me to move the bed back for you?"

I liked the bed in its new spot. "No, I like this new perspective. Let's keep it here." Then I smiled into his neck, laughing at my use of *let's*. I kissed him and then bit his neck, breathing in his warm scent of soap and scalp. I drew an invisible pattern across his chest as we spoke, and after a while began to tell him I wished we could choose our memories. "We can't," I said, "but I really hope I remember this." And as I whispered it, I wondered if he weren't really asleep beside me, just as you do when you tell someone everything you'd be afraid to say if you knew they were fully awake. You secretly hope they do hear you but still pretend to be asleep. I'll even remember that. But I couldn't sleep—the classic rock was too much rock and not enough classic.

When I got up to turn off the music, Oliver jolted upright. "Go back to sleep, honey belle," I whispered.

"No. I'm up now," he said in a half-sleep.

"Good." I clawed my way beside him. "Then tell me a bedtime story." I cuddled up next to him and kissed him on the cheek.

He began one about an oyster shucker named Phebius, but soon his voice trailed into half words.

I remembered how Gabe told bedtime stories, making sure to include Williams-Sonoma gadgets in its telling. Gabe spun bedtime stories about our future together, how our daughter would have red hair like mine and would like for him to carry her around the house, letting her touch each of mommy's kitchen gadgets while he told her how each of them worked.

When Gabe and I fell asleep at night, we'd groom each other. We'd hug, and I'd begin to scratch his back. When I felt something hard, I picked it off. Though eventually, he demanded that I couldn't use my nails while popping the pimples on his back. "No nails!" he'd shout. Then he'd work on my back, navigating the landscape by touch alone. Sometimes he accidentally tried to scrape off a birthmark, so I'd scream. To quiet me down, he'd kiss me. This would lead to my complaining he needed an Altoid.

"It smells like you've been cheating on me with a very tiny man who just pooped in your mouth," I'd say.

And he'd laugh, and say, "Oh come on, say it." He'd wiggle me on the bed. "Say it."

"Okay, it smells like a midget was here." Gabe loved the word *midget*. He made me love it too. Then he'd burst out laughing, like a boy who just heard the word *penis*.

I loved that about us, the things we knew about each other. I hated and loved that he made rubbing his balls and sucking in their smell off his hands a sport, shouting, "OOOhh yeah! It doesn't get any better than this. Everything should smell like these babies." He wasn't kidding, but he made me laugh. I loved that he'd overextend himself sometimes at the gym when he was working his lower body, so for two days, I'd need to help him walk down stairs. And he tolerated me in the same ways. He understood that I needed to "get situated" when I first got into bed, assuming what he called "the goal-tender position," my leg bent, blocking him from getting close. And despite having a king-sized bed, he always needed to sleep right up in my business. He'd let me steal his shirts, scarf, and even his ski jacket if I was really cold, and he'd complain but later tell me how sexy I looked in his things. He said it made him feel closer to me.

I rolled out of my embrace with Oliver, onto my side to scratch my own back.

"I said I'd move it back," he mumbled in dream speak.

"What, honey belle?"

"Your bed. I'll move it back if you want."

I kissed him on his forehead. "Don't worry, sweet boy. I like things just as they are."

"Are you sure?" He stirred and nuzzled into me. His warm naked body had the sheen of Egyptian cotton.

"Believe me, no one is touching my fucking furniture again." I'd already endured my share of unsolicited renovations à la Rome.

ONCE UPON A TIME ROME LIVED A DECORATED LIFE. Okay, she didn't. What she did was study interior design, but to the best of my knowledge, she never actually worked as an interior designer. Though she worked in a store once, which entitled her to a designer discount. So later in life she divided her time equally between Bergdorf's and the D & D building. She helped decorate the expensive homes of her friends, offering them a discount on ampersand fabrics.

Her taste was upholstered and formal, gilded frames around oil paintings of dogs, a cone-shaped basket with dried hydrangeas and silk

flowers hung heavy over mantelpieces throughout Teaneck and Engle-
wood, New Jersey. The basket arrangement was her signature. The thing
looked like a turkey's ass, and I couldn't comprehend why her friends
wanted matching homes. It's like using the same plastic surgeon and
walking around with identical noses.

I should have smelled trouble when I phoned home to ask Gabe what
he wanted me to pick up for dinner.

"Noth-ing," he said, as if I'd just kicked a puppy.

"Are you sure? I'm walking home. I can pick something up on my
way."

"No. Besides, my mother's here." There was no "besides" about that
statement. After a brief silence, he continued in a quiet voice that held an
undertone of distant contempt. "I gotta go. See you when you get here."
He hung up the phone with a slam.

Not exactly in a rush to hang with *The Bulldog*, I retarded my pace,
walking past neat windows of neat lives with chandeliers and built-in
bookshelves. I wanted a warm neat life, too, the kind that smelled of
roasted rosemary chicken and dishwasher. I wanted a lifetime of lazy fire-
lit Sundays.

Gracious Home, the cloud nine of interior decorating stores, was
around the corner from our Upper East Side two-bedroom apartment.
On weekends, I combed through their rectangles of paint hues, weighed
the pros of wireless blinds against the charm of curtains, and haggled
with the saleswoman to retain curtain swatches an extra week. Everyone,
eventually, ends up smelling like their home. I'd find something clean
from a Dyptique shelf. I wanted us to have our own smell, to share more
things than a marriage tax. I read pillars of books on crackling and dis-
tressing, updating flea market finds, and feng shui. I was determined to
make our home comfortable and ours. In my handbag lived squares of
area rug samples layered between the furniture blueprints I'd drawn on
restaurant napkins. I'd finally cleared out my handbag—our first apartment as a newlywed couple was just as I liked it.

When I arrived home, I couldn't open the front door. The key worked, but something was obstructing the entrance. I suddenly felt as though I were about to catch the other woman. "I'm coming. I'm coming!" Rome moaned. I forced a smile. Then the door swung open, and with it, the lid right off Pandora's box. "Surprise!"

The sofa was now set on a diagonal, my books now in the bedroom. Nothing was as it ought to have been. My bedside table, with my vibrator and birth control, had been moved to the other side of the room. I wasn't just mortified—I was livid. My blueprinted napkins were shredding in my mind as I surveyed the transformation. The measurements, the magazine clippings, the time I'd spent—it was all gone. She'd taken over. "Don't you just love it?" I didn't know what, or who, to disband first.

I tried to sound less than offended as I asked, "Wow, what brought all this on?" I was pacing and on my third cuticle.

"Oh, you know, just a new way to look at things." She actually twirled. "Isn't it great?" Rome's hands were jammed into her makeshift waist. She was wearing salmon . . . everywhere. Salmon pants, suede shoes, sweater, and matching eyeglasses. I wanted to skin her alive and sell her saturated fat to her malnourished son.

Had I asked my own mother for help in arranging furniture, she would have at least cautioned, "Are you sure? Won't Gabe get mad? Shouldn't you ask him first?" There are things called boundaries. Clearly Rome didn't know from them, and fucking Gabe, Jesus. Not once did he think to raise some kind of concern . . . you know, "Mom, maybe we should see what Stephanie thinks." Instead I came home to sweat and destruction. Gabe was sweating from moving all the furniture on her command, and I wanted to destroy him.

The last thing you can do when you're infuriated with your husband is fight with him in front of his family. It's like handing your nightmare-in-law a big cardboard sign on her way out saying, "I told you so." She'll wear it proudly each time she visits, and over luncheons, when asked how we are, she'll whisper to the ladies, "Well, they had a big fight last time I was there. Marvin and I never fight. We'll see how long this lasts." Then she'll extend her pinky, sip her tea, and let a sweet meringue dissolve in her acrimonious mouth. So, you thank her for her expertise and fall asleep that night on a saline pillow of frustration. *You are such a momma's boy* becomes the evening lullaby in your head.

In bed, Gabe whispered into the back of my shoulder, "I just thought it would make her happy, but Steph, come on, clearly you're upset. I'll move it all back right now if you want me to. I liked it your way better, anyway."

"Oh, please. Pretty please. Don't go there. Everything is so after the fact with you. You apologize in private and love me secretly. No wonder your parents hate me. You never show them that you love me. This is bigger than the goddamn furniture, and they still don't even know we're married!"

"Oh, Christ. Stop being so dramatic." He stopped touching my back. "I give up. Go ahead, go to sleep angry. I don't give a shit."

"Thanks, Captain Obvious. I could have told you that the minute you moved the coffee table for her."

He left the room, and I sobbed silently, staring at the ceiling. Why hadn't I paid attention to the signs, to how similar he was to Marvin, the way he would yes people to death? I married a momma's boy who double-booked and overpromised our lives, agreeing to be at two places at once. The next day he'd phone with apologies. "Stuck at the hospital," he'd lie. His middle name should've been Afterthefact. Judas, his actual given middle name, wasn't far off the mark. Christ was looking the other way when Judas betrayed him. I was looking the other way, too, staring at the acorn instead of the family tree. "Well, you aren't marrying his parents, now are you?" was a pill I'd hide under my tongue and spit out later. I've since learned not to swallow advice from anyone who has never had to deal with a Roman empire. You do marry the family, and a difficult family is as bad as a man with a temper. Lucky me, I had both. You're signing a contract. His family is the fine print, so make sure you know what you're getting into. Because, soon enough, the family comes into your house and moves your fucking mattress. Just make sure the man you choose to marry isn't doing the pushing, or the "moving of the furniture," without you. Pun intended.

nine

THE RUNS

A BOY CHASES A GIRL ON THE PLAYGROUND, YANKS HER braids, then runs away in a frenzy, yelling that her freckles are uglier than her nose. It's his savvy way of communicating *like*. Unlike Gabe, Oliver never called me names or ran from me, but he did his share of pulling: namely, my teeth. Despite my unwavering declarations of "NO WAY IN HELL," he begged me to run with him in New York Road Runners Club races. "It's because I love you," he insisted.

"No. You hate me," I countered one weekend over a 6 A.M. breakfast in his Central Park West studio apartment. "No one who loves me would ever suggest I run anywhere, or for that matter, wake me this early." Love was being bartered over Brie and baguette.

Oliver would be spending the next two days at the hospital. Pediatrics at Mount Sinai. Meanwhile, I was busy with my own work overload, spending many late nights at the office toiling away on creative executions for inhaled insulin. Oliver thought it was "cute" when our work overlapped, mostly because he felt helpful around me. He'd regularly need to quell my medical fears when I was assigned to a pharmaceutical client. The agency brought in experts to educate us on the diseases for which my client provided medicines, so I often needed to excuse myself from meetings, light-headed and sweating. Conceptualizing interactive advertising solutions for drugs wasn't exactly what I wanted to be working on, but overall, work was relaxed for me. You know, aside from my constant nightmares that some dormant genetic condition would spring into action. I was convinced for several months that I had type 2 diabetes. I'd also recently learned, thanks to the Discovery Channel, that dogs could smell cancer. At night, after the makeup was removed and the triple crèmes were applied, I stripped naked and collapsed on my bed. Oliver thought it was part of foreplay. "No," I'd yell. "Linus goes first." Then I'd let Linus survey my body for The Cancer. He rarely made it past my toes. "That's it, baby. Mommy's got the 'beeties, so enjoy 'em while they last."

"Dear God, Stephanie!" Oliver had said. "Maybe it's your head that needs the examination, not your blood sugar." Then Oliver would try to bite me, just as he would during this 6 A.M. breakfast.

"Let's break bread before I spend days apart from you examining broken everything else," he had said. I didn't mind because his apartment was cave cool, conducive for sleep. I could give him breakfast. That, I could do. Running was another story.

"It's important to me, babylove." He batted his eyes. He was way too perky. "And it's not like I have other races this year." Oliver needed to run his last NYRR race, which would automatically secure him a spot in the New York City Marathon.

"I'm not stopping you," I said plainly as I reached over him for the Brie. "Go ahead and run it. I'll be at the finish line with Linus, lungs intact, thank you very much." He pressed his mouth against my tricep in what felt like the beginning of a warm kiss, then opened his mouth wider, digging his fangs into my flesh. "Ow! Stop biting me!" I said as I snapped my hand back.

"It was a love bite." Then came his snickerwheeze. When Oliver was in a mischievous mood and didn't like what I had to say, he'd mock bite me. Sometimes it hurt. This time it did not.

"Well, it fucking hurt."

"Please, baby? It would be so nice to do it together."

Brie on baguette was nice together. Peanut butter and jelly, Stockton and Malone, rum and Coke are "so nice together." Stephanie running alongside Oliver? Notsomuch.

I understood his point. We were in a relationship now, so the things he enjoyed when he was alone, he'd now have the opportunity to share with me, the woman he loved to love. The problem, of course, was sharing running with me was like sharing gonorrhea. I wanted none of it.

"Hmm, let me think," I said with my finger to my chin. "Yeah, no, I don't think I'd be into that so much."

"Come on, you can walk the whole thing," Oliver whined. "I just have to do the race. My time doesn't matter."

"But I'll be holding you back."

"I just want to share it with you. That's more important to me than how fast we go." I wasn't sure if we were talking about the race anymore. "We'll go at your pace. It's just something nice for us to do together outside."

It wasn't the first time I'd heard these words. Gabe said the exact same thing about golf. It wasn't important how well I did, only that I was there participating in *his important*. I purchased a stack of collared polo shirts in sorbet colors, a Lady Fairway glove. Even did the lessons thing, hoping I'd catch the golf bug and begin to crave that clicking sound when you hit the ball the right way. The only thing I caught was a hatred for the time he spent playing. It's called resentment. I had a case of it. I kept it right beside his case of *en*Titleist balls. How his and hers.

"Oliver, I'm going to say it only one more time, so listen closely. You, my friend, are seriously delusional. Let me explain something to you."

"Oh, dear, here she goes." He pushed his plate in front of him, setting his napkin on it. If he had sleeves, he'd have pushed them up and crossed his arms, ready in his waiting.

"Running, just so you know, was invented to escape. Something wants to EAT YOU. You run for your fucking life. It's not meant to be a good time on paved roads through a park with headphones, okay? Coaches punish players by subjecting them to an extra lap. PUNISH. Hello, are ya gettin' what I'm sayin'?"

"Haven't you ever run toward something?" His shoulders fell.

"Are we still talking about running here? Because it seems to me like you want me to do this just to prove something." It was too early for this, but it was too late to rescind it.

"Please answer me. Haven't you ever run toward something?" He actually wanted an answer, which meant more than wanting an answer. We were now having a talk.

"I don't know."

"I run home toward you every day, Stephanie. I leave work excited, and I literally run toward the subway, knowing I'll get to see you."

"So, we run toward something we fear we might miss, then?" I was imagining his train leaving the station, a brown paper bag skipping on the subway platform, the doors closing just before he had a chance to board. I knew the way I said it sounded heavier, as if I meant our relationship, a fleeting us.

"Wait, what do you mean?"

"Maybe you run toward us, Oliver, because you're afraid I'm going to leave you. Maybe you want me to run in this race with you because you think it will mean I'm more invested in us."

"Okay, hold on. This isn't about us. It's not. I'm just saying that it would be nice to share something with you that I really enjoy. That's all." He said it in a voice that conveyed resignation. "It means more when you're there, Stephanie."

I'd have preferred letting him stick a needle in my hard-to-find veins to running with him. Asking me, an out-of-shape woman whose heart could give out upon orgasm, to run more than a mile, was really like asking me to go hiking in mud, uphill both ways, during mosquito season, if there were such a thing. But I'd do it because I knew it was ammunition for the future.

My running would be something I could hold over him to get my way—The Mistletoe Method. What? Like you've never done it? Please. We all do it from time to time. It's not exactly the mature approach, but I was in rebound mode with someone who met the needs Gabe couldn't. Of course, I know this isn't the reason to do things, to expect something back. I am quite aware that relationships aren't really always equal and severed into fair bits. But with Oliver, I measured things. How often he'd sleep at my place, which of us paid for the last meal, who said "sorry" first. As far as measurements were concerned, the scales were tipped in his favor. I owed him.

"Fine."

"Really?"

"Don't give me a chance to back out of this or I will. Now let me go back to sleep."

Maybe he deserved more than the asshole "fine," but I wasn't ready to give it to him. "Fine" was my compromise. It was all I could manage at the time. I started to see our relationship merits on a system of Stephanie. He was good to Stephanie, stewed Stephanie tea and produced pints of mint chocolate chip for her in the middle of the night. He was patient and loving toward Stephanie. But Stephanie was rarely inspired to make Oliver happy. Shopping at Bergdorf's for a new outfit he'd like was hardly selfless. Yes, I'd cook him dinner, but I liked to cook, so did it really count? Maybe the only way it became about loving him was when it became insufferable, like when my parents forced me to attend services at synagogue. If I were miserable, spending my Sunday afternoon indoors, in itchy tights, God would know I loved him. Maybe this is love: doing the things you really don't want to do just because you know it will make them happy. Just as I'd spent Sunday afternoons on Long Island with Gabe's parents, in lieu of my preferred activity of bathing suit shopping in cruel lighting, I would love Oliver like Sunday school and run in his craptacular race.

On the day of the race, we were running a half hour late due to what Oliver liked to call "the variable." Regardless of alarm clocks, setting out clothes for the next day, everything accounted for, there was always the unaccounted variable with me, which continually resulted in our being late. Sometimes it had to do with having to wait for my phone to charge, or not remembering to fill Linus's water bowl until the elevator was in the lobby. Mostly it was due to my inability to manage time. Everyday rituals were kinetic; my body just performed them without accounting for how long they took.

That morning, I was tightening my shoelaces when something inside me loosened. A very loud noise escaped my body. It wasn't as if it slipped out during a stretch. This was a fugitive fart. I looked at him with a blank stare bordering on mortification, but then, just as quickly, a smile escaped, too. I laughed, doubled over, until I actually gripped a handful of his shirt and tried to apologize.

"My baby just passed some wind," he said, hugging me. "You know, there's always that first moment in a relationship, Stephanie, when you have to encounter stuff like this. And man, you just went for it, no pinky toe in those waters. You just dive, don't you, girl?" He was right, but it had less to do with gas and more to do with life.

"Wait, Oliver, it's not funny, I think I have to . . . make." I'd gone to the bathroom with him around before, but I'd never "passed wind" in front of him, and I'd certainly never corrupted my bathroom in his presence.

"There it is, the frickin' variable." He tossed his hands into the air, smiling.

"It's not like I can help it! Just go without me."

"No, just see if you can go first." What? I wasn't four. I knew when I had to go to the bathroom. "God, we're always late. It's so disrespectful. I know this time it's not your fault, but it's always something. Just put a verb in it, all right?" This was his clever way of urging me to hurry.

"I swear, it's not about disrespect. Everyone always thinks tardiness is about them," I shouted to him through my bathroom door. "They take it personally when I'm late, like I don't respect their time. Hello, this is 'rhea, not respect!" I was grunting and had the sweats. "Why don't you go without me?" I urged sweetly. Please, someone, anyone, make him go away.

"I'm not going. So we'll be late. It's not like it'll be the first time. Besides, worse things have been known to happen." Yeah, like dying with your granny panties around your ankles.

"Are you just going to stand there and listen?" Between rocking in pain and trying to remember if I'd removed Gabe from my beneficiary forms in case I died right there, I had to try to be quiet. "Can you at least play some music or something?" I was horrified.

THE CHICKLETS AND I HAVE HAD MANY A HEATED DISCUS-
sion about the crap we take, or refuse to take, once we're in relationships.
Phone Therapist cautioned, "Sex is the barometer of a relationship. It can
tell you all you need to know about the strength of the partnership at any
particular time." For others, namely Alexandra, it was not about a barometer as much as it was about a barium enema. Shit was the real gauge on
the success of her relationships. It wasn't about how much she was willing to tolerate, but rather, actually taking one.

She couldn't poo in public, not even in a work bathroom. She'd
sooner go home or borrow keys to Dulce's nearby apartment than make a
number two in the offices of her number one publishing conglomerate.
Even when we were in the Hamptons, she'd agonize about how many
people were in the house for the weekend, not in fear of overcrowding,
but because of what she liked to call "The BS," or The Bathroom Situation. Her bathroom was something she just wouldn't share in the sharehouse. If Alexandra ever found a guy she could actually "make" around,
I'm certain they'd make it. I'd begin to plan her engagement party.

I didn't have Alex's problem. I also didn't share in the opposite ex-
treme of my sister who boasted about her BMs as if they were MVPs,
leaving hers in the bowl, dragging an unsuspecting friend in to witness
her creation. I straddled the two extremes. I'm a firm believer that if you
can be intimate with the guy, you've got to be able to go to the bathroom
if he's around. So in the past weeks with Oliver, if I had to go, I'd just
put it out there. "I'm going to make now. So you need to either go to the
other room or turn up the volume." Of course, by doing this you're running a risk, because now he knows what's happening. Now he'll suddenly
be aware he's with a human instead of a goddess. It's a risk I was willing
to take. I just didn't want to take it with him leaning just outside the
door. "Hello, are you putting on music or what?"

"Sorry, love, I was trying to find the right station for the mood." I
could hear him snicker through the door.

"It's not funny! It hurts." It was funny, the kind of funny when you see someone slip on ice. I hated and loved him.

I DIDN'T THINK IT GOT MUCH MORE EMBARRASSING, THE key phrase being "I didn't think." Coming in second to last place in a New York Road Runners Club *Run for Fun* is pretty humiliating. Because we walked the race together, once we approached the finish line, Oliver watched me sprint ahead of him toward it.

"If you're going to lose baby, lose big," he said casually as he walked over the finish line, throwing his fists into the air above him. Then he hugged me and whispered, "Thank you. I'm so proud of my baby. You really got into it at the end, didn't you?"

"Uh, yeah, knowing the torture you were inflicting on me was coming to an end really kicked my ass into high gear."

"Could we not talk about your ass again?" I hit him on the back and tried to wiggle free from his embrace. "I'm kidding, baby. You haff a loffley bum, just loffley."

Something in me opened up during the race, and I actually enjoyed it. I'd never share with Oliver just how much pleasure I derived that day in fear that he'd plan more future mornings on roads, making his important mine. Instead, I ended up goading, "Happy now?" while thinking I was finally just that. Happy now. Not running toward or away from anything, just alongside someone who wanted me there.

GABE WANTED ME NOWHERE NEAR HIM THE DAY WE WERE to tell his parents we'd been married. He was edgy, pacing in our apartment, and when I asked him to help me decide which outfit to wear, he snapped. "Who gives a shit, Stephanie?" Oh grand, this day called for a party dress, something bright with polka dots, certainly.

Okay, fine. It called for a suit. It's important to always own at least one suit you can wear to an interview or funeral. A visit with my in-laws was like both, but none of my suits fit anymore. I'd recently put on twenty sticks of butter. Okay, that's not really fair. You can't "recently" pack on twenty pounds. I mean, it doesn't take a week to do. Its thickness builds gradually, like a storm. When I'm happy, I relax, enjoy myself, and yeah, basically get fat. Thin is usually a symptom of miserable, so when I'm actually slender, I rarely enjoy it. My weight floated from one hundred and twenty-three pounds to one hundred and forty-five pounds by August, which meant I was happy, settling into married life. If the honeymoon phase is anything like college, I'd done what was expected of me. The good wife for two and a half months one-upped the Freshman Fifteen with the True Love Twenty. So all was fair in love. It was time to go to war.

If it were September, I'd have gone military chic in a Balenciaga battle jacket, parachute pants, and a camouflage headscarf, ready for combat. But it was August, too early for head-to-toe olive-green drab. I did have new initials now that I was married. Married meant J. McLaughlin and P.K. Bradley. Sexy had a relief pitcher—her name was Lily Pulitzer. My clothes needed to look the part of wife when we told Gabe's parents I was just that. His wife. They still didn't know. Conservative. Feminine. Polite. Pearls, twin set, capri pants, and loafers. If my clothes were "just so," Rome would have less to judge. When she wasn't starving herself at Bergdorf's, the woman was feasting on a diet of hearsay and judgment and avoiding introspection and accountability as if they were carbs.

Time with Gabe's mother was always an interview with trick questions and sweaty palms. "What will you do, Stephanie, if the only place he matches for a residency is in Kansas?" What do you think I'll do, witch? Scream out for Auntie Em and file divorce papers with The Wizard?

I'd go with him, what the fuck else would I do? Why the hell would she ask a question like that, other than to try to stir something up with her broom handle? I wanted to pull the hair from her chinny chin chin when she said things like that.

"DO YOU WANT TO HEAD TO MY PARENT'S HOUSE BEFORE or after dinner?" Hi. Neither A nor B. It was a test I'd never pass. Maybe

I could dress my way out of it. The confrontation demanded more strength than Pulitzer could offer. I'd need formidable. I'd go governess. Prim, proper, Poppins. Mary Janes, a swan-neck collar, crispy white. Gloves would be pushing it. I brought along a vintage Gucci handbag that had belonged to my grandmother. I'd clutch it for strength. I needed to control something. I could control, at the very least, what I wore, as if Rome's hatred for me would go unnoticed when she saw I was cut from the same Italian cloth. I wanted to fit in, so they'd like me. So they'd tell their son he made a wonderful decision, tell him he's so lucky. Tell him to "never let that one go."

It was Tuesday, August 8, 2000. Gabe still hadn't completed his medical boards; he decided to put them off another year. This meant he could no longer use the excuse that telling his parents would interfere with his exam preparation. And, since still no date ever seemed to align with an open slot in the Rosens' calendars, we decided to end the charade and reveal our actions to them in person. Gabe started in with the excuses as we rounded his parents' expressway exit.

"I just don't think I can do this, Stephanie."

I didn't understand. My father is my best friend. It was always easy for me to communicate with my parents. So it was next to impossible for me to comprehend just how scared Gabe was of the people who brought him into this world. This made it absurdly easy for me to make his issue mine, worrying his inability to express himself to them was a reflection of his love for me. "If you really loved me, it wouldn't be so hard for you to say." Then I'd sit with that thought for a while and realize, no, it really wasn't *our* issue. It was *his*, and that was hard because it meant I couldn't do anything about it. I couldn't improve, couldn't therapy it, couldn't do anything but nothing. And I wasn't good at that then, the letting go. So, really, I should have known exactly how Rome felt. She couldn't let go of anything. No wonder Gabe loved me—I was his mother.

"Do you want a secret divorce to go with our secret marriage, Gabe?"

"No, of course not. I love you."

"If you love me, then why is it so hard for you to tell them?" We hadn't told anyone. I hadn't told my sister, my father, anyone, because I'd made a promise to Gabe.

"Steph, I don't doubt the way I feel about you. I love you. I know that." He took my hand. "Not just 'she's great, I love her' but I really love you, deeply. I love staring at you in bed while you laugh at TV shows. I love kissing you when you're asleep, even though I know you have no idea that I'm doing it, that kind of love."

"Then what's the problem?" I pulled my hand away.

"I just want to handle this the right way. I don't want another mess with them. Everything with them has been a nightmare. I just want to wait until I feel more comfortable telling them. Is that so bad?"

"Yes. Sorry, but yes. It is. We're married, Gabe. You made the decision to marry me, so stop whining about it and be married to me. Be my husband."

I can't believe I was one of those adults, in that car, having that pathetic conversation. After over two months of excuses, boards, "my mother this," "sweetheart that," I had no idea how I allowed myself to get entangled in such a fucked-up situation. Convincing a little boy to grow up: I could add it to my dating resume.

I married a momma's boy. I don't know what's worse, being a momma's boy or the woman who marries one. How do you handle dating or marrying a boy like that? You leave. You invest in some high-tech, aerodynamic running shoes, and you sprint your ass as far away as you can get. You don't stay in the car, alongside him, and try to convince him to open his side. You don't play the understanding, "You poor thing, I know just how you must feel" martyr. You fucking run because he won't grow up. His whole life Mommy and Daddy made everything right for him, and a man who hasn't had to really risk hasn't had a chance to build character.

"Sweetheart, I'm so sorry," he said. "I know you deserve more than this. I just don't think I can do this today." This is the point where red fury replaced any type of compassion I could feel for him.

"Look, you feel sick because your parents have made it clear they're against our being married. You know what? You shouldn't fucking care. I'm your wife. You just turned twenty-six. You can make decisions without checking first with Mommy and Daddy . . ." I knew it wasn't helping, my berating him for still being a boy. He might have defended himself or tried more excuses. I couldn't hear anything anymore. I was in what my father called "the red zone."

A car's tachometer gauge measures how fast the engine is turning in RPM. It enables manual drivers to shift at the optimum RPM for best fuel economy or acceleration. When the tach moves into the red zone, you may be causing damage to your engine. It's a no-no. Welcome to my world.

Growing up, when I became fixed with anger and frustration, my father would warn calmly, "Stephanie, there's no talking to you right now. You're in the red zone. Nothing I can say will penetrate, and you're only hurting yourself." He wouldn't talk with me until I could form full sentences that didn't include the word "hate." But I'm angry, so you're going to listen to me right now! "You're all emotion right now. There's no talking to emotions, no reasoning with them." He would hear none of it, which only revved me up more. Eventually, I'd stall.

I wouldn't stall this time. Gabe wouldn't let go of the steering wheel. His knuckles were white. I felt like a mother, convincing her red-faced son to let go of her leg on his first day of kindergarten. Could I trick him into a round of patty-cake and make for the front door?

"I'm going in now, Gabe, with or without you. Are you coming?" He stared at me blankly. I wanted to rip him from the car and guide him to their front door, my hand resting on the crown of his head. That's it. Thatta boy. Easy does it.

"Okay," he said in a shaky voice, "I'm ready now."

We'd never stopped by their home without calling first, so this unexpected visit would immediately set them into uncomfortable. We needed time to explain, to tell it on our terms, so we took care to slip off our wedding bands. Gabe rang the bell and took a step back.

I wiped my hands on my skirt. On my hips. Folded them together. Let them fall. I reached for Gabe's hand, but he pulled away. This was a great start.

"Well, this is certainly a surprise," Rome said in a voice so tight I thought it would snap. She glanced immediately at my left hand, then to his. "What, what are you doing here?" She kissed us formally. "Marvin, it's Stephanie and Gabe. We still have time," she yelled from the foyer. "The Diamonds are on their way over. We're going to dinner at the club."

"Oh, we didn't mean to intrude," Gabe stumbled. "We were just at Stephanie's father's house and thought we'd say hello." Lie.

"Please, you're my son. It's never an intrusion. Do you guys want to join us for dinner? God, would you look at me?" She patted her head, suddenly aware of the curlers loomed on her head. Without waiting for an answer, she began to walk toward her bedroom.

In her brief absence, Gabe whispered to me, "Why don't we tell them after dinner?"

"No fucking way in hell. You're stalling. I swear to God, Gabe, I'm not going anywhere until you tell them."

"They're rushing around right now. It's not a good time."

"I can't believe you." I wished I were wearing pointy shoes.

"Can I offer either of you a cold beverage?" Rome asked, now back from her bedroom, with sanguine lips and a soufflé of hair.

"Nah. Where's Dad?"

"Oh, he's just putting on his shoes. You're coming to dinner, right?"

"Sure." Enough already. Who cares about dinner? Tell them!

Marvin joined us in the foyer. "Hey, kids." He shook Gabe's hand and kissed me on the cheek. I felt more at ease with him now in the room. "So you're coming to dinner with us and the Diamonds?"

"Yeah, why not?" What was he waiting for? I felt like we were in a three-legged race, our shoelaces knotted, pulling each other in different directions as we raced toward the finish line. I should have chosen the burlap sack race, won, and upturned the sack over Gabe's head and clubbed him.

"Can you two sit down for a second?" That had to be the hardest part, right there, formalizing it. Bad news always follows a request to be seated, as if hearing the news would bring the onset of fainting spells.

"What is all this about?" Rome asked, pretending to look at the time on her watch. "We really don't have time. The Diamonds are—"

"Romina, we have time to sit," Marvin scolded before lifting the legs of his slacks as he sat.

She knew what was coming. She wanted to stall. "Are you two sure you don't want something cold to drink?"

Gabe sat silently for what felt like a full minute. I smiled with a forced face of apology, wishing he were holding my hand.

"As you both know, it has been a nightmare trying to set a wedding date. And it was becoming so much more about the wedding than our marriage, and we wanted you two to be the first to hear it, from us, in person . . ."

"You've set a new date?" Rome interrupted hopefully.

"We didn't want you to say you heard this through the grapevine, and we didn't want to tell you over the phone." He reached for my hand. "We got married on Saturday." I closed my eyes and waited. I was expecting something to explode. I opened one eye, then the other. Maybe they hadn't heard him. They were still sitting. Their legs were still crossed. There was no fainting. It was the calm before the storm, I was sure of it.

"I can't say that we're surprised," Marvin said flippantly. "It's been years in the making." No, this is the part where you hug and congratulate us.

"We still want to have a wedding reception," Gabe added, "to celebrate when it works with your schedules, and we don't want you to think our decision had anything to do with you. The whole thing was just a debacle. We want you to know, it's not about you, and we were worried you'd take it personally."

"Of course it's not," Marvin assured us without getting up.

Rome sat as if she were still waiting for something, rubbing her thumb over her manicured nails.

"What was the date?" she snapped. The thin band of soldiers around her mouth came to attention. Go on lady. I'm ready. Don't let the outfit fool you.

"The date?" Gabe repeated in a slight panic. We had no idea. May twentieth. May twentieth. May twentieth! We had to think quickly, starting to count backwards from Tuesday. "I don't know, what was the date on Saturday?"

"You don't even know the date?"

"The fifth. August fifth," I interjected, really still unsure if I was right. "It was this past Saturday when you guys were away. We wanted to call you," yeah, like months ago, "but we thought it was better to tell you two first, and in person." So you can't find anything else to bitch about.

We were saved by the bell. It was David and Arlene Diamond, waving through the window that flanked the front door. "Please don't tell anyone," Gabe said sharply, "because no one else knows yet."

"Weren't you just at Stephanie's father's house?" Rome asked without standing to open the door. "You mean to tell us you didn't tell him while you were there?" Lady, I know it looks like makeup, but this is war paint. I squeezed Gabe's hand.

"No," Gabe lied, "we didn't see his car in the driveway, so we figured we'd go back after telling you." We were never at my father's house. This was Gabe doing improvisation, with one hand behind his back. I'd give him that—the boy could lie.

Marvin opened the door for the Diamonds. Hugs, handshakes, kiss kiss. "What are you two doing here? What a nice surprise." In a beat, Gabe and I were in our car, following the two couples in Marvin's car to a dinner we never planned on attending. There would be no toasts at dinner, no easy conversation, and no escaping the inevitable: Rome would cry herself to sleep that night in Marvin's arms questioning, "Am I that horrible of a mother that my own son would go and get married without me? And back in Manhattan, I'd fall asleep in Gabe's arms questioning, "Am I that horrible of a choice for your wife that your parents wouldn't be happy for you?" None of us would be able to run from it.

IT'S PROBABLY HUMAN NATURE THE WAY WE ALWAYS think it's going to get better with almost everything, until the tipping point where our health and looks begin to decline. With relationships, I always had a reason why some time in the future would be better for me than it was that day. When I was fat, I thought I'd feel pretty when I was thin, and when I was thin, I thought I'd be happier if I was more toned and muscular and had more money to look more coordinated. I wasn't comfortable in my own skin unless there was a man there to tell me just how radiant that skin looked. I was a victim of low self-esteem and had the Soon syndrome *bad*. I was running toward a brighter future, unaware of the mirages I'd created in the distance.

I thought everything in my relationship with Gabe would be better in our future, because by then his parents would finally take us seriously— they'd treat me like family instead of the redheaded stepchild-in-law who turned their son into some kind of outlaw. By then Gabe would shake his Peter Pan syndrome and become a grown-up, the kind with leather laces and polished shoes, the sort who read the paper and wasn't afraid of honesty. I genuinely believed all I had to do was "just make it through this," like the pain in your lungs when you're approaching the finish line. Our relationship required stamina and perseverance. I thought running along-side him as he lied to his parents would guarantee us a 26.275-mile marriage. I didn't know then we were more endurance training, alternated with speed drills, than anything that would ever approach a marathon.

On our one-year wedding anniversary, the one we celebrated publicly on August fifth, I felt relieved. One year together felt like the "I told you so" of endurance, until, that is, Rome refused to acknowledge it. The rest of her family sent gifts and cards, wishing us love. Rome's own mother confided to me, "Stephanie, I did not raise my daughter to behave this way. I never taught her this." Rome would repeat this exact phrase years later, when I'd confide in her what Gabe had done. "Stephanie, I didn't raise my son to behave this way. We didn't teach him this."

ten

CONTROL ALT DELETE

HE DID IT OVER TOOTHPASTE. IT WAS SUNDAY, NOVEMBER 2, 2003, at the butt-crack of dawn, the day of the New York Marathon, when Oliver asked me to move in with him. He was leaning over my bathroom sink, spitting minty foam into running water while I sat on the toilet peeing.

"And this is how you ask me?" I pretended to be annoyed. If I hadn't just peed, I would have wanted to.

"It seems appropriate. We know we can share a bathroom."

"Can I wipe before we talk about this?"

"You can do anything you want to, baby. I just think it makes sense."

I was thrilled someone loved me enough to want to live with me. It made me feel important, like I'd just checked the wall posting at school and learned I landed the leading role. Oliver and I had been dating exclusively for three months. In that time, he had made a practice of cooking me romantic dinners on hot summer nights, complete with rose petals, candlelight, and Christmas music. Holiday music always makes me happy, so during dinner, in lieu of Billie Holiday, we listened to Billy Gilman sing "Jingle Bell Rock." And once we finished eating, I'd turn up the volume and we'd dance in our socks, slipping on his wooden floors. Despite my pleas, he'd always lower the volume. "I'm saving you from tinnitus." And that's when I knew he really wasn't the guy for me.

I know what you're thinking. Is she fucking kidding me? She wanted to break up with the guy 'cause he lowered her music? I know it's a small thing, and it might sound absurd that I'd want to end our relationship over something so trivial, but it was a very illustrative straw. And maybe I grasped onto that straw because it's what I could hold—it was a reason I could point to. Otherwise, it was just some gut feeling I couldn't explain, and then I'd have to wonder if it was sabotage, wonder if I was gun-shy, wonder if it was me. This way, needling at some inane reason not to be together made me feel like I was in the right. Besides, I really didn't think I could spend the rest of my life with a man who didn't enjoy me singing with my eyes closed at the top of my lungs. When I get to that place, I'm a toothy kid, in mismatched clothes on top of the big slide, doing it all myself, with the whole world out there in front of me. I'm happiest there, and spending eternity with someone who unremittingly lowered my groove, well, he'd always be bringing me down. It was a sign.

He also had horrible breath.

Still, I lingered by his side, ignoring signs, because he told me innovative bedtime stories, and took Linus for runs in the park so I could read, or photograph, or let's face it, just kitty about in a laze. He loved me selflessly, with back scratches, mushroom barley soup, and chick flicks. He wanted to make me happy, and when I looked at him, some afternoons, on his sofa reading, I thought of tea sandwiches and hand-knit blankets. Of lunchtime and buying fresh bread. Oliver made me feel taken care of, like I was in grade school with its organized times for naps and finger-painting. He was my comfortable. I liked him most when he was depressed.

So, I remained because of that, because of how well he did patient and loving and there. I hung on because Phone Therapist said "self-sabotage" repeatedly during our sessions.

"So what do you say? I'll even give you the big closet." He was now in my bedroom pointing to my squeak of a closet.

"Don't you need to go stretch or something?" I answered without answering.

"Okay, sweetie, we'll talk about it later. I'll look for you on the East Side. You're taking your camera, right?"

"Yeah, I have to practice my panning. Don't forget to brush your tongue." He went back for the toothbrush and did as he was told.

"Okay, Mom, I love you," he mocked. " 'Bye, Linus. Be good for Mommy." And he was off to run twenty-six miles of torture.

It was too bright out later that day; it hurt my eyes. Delicate whisps of cloud, layers, and mittens. I couldn't stand it. I hate blinds pulled to the top at any time, but in the morning, it's insufferable. I yanked the blinds down, then grabbed my camera, let Linus lick up my nose, and headed to First Avenue to photograph the runners as they made their way off the Fifty-ninth Street Bridge.

The streets were littered with clementine wedges and crushed paper cups. Barricades, officers, windbreakers, and dogs. Children holding signs, "Go Ted." Some of the kids were attached to their mothers with plastic coiled leashes, connecting their wrists. And I nodded. It made sense. Crowds, kidnapping, missing children screaming for their mothers. Precaution.

Growing up, I was terrified of being kidnapped. I'd dream a stranger snagged me, and when I'd part my lips to release a ripple of a scream, nothing would come out. Today, the Upper East Side of Manhattan paralyzes me in the very same way. The South Bronx or even some disreputable streets south of the Meatpacking District, near the warehouses and twenty-dollar trannyjobs, is understandable. But it's the Upper East Side, home to the Ralph Lauren mansion, Serendipity's frozen hot chocolates, and Bloomingdale's big brown bag that houses my anxiety. It has little to do with East Side rapists trailing unaccompanied quick-paced women to their fifth-floor walk-ups. It's worse. It's where Gabe lives.

But this was the only appropriate place to go for the marathon shots. The lighting was better here than on the West Side, closer to the end of the race. Sure, his friends, the hospital at which he worked, and our memories resided there. Until that marathon Sunday there wasn't much room for all that *and* me. I was on a goddamn island. There wasn't room for rationing anymore. Running into Gabe or one of his extensions would be unnecessary drama, like the suspenseful music, warning the audience something is about to happen. The warning music is nerve-racking; it's the same as the anxiety I toted to the East Side with me in my camera bag. You're just waiting for something big to happen. But the truly scary bits usually happen in silence, as quick as a guillotine. I needed to take precaution—I'd hide behind my camera lens if worse came to worst.

I'll save you the suspenseful music right now. I didn't run into Gabe. I ran into our former doorman, Asa. He smiled at me across the barricade, and as quick as that, I wanted to cry. His smile was sympathetic, the kind you get when you tell someone you've just been laid off. Looking at Asa's face, it came upon me: I wasn't ready to move in with Oliver. I didn't want to share any more people with Oliver. I didn't want overlap, for fear that years later I'd run into *our* doorman and want to cry. I think they call it gun-shy.

It's no wonder. Too many people move in together to save money. "Well, it just made sense at the time. It's stupid to be paying rent in two places." After a few months of dating you're both cohabiting, sleeping together nearly every night anyway. Stupid is moving in with someone before you're married. It's not like it was years ago, when dates were formal and regulated. Now you're aware if he hogs the covers, pays his bills on time, or squeezes the toothpaste from the middle or the top. You don't need to share a lease to recognize if he picks up his socks, keeps the refrigerator clean, or makes the bed every morning. You already know. This whole living together before you get married is absurd. It's a fake precaution. It's a false sense of security, like a frail Juliet balcony. I lived with Gabe for three years before we actually got married, and how well did that serve me? I knew false security all too well.

ON OUR WEDDING DAY, THE RABBI TURNED TO GABE AND me and said, "It's no longer just between the two of you." He looked at each of us. His hands were warm and dotted brown. "Now it's between you, and you, and God."

I loved that idea.

God was my precaution because now, if Gabe screwed up, he

wouldn't just be messing with me, he'd be fucking with scripture and commandments, with the big G. Marriage was a commitment to spend our lives working on our relationship, no matter what. In my mind, the "what" part excluded abusive behavior. If, one day, he abused our children or me, that was a deal breaker. Otherwise, until death us do part, just as it says. I was firm on this. I'm a big fan of the vows.

I believed no one goes into marriage thinking about divorce. Single people confirm, "I don't believe in divorce" early in relationships. It's as if it's something to boast about, like homemade tomato sauce or naturally straight teeth. "Oh, well I don't believe in divorce," she'll say as she folds her napkin and purses her lips. As if "divorce" could fly like Santa or the Tooth Fairy. I've never heard anyone retort aloud, "Oh, well I do. It's fabulous for the wallet and the complexion. All that saline, dear, you oughta try it." Maybe you believe in divorce when you're a child who witnesses his parents making each other cry snot. But then, maybe you don't believe in *marriage*, the way some people don't believe in e-mail or cell phones. You know it exists. It's just not for you—until it is.

It was my understanding that both Gabe and I believed in marriage upon the respective "I do" bits. Even if one of us strayed, I assumed we could ameliorate the situation through communication, work, and counseling. I'd say it as if I were reading buzzwords off a chalkboard. We would rebuild trust by first examining and understanding "why" a betrayal occurred. Then we could overcome it by preventing a recurrence through our newfound understanding. I could make our environment safe for him to communicate honestly with me, while he could identify when he was in compromising situations and act more appropriately. It all sounds lovely and neat, like a dainty tea sandwich. Unfortunately, the only tea sandwiches Gabe cared for were made of bologna.

I knew we would fight, but at the end of the day, we were a team. It was us against the world. Despite my enormous set of lungs, I couldn't cheer enough for the both of us; he'd need to do his part. Otherwise, we'd never win.

Many people I know shrug their shoulders at marriage. "I guess.

Why not? If it doesn't work out, I can always get divorced." It's not ideal, but it's as contemporary as "Come join us this Saturday night as we celebrate my divorce" e-vites. I've discovered a way to spot the ones who really, truly, believe in marriage.

They move your relationship forward.

If you're in a relationship with someone who hasn't been the one initiating forward momentum, question things. If he's the one who only moves things ahead out of fear of loss, then you have someone who'd rather lean toward the water of your sinking boat than grab a bucket and work to stay afloat. Consider this your red and white life preserver.

Before Gabe and I were married, I could forecast my behavior for years. I used words like *always* and *never*. "I will always work through anything with you. I'll never have children just to bring us closer." The truth is, I wouldn't learn how I'd really deal with a situation until the weather actually turned. One day it did.

It was exactly one year earlier to the day. It was Sunday, November 3, 2002, NYC Marathon Sunday. Linus was getting his nails clipped on East Eighty-first Street. My sister Lea was over, reclined on the living room sofa, watching E!, flipping through the pages of *InStyle* magazine. I was in my first trimester.

"Lock the goddamn door, Lea. And no matter what happens, don't open it."

"What the fuck crawled up your pregnant ass?" Lea asked without looking up.

"I just have a feeling." I raced to the front door and locked it with the sliding chain.

"Yeah, whatever."

"No, seriously, I'm fucking shaking. I just know."

"What the hell are you talking about?"

I didn't answer her. I bolted into our office, a small room we were currently converting into a nursery. We'd just put up curtains and a toile valance. I sat at the desk, opened our laptop, and began to dig through the history of visited web pages. There wasn't anything suspect. CNN, ESPN, Yahoo!

Years prior, Gabe had given me the password to his personal Yahoo! mail account to send an e-mail out for him. And since then, unbeknownst to him, I would periodically check his e-mail for anything suspicious. "Suspicious" didn't mean other women—it meant lies. Gabe was the type of guy who would habitually lie to his friends and family. "Sorry, man, I really wanted to make it this weekend, but I was stuck at the hospital" e-mails were issued regularly to his friends. If "the hospital" was a substitute for "on the sofa picking my balls and watching the NY Jets game," then call me Woody Johnson. He never had the stones to be honest with people, fearful of what they'd think of him. Having to work sounded safer than "I overpromised, and ended up going out with Stephanie's family instead." Work implied obligation instead of choice. No one could be offended by obligation.

When I'd see these e-mails to his friends, I'd confront Gabe. Okay, I'd do my share of lying too, telling him I needed an address or number from his contact list, "that's the only reason I was in there. And then I saw an e-mail from Paul, and well, I just wanted to see how he was doing. But then I saw you lied to him. Why?" It was that type of thing. The truth is, I just didn't trust him. I'll say it again. I didn't trust him. He'd postponed our wedding, would lie to his parents and friends, and something in me worried he was lying to me too. I knew, deep down, he was a "yes-man," who would say *yes* even if he meant *no*. And he was a flirt. He'd even flirt with the telephone operator: "Why yes, the address would be lovely, just as lovely as your voice."

"Jesus, Gabe."

"What? It's funny." And then he'd laugh, and seeing him laugh made me happy, so I'd sneak attack him with a kiss. Gabe was an emotional slut. But he was my emotional slut, and we were married, so I'd have to love him for it, and get over the "little things," like his lying to his friends via e-mail. So I convinced myself, "When you're married, it just doesn't matter." Let it slide.

That Sunday, I wasn't in the mood to slide. I checked his Yahoo! e-mail account with the password he'd kept the same, as if to say, "See, we have no secrets between us, sweetheart. See, I have nothing to hide, baby." There was nothing suspect. Then I scoured the web history folder. It was clean of misgivings. He didn't want to get caught. He knew to cherry pick through it and expunge evidence. Evidence of what? I didn't know.

He didn't kiss me any differently that day, wasn't extra nice, or too aloof. He stuck to our habits, the embrace on good-bye, and the quick kiss. He looked me in the eyes when he said he loved me, just as always. They say only a small percentage of our communication is verbal—the rest is spoken in our stance, the way we shift our eyes or flick a finger. We use different muscles when it's a genuine smile. Maybe it was the pregnancy hormones, the nesting instinct to protect things, which propelled me forward, hawk-like, in search of his little cookie trail. I combed the machine, searching through the cookies, electronic fingerprints of where he'd been. My life was a goddamn horror movie. You want to be scared, but you don't. I wanted to find something, but my God, what if I found something? It was so lose-lose.

There was a file in the cookie folder indicating he'd been on his hospital's website, yet in the history folder, there was no evidence he'd ever visited it. The site was a login screen for his hospital e-mail account. I'd need to figure out a way in. For the password, I'd only have three attempts before being locked out. I tried:

the name of his dead dog.

the alarm code for his parents' house.

his social security number.

Holy shit. I was in. I held my breath as a loading bar appeared. My throat had a pulse. I could hear the liquid in my ears. Everything seemed to split apart around me.

An e-mail from missylikeshorses@aol.com had a subject line reading, "On a more serious note." In it, a woman described how Gabe flirted with her on the phone, in their e-mails and text messages. She inquired about moving the relationship further and questioned why he hadn't.

You'd think I'd be relieved to read this. Shock, not relief, is what you feel when you discover another woman is e-mailing your husband, the father of your unborn child, about *their* issues. Someone else needed to have "a talk" about *them*. They had a *them*. It wasn't about whether or not they were intimate. They had a relationship, a secretive *they*. Secretive e-mails. Secretive phone calls. Secretive dates. What was next? The next logical step was intimacy.

I began to shake. I was pregnant, in our home. He was at the groomer, picking up our dog, and he had *this* in his e-mail inbox. I wanted it to be some dream.

In the face of tragedy, some people clean voraciously, unsure of what to do with their nervous energy. Others laugh uncontrollably. I e-mailed.

This is Gabe's WIFE. Do you know that he has one, and that I am pregnant with his child? Whoever you are, I sure hope you didn't know this. Please, out of respect to me, sever your relationship quickly, as I don't think my heart can bear this news.

Then I waited.

She replied a minute later, "Consider it done. Will you tell him or should I?" Then, instead of replying to her e-mail, I used the number from the e-mail and called her. I didn't even know her name. When she answered, I didn't know whom to ask for . . . Missy?

"This is Stephanie . . . Gabe's wife—"

"I'm so sorry. I just can't believe he's married." Her voice sounded older, sophisticated, yet panicked, as if she'd lost a child in a crowd.

"Well, he is." My knees wouldn't stop shaking, even when I pressed on them.

"First of all, nothing happened. I mean we went out many times, but he never even kissed me. Well, not yet." Oh my God, did she just say that? Then, "Listen, I just don't believe you. I don't think he's married." Her not believing me revved me into the red zone.

"Really? Do you happen to have his phone number? You know, something other than his beeper or cell phone? Ever try, I don't know, calling information for his HOME phone number? Why don't you do yourself a favor, honey, and try calling him at home. Then we can finish talking." I went there. The dynamic changes when someone plays the honey card. I was pissed, but I couldn't hang up. I couldn't move.

"Listen, nothing happened. We just go out a lot at night."

"Where?" I said as if she had to answer me instantly. I was surprised when she did.

"Well, we've been planning on attending a black-tie affair together."

"Affair" hung in the air like a thick cloud of dust after an explosion. It was an old-fashioned word in that context—*affair*—one used by grandparents on Sunday nights after speaking of the weekend weather. "Oh yes, it was a marvelous affair. Just marvelous." *Affair* wasn't a word uttered by the other woman.

He was going to functions with her, entering rooms with her on his arm, eating mini egg rolls, and shaking hands with strangers, pretending he had a different life. He'd phone me from the hospital—the number showed up on our caller ID—apologizing that he'd be stuck overnight on a case that hadn't even started yet. "I'll make it up to you, sweetheart. All I want to do is crawl into bed with you and Linus. Next week will be better. I love you so much." I'd cover his dinner with aluminum foil. He'd cover his ass, then leave wearing a cummerbund, slipping his plain little band of gold right off.

I changed my mind. I didn't want to hear anymore. Learning the details of their whats and wheres meant everything as I knew it would dissolve. With each detail she'd divulge, I'd be less proficient at pretending it all away. Knowing what was "theirs" would change my life forever. I wasn't ready to commit to this fortuitous forever over the phone. I also couldn't help myself.

"A black-tie affair?" I repeated.

"Well, yes, but mostly it's been movie premieres . . ." He went to the opening of *Narc* with her. ". . . a Knicks game . . ." He'd said he'd gone with his friend Chip, came home that night, raving to me about their courtside seats. Told me he wished I were there with him. ". . . Oh, and The Bungalow a bunch of times," she finally said about the "private" nightclub Bungalow 8 because she'd been there, and when you've been there, it's "The Bungalow." "That kind of thing. You know." No, but I was beginning to. "But, like I said, nothing happened."

"Um, I don't care if nothing happened." I enunciated "happened" as if I were speaking to a second grader. "What happ-end is he walked around letting people believe he didn't have a pregnant wife at home." I wanted to wake up. Instead, I hung up.

"He's so fucking dead. Lea, I can't even believe this. He has been lying to my face, without any signs of remorse. He's a fucking sociopath!" She was reading the e-mails I'd already pilfered from his inbox and forwarded as evidence. His e-mails complained that he was sad when he didn't receive a new correspondence from her. My God, there was even an e-mail in his "sent messages" folder, dated the evening he'd asked me to go to Barney's with him. A week earlier he'd asked me to help him choose a tuxedo at Barney's. His parents were buying him one for no particular reason, other than his asking. It wasn't as though we had many occasions that called for formal attire, but it didn't seem suspicious. It seemed like shopping.

He was buying it for her, with me. I helped him decide on lapels and buttons, spent an hour narrowing it down, pinching shoulders and watching sleeve lengths. It was all for her. His e-mail to her that night was signed with xxx. My heart hurt. I forwarded that message to my personal e-mail account. Even when I caught him cheating, I was taking precautions for an uncertain future. Now, I had proof.

DESPITE THE PROVISIONS I MADE, KNOWING HIS E-MAIL password, and checking it twice, he still found a way to lick icing and eat out the cake. If someone wants to lead a double life, they will find a way to do it. And they can promise you things until your nerves unfold and you can finally put your feet up. But it can all be a lie. There are no guarantees, even when people mean what they say at the time. People change their minds. People die. And the hurt is as real as a baseball bat.

At the end of the day, you can take precautions every step of the way, play it safe, do it right, be as structured as DNA. We try to prevent bad from assaulting our lives. Keep your kids on a leash, keep your husband on a leash. It's all control, and no amount of it will be real, none of it will give you safety. That little gold circle isn't safety, it's a promise to work on the relationship for the rest of your life or until the divorce goes through. Safety is something you have to find within yourself, like willpower. And I knew it.

Growing up, I was the fat girl. When the bottle landed on me during Spin the Bottle, the boys chanted, "Do over." I didn't get to choose boys. Gabe was the scholar and athlete of the year growing up, and he chose me. His wanting me made me feel special. His cheating on me was worse than being told you'd outlive your children.

After the divorce, I finally got to a place where it was my choice: what color to paint my new apartment walls, where to eat, and whom to date. And I chose safe. I found safety in Oliver, instead of finding it within myself. He'd fall over himself trying to make me happy, and whenever I thought of ending it with him, I'd remember Hallmark, those rows of sympathy cards. How horrible things can happen in our lives, and now that I've found someone worth something, shouldn't I hold on? I'd think of the times I was in pain, curled in the fetal position, crying for my grandmother Beatrice, the one who died a long time ago, to please take the pain away, please protect me, watch over me, please give me strength to get through this, please. Then I'd swallow and let the tears go, thinking safe was better than that. Oliver was a rest and exhale, and I knew in my bones he'd never reject me or deceive me. So I'd hold on tight even though I knew Oliver was the wrong choice. Because he was safe. And safe was something I didn't know how to give myself.

I needed to learn how to create safety from within, how to string a yellow reminder ribbon around transience. Knowing how to nurture myself, trust my instincts, and believing in my body were the keys to finding safe. These lies we tell ourselves, "Well, he did say he missed me," "He got me a diamond the size of a walnut so he must love me," "When I threatened to leave, he did, after all, come after me and ask me to move in with him," are false security. Rationalizing our gut instincts away, we try to convince ourselves because we want what we want. But after you've been hurt enough times, you realize sometimes you have to just let it go. It's the only precaution you can really take.

We all suffer, and we all want someone safe to catch us, wipe our tears, bring us the mint chip, and hold our hand. Oliver loved me to death. But that can't be everything. You have to love yourself to death first.

I had to let him go. I cut the cord.

eleven

THERE'S NEVER JUST ONE COCKROACH

MY MOOD WITH OLIVER TOOK A TURN BEFORE OUR CAB driver even signaled. We'd gone out for dinner, but I couldn't work up the nerve to end things aloud. I thought maybe I could just distance myself, and in our cab ride back to the Upper West Side, a centrifugal force pushed me closer to the door, away from him, my shoulder a new weapon against intimacy. I grew silent and felt alone. I looked out the cab window, streaks of steam, beads of rain joined and pooled into tiny rivers. I felt closer to them, to the rectangles of light from sleepless apartments, to the short-order chef with his fold of a hat as he stubbed out his cigarette on a square of sparkling sidewalk, than I did to Oliver.

I'd felt that, against a cab window, so many times before him, in that thick heavy silence where I'd wonder what was next. My movements no longer felt casual. Everything was heavier. I waited for him to ask what was wrong. Instead, he reached his hand out toward me. I didn't hold it back.

When we entered my apartment, he broke the silence. "Are you going to tell me what's wrong?"

"Ugh, I don't see why you put up with me. I'm all drama and difficult." I put it on him. Maybe he'd end things. It would be easier that way, with less to regret. It was Projection, full on with a capital P.

"I like you difficult, and I'm here because I care about you." He brushed his hand against the back of my head. "Stephanie, we're great together." He sensed it; he knew what I'd been thinking.

"Can I ask you something?" I looked up to make sure I had his attention. "Don't you ever get tired of defending us to me? Isn't it exhausting?" I knew what that was like. Cheerleading isn't just tiresome—it's embarrassing.

"I guess I don't see it that way. I see us as 'us,' and sometimes my babylove just gets sad. So I'm here to listen and do what I can." I hated how agreeable he was being. "Linus, do I need to remind Mommy how great we are together?" I hated when he asked Linus rhetorical questions. Anything he did was going to piss me off. I was pulling a Gabe on him.

Pulling a Gabe involved assigning the role of "the heavy" to your significant other. It meant staying because it was easier than leaving. It made lazy acceptable. See, Gabe stayed in our marriage and agreed to start a family because he knew how much I wanted it. That had to be it. Maybe he thought I could want it for both of us, and seeing me happy would make him happy too.

After months of trying, and fainting at the gynecologist—fearing I'd hear the doctor say, "Sorry, you just can't have children"—I had to take fertility drugs. Clomid. Gabe dutifully came home every fertile day to procreate the shit out of me. And then it happened: two pink lines. I had everything I wanted, everything on my love list. Then all the Betty Crocker products hit me on the head when I discovered the rogue e-mails.

Gabe wasn't strong enough to be honest. I speculate he knew I was a good person and didn't want to hurt me, so he concealed parts of his life from me. I force myself to speculate it. Otherwise, he's venal. Otherwise, I married someone ruthless. It's one thing saying you've fallen out of love. I can understand that. But to come home every day and try to impregnate me, spilling lies on my cervix, knowing the whole time he was running around pretending not to be married—that's a snake. It's someone without character, without virtue, someone who never had to account for his actions because Mommy and Daddy would always make it right.

The problem is, *he* shouldn't have been okay with that. He should have felt remorse, not because of how I'd feel if I ever discovered his lies, but because he knew what he was doing was wrong. Yeah, it's got a name. Try morals. Integrity. Go ahead, for shits, throw in strength of character.

He stayed for the wrong reasons, with one foot in, because it was easier than leaving.

I was staying with Oliver for the same reasons. The difference was I didn't need to do it for years to know Oliver deserved more, to know, really, at the end of the day, I deserved more, too.

"I'm sorry, Oliver. I *know* this isn't what you want to hear, but it's something I won't change my mind about." Deep breath. "We need to break up." I exhaled and waited.

"I guess I knew this was coming," he said more to himself than to me. "I just need to know why. Do you even know why?"

This would hurt. "When I go out at night, I find myself looking at other men." I couldn't look at him. "I guess that'd be fine by itself, but it's more than looking. No, I mean, I haven't done anything. I've just been feeling like I've wanted to, and that's a sign. I mean, you deserve more than that."

Truth: that was the symptom. The *real* problem was his personality. While he really was a gentle and very good man, he annoyed the shit out of me. I loved him, but I didn't really *like* him. I didn't want to hear about his work or friends, about the trees he liked in the park. You know that question, "If you were stuck on a deserted island, which three movies would you take with you?" Replace *movies* with *people*, and Oliver would not have been on the list. That was all I really needed to know.

"I'm sorry," I said, and I really was. "I know, believe me I know, this isn't easy, but it's better now than—"

"I get it. I'm going." He lingered near the entrance of my apartment, just looking at me. "I hope you find what you're looking for." Then he closed the door behind him.

IT IS MY ESTIMATION THAT CENTRAL PARK SHOULD ONLY be visited to photograph old people or to mourn. I'd be doing both, which called for my Nikon SLR and a pair of dark rectangular sunglasses, the ones old people wear that look like pimped up Volvos for your face. Perhaps I'd lift a pair from the first slow old man I encountered.

Okay, I was having a mood. It's called a breakup. Welcome to a too sunny and unseasonably warm November afternoon in my life.

When a relationship ends, you're forced to deal with the equitable distribution of assets. You return CDs and faded T-shirts. Oliver left a box with my doorman, crammed it with printouts of every e-mail I'd ever sent, every card, every matchbook or business card from the restaurants at which we'd dined. It was a bit much, but it's how he dealt. Still, there was more to divide. It came down to real estate.

That was really my restaurant because I went there before we were a we. Okay, he liked that bar more than I did, so he could have it. We parcel places in our minds before we plot our days. There was no mistake—Central Park was Oliver's. He knew the names of statues, paths, and trees, could tell me the beginner rollerbladers practice near the azaleas at Cherry Hill, and that I'd get good photos of horseback riders as they passed beneath the Pine Bank Arch. I was about to violate his territory.

I grabbed my knapsack, journal, and camera and headed toward his park. I needed to stew in my sorrow, and since I knew the park and its inhabitants would make me miserable, it was the perfect destination.

I despise shiny, happy, REM-like days in Manhattan, especially near the park. Central Park serves as a reminder of what I don't have. It's filled with people doing things they should be doing indoors. Like holding hands and wearing their mop-headed children as necklaces. Worse. There's running going on. Isn't that what the frickin' treadmill is for? I don't want to be near runners or families or stick figures lying around in bikinis thinking they've got it good. You're sharing an immense space with too many strangers, and you're stripped down to underwear alternatives doing it. There are available rooms in this city beyond the Pierre Hotel. Note to you: get one.

Okay, so my hatred for the park isn't really about the park. It holds my history in its canopy of trees and blanket of leaves. My mother tells me she spent my childhood crying in parks. "I felt like a single mother, always alone with you in the stroller, watching all the families, wondering why my husband wasn't with me." It didn't matter if he was working. It's not what she'd signed up for. I'd heard this for years, my mother's unhappiness with the lack of time my father spent with her on weekends. It felt like a warning. I didn't want to be alone on weekends, crying in parks feeling single, either. Of course, that's exactly what happened with Gabe.

Once upon a *Oncewife* life, I frequented the park while Gabe was working long weekends. At first I didn't mind it so much, knowing he'd have preferred to be with me than at work. He was sacrificing for us, or at least that's what I told myself. However, it was all about his career, and not at all to do with "our." Still, I sat in the park with a book and a blanket, alone, wishing my picnic for one could eclipse loneliness and envelop him. Do that enough times, see enough Maclaren strollers, and you learn to avoid the park altogether. That, or you revisit it when you want to feel sorry for yourself.

I was wearing lament like a shirt. Misery made me feel. I felt more alive. Like shit, but *alive*. My body liked highs and lows because of their intensity. When I felt something intensely, I experienced a more human condition. Everything was *er*. Sharp*er*. Bright*er*. Deep*er*.

Healthi*er*? Ah, no. I didn't want healthy. I wanted passion and mess because that's what I thought living was. It drips and oozes all sloppy and delicious because we're here. Now. Alive. Living. In Latin, *passion* means "physical suffering, martyrdom, sinful desire, an undergoing." Oh, that was so me.

Ahem.

I use the word *was* loosely. It's still part of my wiring, but now I keep it in check and assure myself that the *ity*'s trump the *er*'s every day and twice on Sundays. Stabil*ity* and longev*ity* are more important than the slop. I'm beginning to realize life should be lived not just with passion, but also with compassion. It should be less about shouting and more about listening.

As I approached the Tavern on the Green entrance to the park, a woman who clearly got her fashion sense from a film noir crime scene asked, "Excuse me, please, where to find Green Tavern?" I smiled and pointed just over her beret. "Ah! Thank you." Then she and her navy sailor pants hurried toward a bearded man with a baby strapped to his chest in a paisley scarf papoose. I kept smiling, watching her point to him and adjusting the knit hat of her infant. I wanted that, the baby and the man with whom to get lost. I wanted to ingest her life. I took their photograph while they were preoccupied with a blue and beige map.

Maybe my spirits would lift if I pretended I was abroad in a European city; I could ask for directions with an accent. "Eh, zee meadow de sheep? Here, no?" I could cross my legs at a nearby café, read my photography books, rig a twist of patterned silk around my neck, and sit in observation mode, stirring espresso, watching my breath disappear in the cold air. When I finished with espresso, I could move on to a Euro café full of racing leather, numbered shirts, and midriff, where I'd sling back Sancerre and gulp orange mussels, dipping crusty bread into a lake of Thai-spiced coconut milk. I could stab a tub of mayonnaise with salted fries, then indulge in dessert and the syrup they call wine to go with it. And the sad fact is, I still wouldn't feel better. I'd only feel full. Fear and full.

I entered the park and headed toward Sheep Meadow looking for a subject to photograph. I was first drawn to photography when I was married. Rome had a collection of Nikon cameras stowed away in her basement "junk room." Most people have a junk drawer. She had a room, and I couldn't believe her Nikons were part of it. If they were mine, I'd display them against a wall interspersed with silvery black-and-white photos when they weren't in use. One afternoon, while Gabe was off golfing with his parents, I borrowed a camera and photographed Linus, lounging poolside in their backyard. Through the lens, there was a moment of clarity where I just knew it was going to be a luminous shot with the right amount of gesture and story. It was. I loved the idea of documenting my moments, my memories, keeping them there, in tight modern crops, the kind I looked for in the art I chose for my advertising clients. So my buying the camera was as much for filling my spare time as it was for honing my art selection skills. I didn't dream it could lead to a source of income. I just dreamed of finding something I loved to do for myself.

The camera accessory added to the whole tourist look I was sporting. Sneakers, knapsack, and mandatory camera. I entered the meadow thinking how in foreign cities I move without direction, in sneakers, inhaling architecture. I see fashionable men and question if their wives chose their ties, see nuns and wonder what their hair looks like, and who, if anyone, cuts it. I hear small girls, with small folded white socks, ask for small things: a scoop of ice cream, some change to toss into the fountain, a balloon.

A hotel doorman escaped to Sheep Meadow for what I imagined to be his break. His face tilted toward the sun, eyes closed. I wondered how many tourists asked him to suggest a place where the locals go. "Nothing touristy," a woman in shorts and a fanny pack would ask him. It's exactly what I'd ask when I traveled. But I've quit asking, and instead stroll without direction, hoping I'll stumble upon a secret gem of a restaurant.

Not unlike a new love, there are few things more rewarding than believing you've found something amazing that no one else has gotten wind of yet. For that moment, it's your secret delight, and it feels warm. Your wine tastes better there, and the spaghetti is unlike anything you've tasted. You're certain this music you hear will follow you in life, and when you're back in the U.S., you promise to go to the Tower Records international section. You'll load up on this music and play it when you're cooking. When you are back in America, though, you have new to-do lists involving film development and phone calls. When you meet with friends to speak of your trip, of the weeks you were gone, you do it in minutes, speaking of the beach you discovered and were on alone, of the fish you almost caught, of the guy with whom you danced until morning. You suddenly have less to share—it wasn't for them. They won't understand how you felt near that fountain, how you remember the face of the gypsy who blessed you more than the entire face of a city. They won't comprehend the small moments you felt on the train, as you passed rolling farms, wondering about the hands that tended to them. They will compliment you on your new silk scarf, and you'll thank them, wishing you could remember more.

Seeing that doorman in the meadow brought it all to mind. It's exactly how I felt about my relationship with Oliver. When it came down to it, there were moments I couldn't quite remember or express, and I was left speaking about my feelings for him as if they were a flimsy pair of sunglasses. It took me months to accept that we weren't suited for each other, and even knowing he wasn't right for me, I still questioned my decision. What if I was just sabotaging any chance at happiness?

I paced the park, but nothing seemed worthy of a photograph. I couldn't find a gesture or expression in anything I saw. Small uniforms with leather gloves children will outgrow and younger siblings will inherit along with reputations. Friends jogged and gossiped. I watched a red-headed girl make piles of grass and sprinkle the blades into a soda can. New lovers licked each other in violet shadows beneath ancient trees. I didn't want to photograph any of it. I wanted to call Oliver and take it all back. Instead, I found a patch of dry grass, set down my camera, opened my journal, and began to write.

"When am I going to get this right?" I was frustrated and worried this would be it for me. I stopped writing, then thumbed through my journal and began to read entries I'd written while living with Smelly, after Gabe had canceled one of our many weddings.

> If I learned anything over the years, it should've been how to walk or let him walk away. I haven't learned how to let go yet. I hope I get there one day and remember that I'm an individual. Remember the days when I was younger and didn't know to recognize any of my imperfections. I would write "famous notes" when I was eight years old, looking in the mirror, saying I was destined for something. I've lost that girl, and I want the strength to find her.

> I've never been so devastated, but it could be worse. It could be divorce with a child and a house. I could be sick. I could find him with someone else. This is not the worst.

This is what happens when you don't learn to let things go. This is what comes from control. I was doing the same thing with Oliver. I took out my red pen and added to the entry:

It's years later and I still haven't learned to let it go. Stephanie, you can't control everything. If anything, you should realize this is what will set you free. Practice it now. Let go. It doesn't matter if he calls, whoever he is. Something, some power will take care of you.

I didn't know yet that power would be me. In the park that day, I knew what I had to do, saw it in the pages of my journal, in my patterns and habits. I was still very frightened of alone. I was terrified of what it meant. "Oh, she's alone because no one likes her." "She's alone because she's a pain in the ass." "No one wants her." "She's fat, ugly, and deserves to be alone." I thought alone was a punishment. I'd sooner grip onto the wrong relationship than "let it go" and see what would happen if it was just me.

I phoned Dulce with one hand as I flipped through the rest of my journal in a frenzy.

"I'm having a panic attack." I sounded like Smelly. I'd call her next.

"Like you can't breathe and you want to go to the hospital? Where are you?"

"No. I'm in this crapass park! I came to take photos, but I can't focus on anything. I know I should be using this time to focus on what will make me happy, but I can't do it, Dulce. I just can't. This is too hard." I was whining. "I tried writing in my journal, but then I ended up reading. My God, I'm so fucked up. You know, I saw a list written in there about everything I should have now." I was ripping out grass by the handful. "You know, that list we make for ourselves, the one about a house in the suburbs, diplomas from good schools, husband, and three kids? I was there, on that path, and now, it's like I'm suffering from whiplash. I look around now, and what do I have? What have I accomplished? I'm living in a cramped one-bedroom with a dog that shits on my floor." I laughed until it became crying again. "I hate myself, hate how I ruin everything. All I want to do is call Oliver, take it all back, and just move in with him. Tell me again why I shouldn't be with him?"

"Stephanie, how are you feeling right now?"

Ew. Why wasn't she answering me? This was her way of getting me to slow down. I had to take a moment to switch gears and respond. "Anxious and scared."

"Why?"

"Because I'm afraid I'm making a mistake."

"Why?"

"Because I'm frightened I won't meet anyone."

"Why?"

"Because maybe I'm not worth it. Maybe there aren't really smart men out there who will love me so much."

"Why else are you anxious?"

"I'm facing my fear of being alone and it's scary."

"Why?"

I wanted to hit her. "Why the fuck why?"

"Just answer me. Why are you facing your fear of being alone now?"

"Because I know that facing it will take away its power over me, but it's still scary."

"Stephanie, if you weren't afraid of it, it wouldn't take courage. I know this is hard for you. I know you're scared. That's why it takes strength. And, please, you've had to be courageous about much harder things." This is why I phoned Dulce—she was cheaper than my therapist.

"I know, but I've never just faced alone, and it scares the shit out of me, Dulce." I was whining again.

"Why? Think before you answer me. Why really, Stephanie?"

"Because I don't want to die alone and not have a loving family or children."

"Stephanie," she said quietly, "we all die alone."

I WAS HAVING A HARD TIME ACCEPTING THERE'S NO GUARantee in life, that at any moment the things we hold dear, the people we love, can be ripped from us. I knew I needed to acknowledge it, but it's grueling to work for something, to believe in it, and also accept that it can go at any time. It's a very scary thing realizing you can't control. I knew the people who don't fight it, who just accept transience, will have an easier time coping with loss. I wasn't just terrified of my new independence without Oliver. I was grieving the loss of another relationship that I thought was headed where I wanted it so desperately to go, and with that loss, I also had to give up the idea of guarantees and permanence. I was dealing with it all over again now with Oliver.

I said it aloud to Dulce. "Maybe I'm not worth it." I didn't believe I deserved happiness. Deep down I couldn't understand why any man would want me when I wasn't a whole person. I feared I wouldn't make my dreams happen, that I wouldn't have the courage or the strength. I didn't want to die alone. Then the tears stained everything, leaving rings, like the insides of ancient trees. I didn't need to call anyone to talk about it anymore. I knew what I had to do: I needed to tear up the life list, the one from my past perfect life of *had*. I also needed to get the hell out of the park.

Then the inevitable happened. No. It wasn't Oliver. A slip of paper slid loose from the pages of my journal. It was a yellow card I'd made when I first learned I was pregnant. I'd glue-gunned a gingham ribbon on its front. Felt shapes of a diaper and baby jumper were glued inside, flanking these handwritten words:

Locking out Linus was not done with ease.
Gave him a flossy, not too hard to please . . .
Still scratched at our door, for all but an hour
As we tried so hard, we needed a shower.

Harder we tried for eight crazy nights—
Hanukkah it wasn't, but we tried with our might.
Asleep in your arms, so tight, so close,
Could I wake up, with more than our pup?

Who knew what it meant, two thin pink lines—
A new baby Rosen—it's the start of new times.
A family we'll be; Linus, you, and me
Plus our new baby—a new family tree.

No words can express the elation I feel
A new life is among us—this is the real deal.
So dizzy with happiness, from my face tears do fall
Get ready for summer—our new child will call.

Ice cream and pickles, don't laugh just yet,
From car seats to diapers, we'll soon be in debt.
Inside me now, grows more than my love—
It's our new little baby, thank the heavens above.

Grab my hand, hold it tight, 'cause we're in a new place.
Soon you'll be a father, a child with your face.

Gabe had cried when he read it, pulling me close to him. The next week, he went shopping and bought me a new handbag. "I wanted the mother of my child to have something nice."

I was having a pity party in the pit of Central Park, and I was the hostess. I wanted to torture myself. "Okay, Miss Melodrama, get off your sorry ass and say good-bye to this shit. It's time for new." I might have clapped. Oh good, everything was back to normal—I was talking to myself again.

I yanked my knapsack up, slung the SLR camera over my shoulder and headed north. I could do this. It would hurt now, but I'd be happy for it someday. It's like dieting and sunblock. One day it would be worth it.

As I made my way toward the Seventy-second Street exit, I saw a familiar face. It was Jaimee Lowrey with her husband David and son Neil. Jaimee and I had been friends, inseparable friends, through work, back before I was married. We planned our actual weddings together, got pregnant at the same time, shared our recipes from *What to Eat When You're Expecting* and our anxieties about childbirth and spina bifida. She had the life I was supposed to have, right there in a stroller and in her husband's hand. I was staring at them with a forced smile. This was not my day. I mean really. Come on. Who has this shit happen?

"Oh my God, Stephanie, you look wonderful." This had to be a lie. Maybe she meant thin. I couldn't eat when I was anxious. Surely I weighed less, but wonderful was a stretch. "What are you up to these days?"

We hugged, and she felt warm. I didn't want to let go. I missed her. I mean really *missed* her. Seeing her, feeling her, I suddenly felt it. I wanted my life back, the one I thought I had before learning the truth about Gabe. I dropped from our embrace slowly and told her how much I missed her with tears in my eyes. We'd been inseparable, until we weren't. It would be easy to say we grew apart because I became single. Fact: you see less of your married friends once they have children. I'd want to meet for drinks, she'd need to feed Neil. We didn't grow apart. We just grew.

I've heard married couples oust the single girl because maybe now the wife sees you as a threat. I've never encountered this. None of my close friends whom I actually see and spend time with have kids. I think those with children make new friends at the mommy park, through play dates and Gymboree, the same way single women find other women to play with. Beyond our love for each other, Jaimee and I had less in common.

Neil began to scream when the pacifier fell from his mouth. "He's addicted to this thing," Jaimee said as she fetched him a new one.

"Yeah, I know how he feels."

As an infant, I was once addicted to a discontinued pacifier. My parents tried to replace it with new brands, but I'd just spit them out. "So what did you do?" I asked them.

"We purchased every last one," my mother had said, "and once they were gone, we just let you cry. Eventually, you gave up."

I'd like to say I learned my lesson then. I'd like to say that's as close as I ever came to a security blanket, but please, this is me. Instead, I opted for a serial string of monogamous relationships to shut me up. Obviously, my parents didn't discover the "boyfriend" brand in pacifiers.

"What's up with that camera, Stephanie?" Jaimee's husband asked.

"Oh, this is *my* baby. I just bought her a few months ago. You know me, always got my hand in something." I patted the camera and turned toward Jaimee. "I'm just so sick of putting all my energy into some guy who probably won't be there in the end. Ya know?" Of course she didn't know. "So I figured I'd put my energy into something else. Me. Ya know?" She didn't know that either. Her energy was spent on raising her son and loving her husband. That would have been my life. Instead, I had to create a new one.

"GET READY FOR A WHOLE NEW LIFE GABE, 'CAUSE YOU fucked this one up real good," I had screamed through the front door of our apartment when Gabe had returned with Linus. "You clearly don't give out your home phone number, so I guess you don't live here."

"Don't be retarded, Stephanie. Open the door." He had no idea that the door was his friend. It was keeping me off him.

"There's no more room in here for you." When I said, "in here," I smacked my hand on my heart.

I imagined him on the other side of the door, shifting his weight, not entirely knowing about what I was speaking. Still, he must have had a pit in his stomach, knowing I might have discovered something. I wanted to see his face, to watch him try to lie to me so I could learn to really hate him. Before opening the door, I glanced at my sister on the sofa. "I can't believe this, Lea. I'm so sick." She looked back at me, and for the first time in as long as I can remember, she was silent.

When I opened the door, Linus shot toward Lea's lap.

"I've got no more room for this. I deserve more than this. *HOW COULD YOU?*" I was screaming, my finger pointing at him.

He threw his hands to his sides and waited. I didn't know for what.

Then he shifted his weight and screamed, "Will you lower your voice? I have no idea what you're—"

I began to pound on his chest. They weren't punches as much as pushes. It just seemed like the thing you do when you catch your husband. You scream and hit him. I didn't want to hit him, but I didn't know what else to do.

"Lea, you better stop her, or I'm going to hit her back."

"Oh, because you haven't fucking hurt me enough?"

"What are you TALKING ABOUT?" As he enunciated his words, spit hit me. He pulled my wrists off him and pressed them into my chest.

"Who is Bernie?"

He looked confused and let go of me. "Bernie? I don't know a Bernie. What are you—"

"This," I grabbed the e-mail printout I'd made and shoved it in his chest. "This is what I'm talking about!"

He took a beat to measure the words I'd found and printed for him.

"Answer me! Who's this Bernie person?"

He became quiet, as if I'd just slammed a door.

"Her name is Bern. The *i* and *e* are silent."

"Burn? As in burn victim? You're fucking kidding, right?"

"Nothing happened, Stephanie."

"I'm pregnant, you asshole!" I was screaming, the kind of scream reserved for a mugging. My throat rattled. I ran to the front door and opened it, "Gabriel Rosen, you are a liar and a snake. Get the fuck out!"

"Shut up, you stupid Spic! Everyone doesn't need to hear this." His face was red and a vein pulsed near his eye.

"Gabe, that was uncalled for." Lea was now standing between us.

"I'm sorry, Lea. You're right."

"Is it that easy?" I shouted as I pushed his shoulder. "Should I just tell you you're low, then you'll apologize? No, fuck that. I don't want your sorrys. How could you, Gabe?" I was sobbing now. "How could you?" I whispered. My mouth turned sour and I stood shaking, my chin on my chest. He held me.

"Stephanie, I'm sorry," he whispered, "but nothing happened."

"Don't you dare. I already spoke with her. You were going to go with her to a black-tie party! You tucked me into bed, your pregnant wife, then went out with her and your hospital friends. You introduced her to your fucking coworkers! Do you know how humiliated I am? They all must think I knew about it or something. You never even let her know you were married. And you'd come here and write her e-mails telling her you missed her! How could you do this?"

I know humiliation can be a pretty shallow feeling with everything I was up against, but it's the one that chose to bubble up within me. I didn't want to care what I looked like to anyone, but I did. Being hurt is messy that way.

"Really, Stephanie, you're making a big deal—"

"If nothing happened, then give me your phone." I sounded professional suddenly, as if I were asking for a stick of chalk.

"Stephanie, stop it!" He grabbed my wrists as I lunged for his cell phone.

"Well, if you have nothing to hide, then give it to me. What? Are you afraid I'll find her number in there?"

"Her number isn't on my phone, Stephanie. I'm telling you. She always just paged me at the hospital."

Turns out he'd met Bernie when her son, only two years my junior, had an infection. Gabe examined him, and when he finished, The Burn wanted her turn. "Let me thank you." I imagined she touched his hand softly. "Come play golf at my country club with me." He obliged. And he continued to oblige her day and night, right after apologizing to me. "I'm sorry, baby. The hospital has been grueling lately. It will get better soon. I promise."

Once I got hold of his phone, I ran into the bathroom and locked the door. He chased after me, but he was too late. He pounded on the door as I thumbed through his call log and text message history. He'd texted her from the Barney's dressing room, while I was there with him. He was looking forward to the "affair." I'll bet.

While I was in the bathroom, I found her numbers on his call log.

I opened the door to the bathroom. "Yeah, I found your girlfriend's numbers, you know the ones you don't have." I threw his phone at him.

"Okay, I lied about that."

"Yeah, ya think?!"

"But listen, Stephanie. I love you. I want us." He wanted to do or say anything he could to stop me from crying.

"Why her?" It was a small voice I didn't recognize as my own.

"Look, I'll never talk to her again, I swear." He moved his hands from the small of my back to the nape of me. "I want this, Stephanie. I really do. I love you."

I wanted to believe him, to believe that this was all some mistake, that I was overreacting. But come on, this was just the one I found. I knew, deep down, there were others, women who made him feel important, and I knew he was more needy for attention than he was for me. But I didn't want us to be over. I loved him in our bed, his body and breath in the middle of the night. I wasn't ready to let go. So I told myself maybes. Maybe he was just panicking because he had to be so responsible at his job. Maybe he had to act out in his life. Look what he'd done with the responsibility of marriage. Maybe this was how he dealt with change. Maybe he just needed therapy.

"I'll do whatever it takes to make this work," he'd said, "to earn back your trust. I will tell her that I want nothing to do with her. Then I won't speak to her again. I swear, sweetheart."

"Why her?"

"Honestly?" No. Lie to me. "She took me to impressive things. Things I'd never have the opportunity to go to. I didn't think you'd understand."

"No. You want to be single is what you want. It isn't about my not understanding. Otherwise, you would have told *her* about me. You didn't tell me about her, and you led her to believe you were single. That's not about my not understanding." He just stood there with his arms crossed. "You know what? You're a fucking asshole." I said it simply, as if I were asking a butcher for a leg of lamb.

"I'm your wife. I *shouldn't* understand why you want to go to night-clubs with another woman. Sorry. It just doesn't work that way. Wow. It's amazing. You really are a piece of shit." I began to count with my fingers. "You e-mailed her from our house, texted her while you were with me, lied to my face saying you had plans with your friends when you were really out with her! All this time you've been telling me you didn't have time to spend with me, how you missed me, how hard work was. All that time, she was 'work.'" I turned from sad and wanting to hear every detail to angry again. "GET THE FUCK OUT." He did as he was told.

As soon as he left, I cried to Lea, "I can't believe he just left. He doesn't care about us. Lea, I hate him. I Hate. Him. So. Much." I couldn't breathe. I cried into her lap. Linus licked my tears. This was now my family.

IN THE WEEKS THAT FOLLOWED, STILL IN MY FIRST trimester, I didn't know what to do. I called everyone asking for advice. My mother told me to just have the baby. "He's just scared of being a father, and he acted out. Once he sees the baby, everything will be fine." I might have flinched when I heard her say it. "Who knows when you'll have a chance to be pregnant again. I'd just have it because I know how long it took you." It didn't sound healthy, what she was saying. I heard her, but I didn't feel her. She didn't know the kind of person I married. I was beginning to.

I called Gabe's parents' house. Rome and Marvin said "Hello" at the same time. I might as well tell them both. I felt like I was tattling. It was my, "See, I'm not the bad guy. It's been him all along. Now you should be on my side!" call. I wanted sympathy, even from them.

"I knew something was going on," Rome said after I used the word *pregnant* followed by "seeing an older woman." "I just knew," she added again after a long silence, "because I heard from my friend Myron that he'd run into Gabriel at a Knicks game with that Bernie woman. I asked Gabriel about it, but he looked at me like I had two heads. I mean, I warned him. I told him to be careful, to really know what he was doing.

I mean really. He should be more careful about who he associates with."
Holy fuck. I didn't know if Rome was disappointed in her son's behavior
or in his taste in women. I couldn't believe his parents knew something
was going on. The conversation made everything feel more real.

"What are you going to do about the baby?" Marvin asked.

"I don't know, but if I do decide to keep it, I promise you can both
see your grandchild as much as you'd like." It's what I was supposed to
say. I used the word *grandchild* purposefully. I wanted them to feel the
real in all this, to know their son fucked with forever. I wanted them to
feel guilty for raising a son like Gabe.

"I'll call you later, okay, sweetie? We will check up on you." And
Rome did call, just as she'd said. She called every day to see if Gabe and
I would be working things out. To see if I'd go through with our mar-
riage. To see if she'd have to be connected to me for the rest of her life.

"LET'S GO FOR A DRIVE," MY FATHER SUGGESTED. "IT WILL
be good for you. You need to air yourself out." Thirty minutes later, he
picked me up, and we drove for an hour to Nyack, a charming spot of a
New York town with Victorian homes and antique shops. My father and
Carol were in the market for "old" new furniture.

Dad searched in mothball antique stores for a dining room table. I
searched for answers in antique armoires, tried to feel the meaning of life
as I fingered handmade afghans, awaited answers to the "why me's" in
chandelier reflections. I sat folded into myself in a leather chair wishing it
were a bed, so I could crawl into fetal position and just weep. Weep, without someone judging me thinking, "Oh dear God, not again," as he rolls
his eyes. Gabe had been doing a lot of this over the past two weeks. Said
things like, "I'm going to fix it. What more do you want from me?" He
was annoyed I hadn't recovered from devastated. I didn't want a solution-
oriented man to walk around with a tool belt and corkscrew to fix things.

Dad saw me tearing in the patina of a final-sale mirror. "Steph, you
can do better," he said pushing the tears into my hair with his thumbs.

"Dad, I'll never do any better. He's smart and funny and good-looking . . ."

"Stephanie," he took both my hands, "how could you do any worse?" Best rhetorical question ever.

"No one can tell you what to do, Stephanie," he said. "Only you know what's in your heart. You have to be true to what you feel. No one else knows what's good for you." Then he told me he was always worried. "Somewhere in my gut, I worried this would happen. Don't get me wrong—I liked the guy enough, but every time the phone rang, and you called me with panic in your voice, I always feared either you were laid off from your job or something happened with Gabe."

"Nice to tell me now, Dad."

"I asked you right after you two got engaged, asked if he'd sown his oats." He did ask me that, and in turn, I asked Gabe, who rolled his eyes, grabbed me, and said, "You're the love of my life." It didn't matter anymore.

On our drive back to Manhattan, my father turned up the volume to The Temptations' "Ain't Too Proud To Beg," and pointed at me each time he sang, "sweet darlin'." Gabe wasn't interested in keeping me any way he could, the way the song suggested a man in love should. And that wasn't good enough.

Gabe *said* he'd do whatever it took to show me he wanted us. But when I asked what that meant, he didn't know how to answer. "Therapy?" he said, wondering if that's what I wanted to hear. He swore nothing physical happened, that he knew what he'd done was very wrong, and he wanted to learn why he lied and snuck around. "I promise, baby. I love you so much, and I know I've been a jerk. I will show you. You'll see. I will make this right."

I was anxious about everything, but I decided I'd give it a few weeks to see how I'd feel before making any emotional decisions. Two weeks after finding out about Bernie, while Gabe was in the shower, his pager vibrated, loud against the dinner table. My stomach fell. What if it were a woman?

Was this the way it would always be? A life of stress and pitfalls, of looking behind my back, waiting for something else to drop? Maybe it would just take time to be at ease again? Yes. That's it. Time, the great salve.

I'd just made dinner and set the table. Linus began to bark when the pager vibrated again. It was a hospital number . . . it had to be. Go on and look, you fraidy cat. Open your eyes. I knew it. I returned Bernie's call immediately.

"I thought he told you it was over, that he didn't want to speak to you again, that we're trying to work things out."

The line was silent, and for a moment, I worried it wasn't her. What if I were seeing things and it really was the hospital? But then I heard her voice, calm and demeaning. "Actually, Stephanie, that's not at all what he's told me. He tells me that you two have been separated for months, and that you're living in denial." Yeah, well, denial must be made of tomato sauce with crinkled noodles and housed in a lasagna pan because we're just about to have fucking dinner!

"That's really what he said? I mean he's obviously here with me now. That's not very separated, is it?" I believed her. I knew as soon as I asked that she was telling me the truth.

"Well, he said his clothes were still in your apartment, so he has to go there. He said you just wouldn't accept that it's over."

I began to shake. "He is lying," I finally said. "He's been here telling me he wants us, loves me, and that he wants nothing to do with you. He told me he only hung out with you because you got him into events. He said he used you because of your connections and that you're a jealous person. He said I should be glad he went out with you because you'd freak whenever he spoke with anyone else." I wanted to hurt her, to make her hate him too. But when I heard myself, I hated him more. He'd actually told me I should be happy he was with her at night because she prohibited him from flirting with other women. This was my husband saying these words, *happy* and *other women* in a sentence constructed to make me feel better.

"Look, I do great things, and I have a nice life. I don't blame him for wanting to spend time with me." Was she kidding? Did she not understand the word *used*? "Stephanie, why would you even want a guy like that? He clearly doesn't want to be married to you. He continues to speak to me, and he told me his parents can't stand you. Is that the life you really want?" Why would *she* want a guy like that? If she knew all these intimate details of our life, details he clearly shared with her, then why would *she* want to be involved with *him*? Even if she only saw him as a boy toy, she still wanted to be mixed up with someone who clearly lied to his wife and caused so much pain. I didn't understand.

I hung up the phone with Bernie.

When Gabe opened the bathroom door, I threw the phone at him. He caught it and his towel dropped to the ground.

"Your girlfriend just told me we've been separated for months and that I'm in denial!" I was tapping my foot, certain I'd trapped him.

"She's not my girlfriend," he yelled as he plucked his towel off the floor.

"Is this denial?" I used my finger to measure the space between us, then pointed it toward the set kitchen table. "How could you? All you do is lie." There's never just one cockroach.

"I guess I said it because I didn't want to burn a bridge. I'm embarrassed by the way I handled things with her, and one lie turns into another. I didn't want her to know . . ."

". . . what a fucking asshole liar you are?" I finished his sentence. "I just love how you're so concerned with sparing her feelings while your pregnant wife, the life you've had for the past five and half years with me, means nothing to you. You'll break your promise to me of never speaking with her again, just to spare her feelings?"

"I'm sorry, sweetheart. I'll fix this. You'll see." No, I wouldn't. This was it. It was the last time I saw him until our divorce proceedings.

The next afternoon, I looked in the mirror and began to tear up. I really looked. It was a silent moment. I hadn't showered in days. A quiet yet strong voice erupted in the mirror. "Stephanie, you deserve more than this, and you will find it. You *deserve*. And you can do better. How could you do any worse? Dad's right." I knew it would be the hardest thing I'd ever done, but staying with Gabe would have been harder. I'd always wonder and suspect. I couldn't live like that, always wanting to check itemized lists of his phone calls and American Express bills. I'd never trust him again because every new day might reveal fresh lies. He'd looked me in the eye and told me he'd never let anything bad happen to me. "You are going to find happiness. You will," I said squinting at myself. "But it won't be with him. Ever." That's the moment I vowed to stop loving him.

"I'll never forget when you told me that," Alexandra sometimes tells me now. "I asked you how you could be dating again, and you told me that when someone is that unspeakable to you, your brain won't let you love them anymore. As much as you thought you'd never stop, when someone disgraces you, something in you would die if you stayed. That's when I knew how strong you were."

I don't think of myself as strong, despite what I've been through, yet people constantly make a point of saying it. I was doing what I had to, to get by, to exist. Screw it. It's not about strength. That's the wrong word. It's courage. It took courage to listen to my gut and leave the comfort I'd known. And courage can't happen without fear. I was terrified. It's why strength never seems to be the right word.

I saw a freckled sixth-grade Stephanie in that mirror, and I asked her to tell me what to do. "Run, don't walk. Pass Go. This is your get-out-of-jail moment. A life with a man like that would be a prison sentence. Fucking run!" And that's exactly what I did, and we all know how I feel about running.

twelve

THE BUTTERFLY EFFECT

"I CAN'T BELIEVE THIS IS MY LIFE." I FELT MY FACE TURN to ugly, my eyebrows pinching, my mouth so filled with pain, I couldn't feign a smile. My father rubbed my back in circles, his eyes red and teary. "Dad, I hate this."

"I know, sweetheart. I know," he said shaking his head in disbelief.

"How is this my life?"

"I know, sweetheart." And he held my hand. And we cried together in a brown windowless waiting room.

When I told my gynecologist I needed an abortion, he said, "We don't handle extractions, but there's a clinic . . ." Aren't extractions when the Russian lady at the salon pushes the pores of your nose during a facial? Maybe he said, "We don't handle terminations." Either way, I was terrified of the word *clinic*. Clinic. It was scribbled on a yellow Post-it note with a date . . . December 12, 2002, the last possible day I had to abort. "But obviously," he said sternly, "the sooner the better." AB+ was scribbled beside the date. "You'll have to tell them your blood type." I hated this.

Clinics were for girls who still played music on their outgoing answering machines, not for twenty-seven-year-old wives. But there I was with a planned pregnancy in my lap, waiting for a woman with a clipboard to call my name.

When I heard, "Stephanie Rosen," I pulled my knees to my chest. My father waved to the nurse and whispered to me, "It's going to be okay."

I stared at him for a moment, then said in the frailest voice I've known, "I'm scared." He shook his head to say Yes, I know sweetheart. He became the father, once again, of a little girl, the one who came to him crying after a tumble on the playground. The one with gummy white scars on her knees. I hated how I still needed him.

I wrinkled my nose and shook my head, then pushed myself into a stand. "It'll be fine." I didn't know if I said it more for him or for me.

The nurse led me into a room to take some blood, and I was frightened they'd impose counseling. Lecture me, using words like *risks* or *options*, as if I were a reckless teenager who'd shoved the results of her test into the back of her knapsack. After the blood tap, I landed in a small dressing room. "Put all your items in the bag." I was handed a pink paper robe and black garbage bag.

A garbage bag.

I trembled as I disrobed. It was as if the paper robe were made of black-and-white jail stripes. After parting with my possessions, I worried they'd want fingerprints or a mug shot. I was right—well, almost. I was led to a room for a sonogram.

I saw the heartbeat. A white blinking dot. *"I'm sorry, baby"* chanted in my head so many times I worried I might have said it aloud. *"I'm so sorry."* The woman who'd had the clipboard moved the electronic table to a seated position. "Now don't get up too fast. Are you okay? Any dizziness?"

No, I'm fine. Leave me the fuck alone. Leave.

"I'm fine."

I finally stood. The groin towel fell, damp with my sweat. I gulped air as she led me out of the room, her hand on my lower back.

"Are you sure you're okay?" I wanted to be silent. There was no use for language. I didn't care to explain to anyone how I felt about anything. I lost interest in speech, nodded my head, and went mute.

I joined a narrow hallway where other women in other pink paper gowns stood, biting fingernails. I walked it with my hand gliding along the wall for support. I wondered what my father was doing in the waiting room alone. Was he reading *Newsweek* or pamphlets on how to support a friend after an abortion? Did he look for one targeted toward men? Did he start to read it and set it down because it was too upsetting to think of his little girl, the one he used to set on his belly when she was upset? Being put under, strapped to a table, a life she wanted being removed.

"Are you still with the guy that did this to you?" a woman with blue eyeliner asked me after a few minutes. I didn't know how she got dressed that morning and was able to apply makeup. I could hardly breathe.

"No, he's a fucking asshole. His name is Gabriel Rosen, so don't ever end up dating him." I went from mute to mortifying in less than fifteen seconds. I was RPM in a robe.

"Yeah, this is my second time here," she said while examining her cuticles, "with the same guy. Is this your first?"

"It's my first everything," I said, fingering the opening of my gown.

"Is he out there?" I knew she meant the waiting room, and as soon as I thought of it, I felt nauseous again. I imagined my father looked empathetic, his blue eyes welling at the sight of other young pregnant girls, a pamphlet curled in his hands as he waited and prayed. Maybe he wondered what he'd say to me when it was over. "Mine's not out there either. I came here alone. So what happened to you?"

Normally I would've asked to see her tax return so she'd learn from inappropriate. Instead, I began to spill, "My twenty-eight-year-old husband came home every single fertile day for months trying to get me pregnant, and the whole time he was off running around with an older woman. And that's only the one I found out about." I imagined there were others, hiding in his hospital walls. Clicking their heels, shuffling, crawling for what he had to give. "I can just picture him cruising his hospital hallways and the nightclubs with his wedding ring in his pocket. The boy would whisper how much he adored me before kissing me goodnight and attending to his beeper. Little did I know that 'beeper' is forty-three years old and lives in a luxury Fifth Avenue duplex overlooking the park." I said Bernie's age in a low tone reserved for deviant behavior, as if I were saying Gabe had sex with a horse. Who would be with her when he could be with me? Just as I'd ponied up to thoughts of mommyhood,

Gabe saddled the idea of another woman. Mrs. Robinson didn't just rob the cradle—she stole away with my rattle, bouncer seat, and designer diaper bag.

I didn't care that my vagina was now showing, as I heaved into my knees, grabbing handfuls of my gown. I began to cry.

"Don't worry, sweetie. You're still young. You've got plenty of time to meet many more assholes." She didn't seem surprised by my tears.

"This wasn't an accident. We tried to have this baby. We tried for months, and the fucking piece of shit coward is probably playing golf right now." I wanted everyone to hate him.

"You can change your mind. You don't have to . . ."

"No. I didn't want a baby," I said through the snot, "I wanted a family." I crossed my arms around my shoulders, and began to rock myself out of the sobs.

I was wearing paper, in a hall full of girls with socks, all of us having abortions. Gabe never offered to be there. He knew the day, knew exactly what was happening. Said he wasn't ready for a child. He was a urologist. He did office hours, not clinics.

The night before the abortion was scheduled, I called Gabe. "Are you sure this is what you want?" I wanted less to regret, and if he didn't argue, it was what he wanted too. What he decided he wanted was to be single again. He wasn't ready to be a father, and he was tired of being a husband.

Gabe tried to get me pregnant and then realized he didn't love me enough. Our apartment, our life, didn't make him happy because there wasn't a velvet rope outside our door. He said he just didn't love me enough to stay married, that when he thought of "us," he thought of "a long time ago."

"We want different things," he had said. "You're happy throwing dinner parties for our friends, that whole wine and music thing, but I don't want to be settled down now. I want to be on Page Six and go to the places that are hard to get into." Suddenly I was the club he wanted no part of because I wanted him as a member. All of our relationship, he'd tried to convince me of just the opposite, saying he didn't care about those velvet-rope places. Said he wouldn't go anywhere with a line whose dress code wouldn't allow for flip-flops. He'd spoken of people who wanted a boldfaced lifestyle with disgust and contempt. We always hate in others much of what we detest of ourselves. So really, at the end of the day, Gabe hated that he was one of those people, hated that it actually was important to him, where he went, and what people thought of him. He said he wanted to be a famous doctor, the kind that would land him a spot on television or, at the very least, in a Ralph Lauren advertisement. He said he wanted fame. He said it aloud. I can't believe I married him on purpose.

Rome called the day before my appointment at the clinic. "How are you feeling?" was code for "Are you still going through with it?" She told me it was no big deal. "I had one in between having Gabe and Jolene," she said. "I know how you feel." No she didn't. This wasn't just the end of a pregnancy; it was the end of a marriage. "Who's going with you?" she asked hesitantly.

"My father." Gabe didn't offer.

"It's just horrible. I swear, Stephanie, we didn't teach him this." Then, with those almost-famous almost-last words, she added, "I'll call you tomorrow to see how you are." Also code for "to make sure I'm not a grandmother of this divorce." And she did call. It was the last time we ever spoke. "Okay, sweetie, I know it's sad, but you'll be okay. I'll call you tomorrow to see how you're doing." I never heard from her again.

I was terror-stricken when the nurse said I was next. I shuffled to the bathroom and began to vomit in the toilet. I didn't know if it was morning sickness or mourning sickness. I thought I'd faint. They made me keep the bathroom door open. Then came straps.

I stared at the ceiling, my thighs strapped to a table, my feet hoisted in stirrups. A wooden butterfly hung between green fluorescent lights overhead. They pulled a string, and the wings began to flap. I wouldn't look at faces. "I'm doctor so and so . . . I'm here to administer your . . . I'll be beside you the whole time . . ." I stopped listening and interrupted with talk.

"Do you know I was on fertility drugs trying to have this baby, and my doctor husband came home every single day from the hospital trying to get me pregnant? He lied. He looked me in the eyes and lied." For some irrational reason, I wanted these doctors to know I was married to a doctor, that I wasn't some irresponsible girl from a poor home, the ones I imagined they were used to seeing. I wanted to prove myself, to save some dignity, and his being a doctor made me feel more important. "His name is Dr. Gabriel Rosen." I whispered his name as if he were responsible for leukemia. Any chance I got, I'd tell people his name, as a warning. As if a plague were coming, I'd flash my headlights toward oncoming traffic. Listen to me. He's horrible. The end is near! The people who surround a surgery table right before the drugs are administered must witness more confessions than a priest after New Year's.

When they woke me, they used my married name. "Stephanie, Mrs. Rosen, do you hear me?"

"It's Klein. It's Klein." I pushed aloud through the cramping. "Will I still be able to have children?"

"Stephanie Klein, yes. Yes."

Tears slipped from the corners of my eyes.

Those Germans got it wrong. Klein doesn't mean *small*, it means *strong*. From here on out, I'm keeping my name.

thirteen

*S*OMEBODY LANGUAGE

GOODBYE OLIVER. HELLO OVERINDULGENCE. I WAS NOW single, which would mean drinking. A lot. Everyone is suddenly parched come mid-November, thanks to the approaching "Triple Jump." Thanksgiving. Christmas. New Year's. 1-2-3, drinks on me! Okay, *for* me. Same difference. It's less to do with the stacks of red polyester blends or heat-blasted stores, and more to do with nerves. Oh, and you can bet our treasured Starbucks would be monetizing on our jitters.

My cherished "Fourbucks" went ahead and busted out with the Gingerbread and Eggnog lattes, at four bucks and change, planting the early morning pumpkin seed that they'd be there to comfort and console, the salve of the season. I was about to start spiking my A.M. latte with hot, buttered rum. The commencement of the holiday months made me more nervous than my quivering dog. It meant plans. "Actually, make that a decaf."

When you're in a relationship, come the Triple Jump, no matter how bad it is, you grind it out and wait for the last string of lights to return to their box before ending things. You bide your time fretting about gifts. You stress over how much to spend, what's too extravagant, and what kind of heft your plastic can bear. You worry about thank-you notes for his parents, or upsetting relatives if you choose one family over the other to celebrate the festivities. If you're female, you search for touchable outfits dressier than sweats. Cashmere pants and sweaters, ladylike silk, rabbit fur, and mesh panties. You want to wear a wife beater with no bra, but it's too cold. Sexy isn't about visibility, it's about accessibility. It's not about cleavage if you're in a corset with strings that looks too complicated to get at the good bits. That's work. It's about accessible and touch-able. And when a guy sees you in a wife beater, he feels as though he's be-ing let into your world. He's in a zone, behind a curtain, and he likes it. So you wear one beneath the angora sweater.

The stores sing to you, luring you inside with their music, cheery mannequins, and twinkle lights. Each small shop looks as if it smells of pine and wraps its goods in brown paper with red ribbons and old-fashioned wax stamps. Suddenly, you're asking, "Do you have a box with that?" even though it's for you. You're wearing red, for chrissake. Too many holiday outfits are embellished with sequins. While they ignite a bit of holiday sparkle and delight, they're dreadfully untouchable. Holidays are for mittens and snuggling, for Maker's Mark–spiked hot cocoa and seeing each other's breath. Holidays are not for the single. And they're certainly not designed with the recently broken-hearted in mind. 'Cause there's nothing quite like breaking up with someone just before the holi-day season. It's like asking for an extra serving of poop, left only to de-cide which fork to use to eat it. Though it can always be worse. You could, for example, during this harrowing holiday season, have a therapist whip out the word *rejigger* and place it beside *your habits*, shrink code for, *you need to change*.

"I hear what you're saying," I responded to Phone Therapist, "but I don't know how to do that. I mean, I don't even want to leave my bed. Rejiggering sounds like a gym class."

"Stephanie, you've survived much worse than a breakup," she re-minded me. Yes and no. I never fully dealt with the end of my marriage. I was dating a month after the abortion. Now, after my break with Oliver, the "deal with it" part meant me. I had to make me whole, figure out who the hell I was and what would fulfill me. And I'd need to do it alone, which scared me more than the word *malignant*.

So how do you begin to face something so scary? In a word: therapy. Oh joy. I upped my sessions with Phone Therapist to twice a week. Dou-ble joy.

"You have to learn to love yourself," she said plainly, as if mentioning there was a ninety-five percent chance of precipitation. Okay. "Love yourself." Sounds as simple as rain. Who can't do that?

"I'm too sick to love myself," I sniffled.

"Sick how?"

"My body feels shut down, like I'm just going through the motions every day. Like I'm sleepwalking through my life. I'm sick of this, all of it."

"You know, you're right."

"What?"

"You're right." What in the hell was she talking about? "You just said, 'I'm sick of this,' and you're exactly right. You are literally sick of *this*." I imagined if we were together in person she'd point at my body, up toward the thick arteries running through my heart. "Your body is telling you something, Stephanie. During our past few sessions you've been complaining about your health—about colds, the flu, you name it. It is my estimation that your body is literally breaking down to stop you from running out there and dating again." Oh, come on. My sickness wasn't about a polluted aura or misaligned chakras. "The mind is very powerful. And yours is very stubborn. Your body is breaking down, so you'll wake up. You need to try something else."

"Something else? Like what? Look, I like taking care of someone, cooking, and doing sweet things for them." As soon as I said it, I knew she'd hurl back a "and why can't that someone be you for a change?" Yes, I knew I could now do that for myself, but the idea of Cooking for One had me running toward the knife block, and it wasn't to quarter a chicken. I was on a mission. I had to learn to comfort myself, to see what others saw in me and believe it. I needed to discover what the hell made me happy other than being in love. Mission impossible.

When did figuring out what makes you happy become work? How had I let myself get to this point, where I had to learn *me* at twenty-eight years old? It was embarrassing. In my college psychology class, I had studied theories of adult development and learned that our twenties are for experimenting, exploring different jobs, and discovering what fulfills us. My professor warned against graduate school, asserting, "You're not fully formed yet. You don't know if it's what you really want to do with your life because you haven't tried enough things." Oh, no, not me. I went ahead and got married at twenty-four years old. "And if you rush into something you're unsure about, you might awake midlife with a crisis on your hands," he had lectured. Hi. Try waking up a whole lot sooner with a pre-thirty predicament worm dangling from your early bird mouth.

"Well to begin," Phone Therapist responded, "you have to learn to take care of yourself. To nurture and comfort that little girl inside you, to realize you are quite capable of relying on yourself. I want you to try to remember what brought you comfort when you were younger."

Bowls of cereal after school, coated in a pool of orange-blossom honey. Dragging my finger along the edge of a plate of mashed potatoes. I knew I should have thought "tea" or "bath," but I didn't. Did she want me to answer aloud?

"Grilled cheese?" I said hesitantly.

"Okay, good. What else?"

I thought of marionette shows where I'd held my mother's hand and looked at her after a funny part to see if she was delighted, of brisket sandwiches with ketchup, like my dad ordered. Sliding barn doors, baskets of brown eggs, steamed windows, doubled socks, cupcake paper, and rolled sweater collars. Cookouts where the fathers handled the meat, licking wobbly batter off wire beaters, Christmas ornaments in their boxes, peanut butter on apple slices, the sounds and light beneath an overturned canoe, the pine needle path to the ocean near my mother's house, the crunch of snow beneath my red winter boots, bedtime stories. "My parents," I said. Damn. I felt like she made me say the secret word and just won extra bonus points on the Psychology Game Network. It always comes down to our parents in therapy.

"Okay, good. Before our next session, I want you to pick up the book *Finding Your Own North Star* by Martha Beck. Are you writing this down? Write it down. You can find a lot of these exercises in the book, so it will tide you over until our next session. Remember to think over what has comforted you in the past and see if you can recreate that comfort on your own without refreshing your online dating profile. Okay?"

Shit. She had to go there. "Yes," I responded aloud, but truth be told, before our session, an intriguing nerve.com e-mail arrived in my inbox from a thirty-seven-year-old man with the handle, "AperturePriority." I *had* to respond because he'd suggested a photography outing as our first date. I thought it was a sign, and was about to respond with a "What the hell, why not?" But then I thought better of it and replied, "Too busy right now, but how about a rain check?"

"Stephanie, that 'yes' doesn't seem very convincing," Phone Therapist said.

"No, I know I can't be dating right now. I know because I'm sick of this pattern, sick of cobbling esteem from one date to the next."

"It's so important for us to listen to our bodies. I also want you to think of situations where you've suddenly felt sick." Yeah, like that would be really tough to do. Just mentioning Rome's name gave me the spits.

"The morning I had to run in a race with Oliver, I got 'rhea."

"Good. I want you to think of two different situations. First, remember times when you've felt your best, at the top of your game, alive and vibrant. Pay attention to your posture, the muscles in your face, your breathing. Then, I want you to think of occasions where you've felt sick or anxious. Don't just think of people. Think of activities. This will help us reveal what makes you happy. Pay attention to how your body responds to these scenarios—it will serve as your biggest indicator in the future when you're actually doing things." This woman was damn brilliant. "And remember, it's okay to feel sad, but just try to limit your bouts with it to an hour a day. Let it all out, give yourself that time to heal, nurture, and comfort yourself. You won't heal unless you grieve. Grieving is good."

"Good grief?"

"Yes. It takes courage to grieve." She might have added, "The only way out is through." Good grief, indeed.

After hanging up with her, I began a list. Okay, I'm lying. I began with the very new, very now, and not at all cliché, but oh so chic, Weep, Whimper, and Wail. Full blast. The list would come later. This time, instead of scrambling toward the laptop for a bit of man shopping via dating sites, I lunged toward my sofa and wrapped myself in the cashmere throw Smelly had given to me as a wedding gift. The tags were still on; I'd been saving it. Too good, I thought. I'll keep it for when I have a house. Fuck that noise—too good was NOW. I snapped those suckers off, adiosed them in the trash, then culled the most rueful music I could find and played that shit loud. Yours truly hammered out an off-key rendition of Carly Simon's "Nobody Does It Better" until my throat hurt, until Linus pinned me down to lick my tears, until the neighbors complained. Okay, really? Until the nobody who'd do it better became me, on my way toward becoming a somebody. All right, it was the drama in me. Get over it!

I DID.

The comfort homework helped. I hugged my knees to me and withdrew into thoughts that made me feel less alone.

Every morning of my life in my parents' house, I awoke to the sound of my father's footsteps. He drummed down the stairs, deactivated the alarm, unlocked our front door, and then I'd hear his weight in the gravel driveway as he claimed the morning paper. I didn't see him but knew he was in his sweats with the brown boat shoes he never wore on boats.

In the evenings, I'd know his return with the sound of the garage booming open like a heavy crane, swallowing his car whole. His voice would charge up the stairs and fill the blue kitchen. "Hello, anybody home?" Upon seeing me he'd ask, "And how was school today, Miss Stephanie Tara?"

"The same," I'd say, shrugging.

And I'd follow him to his room with my half-finished homework, clawing my way up the carpeted stairs. I'd finish my homework beside him as he watched a ballgame on the television.

On my sofa, wrapped in a wedding present, I wished I could regress and climb into his closet of warm brown leather and starch smells, or lie on the floor near his bed with a pillow and a blanket listening to sports as

I fell asleep. But wishing is for little girls with magic wands and chests filled to the brim with pretend. Fairy tales are for children.

I turned off Carly and clicked on the Giants–Redskins game. Don't go getting ahead of yourself. I don't follow sports, but the sound of them puts me at ease, even football, a sport that deeply wounds me. My father claimed I despised football because I didn't understand it, but please. I knew the rules, had to learn that crap with a dose of powder-puff football in high school. I knew "the kickoff" wasn't a rejection technique, that "fielding the punt" and "letting the ball go" weren't positions I'd find in my Tantric sex book, and that a "snapped ball" wasn't nearly as painful as it sounded. What I didn't know was why anyone would watch it. It's clumping. Nothing ever happens.

"Oh my God! Did you see that fucking pass? Jesus Christ!!" What happened? Oh, someone threw a ball, and someone actually caught it. Wow. That's the big excitement? East Coast football is defensive, all right. No one moves. It's like watching George Foreman. He's cumbersome and heavy, moves like a slug on slow. Give me a lightweight fighter who darts and makes you look. Jab. Jab. Now, that is interesting. There's movement, gesture, and play. Watching East Coast football is nearly as absurd as Carly Simon shot up to the loudest decibel. So the boys have theirs. I have mine.

"HOW ARE YOU FEELING, CHICA?" IT WAS DULCE, AT MY door with a container of matzo-ball soup and a stack of Meg movies.

"Oh, come on in. Apparently, I'm not contagious, just corruptive."

"Clearly you're just off the phone with your shrink. Very nice mood you're having." She twirled in and set the goods on my coffee table. Dulce loved hearing what Phone Therapist had to say to me. Regularly, she'd ask me to share my session findings with her. It was her idea of cost-effective therapy for herself. "I love your hair curly. It's so much more you."

"I'm sick. I don't have the energy to straighten it. And you only think it's more me because it's so unruly."

"Ah, so it was a good session, I see."

"Do you find it at all pathetic that our conversations are mostly about my mental health lately?" I poured our soup into bowls. "Thank you, honey. This was nice of you. You're officially my new boyfriend."

"Well, then I'm the lucky one." When Dulce spoke, her tone always sounded as if she were having a discussion about lollypops and gobstoppers. I think they call it carefree.

"Hardly. Want to know what I do to my boyfriends? Apparently I make 'em responsible for my happiness, and thus responsible for my unhappiness. I let them wrap my whole world in their hands like that damn gospel song."

"You know that 'damn song' is about God, and how we really don't have control over our lives."

"Yeah, well, if that's true, I'm throwing away a whole lot of money in *ther-rape-me* sessions."

"Nah. You're just learning to control what you can."

"Lovely. I'm a walking twelve-step program." I swallowed half a matzo ball without chewing.

"So come on," she said, "tell me about your session," Dulce giggled as she tried to slurp up a particularly long noodle.

"I have to make a list of situations that make me happy. Perhaps I'll add noodle slurping to it and hope it works?"

"Why do you have to make a list?" She set her bowl down, tucked her knees up, and knotted herself into what she considered "comfortable" on my sofa.

I turned my head and stared for a moment before asking, "Can't you sit like a normal person?" Dulce is double-jointed. I've never understood this concept of joints. Meathead, the spastic guy from our Hampton's sharehouse, had nicknamed her "Stick Bug" because of her movements and long thin limbs. When she drank too much, she'd display her jointed talents for all to see, showcasing her ability to touch her knee to her nose while wearing her minute of a skirt.

"You can also work on being more flexible by stretching, you know."

"Yeah, I'm working on flexible. I'll try stretching when therapy renders useless."

"So why the list?" she asked again, this time sitting on her heels.

"Because, other than being in love, I don't know what makes me feel good. Not really, not like that."

"What is it about love, do you think?"

"When I'm in a relationship, I'm usually told by the guy that I'm sexy and talented, and I believe it when he says it. But when I'm alone, I don't feel any of those things. I know I have to be those things or they wouldn't see them. But I don't see them in myself. My therapist told me I need to learn to love myself. It sounds easy enough, but really, how do you just wake up one day and learn that? It feels like something you should just do involuntarily, like swallowing or blinking, but now I have to work on it. It feels so forced. I mean, I know I went to a good school, and people tell me I'm smart and creative, but I don't KNOW that. I don't know how to make myself *feel* that."

Since moving to New York from Baltimore, where she'd gone to college, Dulce had four different jobs in finance. She was currently employed at Merrill Lynch, working as an analyst, making a great living, and she hated it.

"I always look forward to coming here," Dulce continued, "because you make me feel alive again. Work is so anesthetizing. It's like some antidepressant that numbs you out. Carter doesn't understand why I'm always so tired. But when I'm around you, you remind me of the old me, the creative me, that I've seemed to have lost somewhere along the way in my own life struggles. It's like I feel hope in myself because I can at least get excited about your passions."

"Yeah, how are things with *The Glenn*?"

I nicknamed her new boyfriend Carter "The Glenn" because he was fatally attracted to Dulce. He referred to her only by her given name, Allyson Reese, just so she would one day say, "Oh, the only ones who call me that are my mother and Carter." He wanted the in on being important any way he could get it. When Dulce spent time with me, The Glenn had her on the clock, phoning her cell on the hour, wondering when she'd be coming over. His ears must have been ringing. Dulce's cell phone did just that.

"Hi sweetie . . . no, I told you . . . well, just a bit longer . . . we're in the middle of a project. No, sweetie, don't be silly . . ." I cleared our bowls from the coffee table and gave Dulce the illusion of privacy as I headed toward my adjoining kitchen. I listened as she tried to pacify him, cooing "I love you"s at him in an *infantimbre* I thought only Gay Max had mastered.

When I returned, she was off the phone. "Let me guess. He can't live or breathe without you?" Dulce smiled and rolled her eyes. "Why do you tolerate him?"

"Well, he's not always like that," she said. "I mean, he has redeeming qualities. Like, he knows how much I hate having to wake up so early for work, knows how much it stresses me out, so he gets up and rides the subway downtown with me just to keep me company. It's completely out of his way, but he does it for me." That was sweet in a mildly needy and maniacal way. Hence, The Glenn.

"You know, Dulce, there is such a thing as too giving. I mean, I know he does that to make you happy, but I suspect he's willing to do anything for you, except if your being happy involves time away from him." Oh, I would know. I'd lived a lifetime feeling that way about Gabe. "What does he do with himself when you're not around for him to shower with affection and praise? I mean, does The Glenn have any hobbies? A sport, anything?"

Dulce blinked at me, biting her lower lip in thought.

"Exactly," I said. "He needs to get a life and figure out what makes him happy besides being in love and making you mixed tapes. Shit, you should've invited him here for our matzo-ball soup for the soul session, after all. He could use a little list-making loveliness in his life."

"Yeah, okay, Steph, get out your journal and make the list now. I'll make one too. Hopefully, we'll figure out what we should be doing with all of this pent-up energy, aside from analyzing it."

WHEN YOU'RE MARRIED, YOUR ENERGY HAS A CHANCE TO roam. You can choose a hobby—raising a dog, fertility, painting. Your Google searches have a theme. You are no longer aimless in the bookstore. You have found something to invest all the energy you had previously spent on planning the wedding, or before that, planning your life. Unfortunately, many of us, when we're single never-been's (as in never been married), don't really think we've got an adult life until we're married. So we obsess over the meanings of IMs, e-mails, and lack of calls as a hobby. We can almost spreadsheet the interactions with our respective dates.

E-mailed him twice, called once.

Returned his call. Ball is in his court.

He asked you out. Up to you to respond.

We could try to elaborate, adding which story we told to whom, but it would require more typing than it's worth. And when there is no guy, we create them or resurrect the older ones because we don't know what to do with the available energy we still have after our yoga, spinning, and elliptical efforts. When you get married, you can exhale and start your life.

That's what I thought. So many women do it, let themselves obsess over someone because it gives them something to do. Carter did it with Dulce. I did it with Gabe, Oliver, and a host of others in between. Now, though, I reviewed my journal entries, examined the scope of my conversations with friends, and I thought, "Is this it? Did you really let it become this, just this? Fuck. You're more than this."

I knew I had to start making my hobbies, my passions, about me. It's a way better investment than some random guy who wouldn't be around the next week. I'd find something I could do, just for me, which made me happy. It would be something no one could ever take from me, on a par with education. Learning to make yourself happy, without another person, is just as invaluable as learning from the past. And masturbation is not a hobby, it's a sport. But I tested it out anyway.

I drew myself a bath after undressing, and as the tub filled, I watched my body, not with a critical eye, but with the eyes of a lover who doesn't care about the distended or aged. He's too focused on what's next to notice about "enough." In the looking, I decide I have a beautiful stomach. It's not muscular or flat enough, but I've stopped giving a shit about "enough." It's what a stomach should be. It's smooth and sinks concave when I pull it up in a breath, exposing a shallow bowl of skin, hollowed to my hipbones. I lie on the bed, feeling desire so strong, it masquerades as hunger. I can feel it there, warm and purring. I like watching it move, pulsing in pleasure. I smell my odor. The deodorant has worn thin and ineffective as I rub myself. Harder. With two hands now. No, not like that. This is better. I pull one arm over my head, covering one nostril, making it harder to breathe. Harder. I'm angry. That's it. Harder. It's not enough. I have to think of something. A strong hand presses into my back. I can't see it. I only feel the warmth and strength in it, as though I could collapse my weight into the palm, and it would still catch me. Salt and pepper hair, an older man. I fantasize about safety. Even in my sexiest thoughts, I conjure security and crave for it to press into me.

I anger-fucked myself to sleep again after my bath. I hated that I needed therapy, hated how broken I felt, hated that I couldn't set everything right immediately. My rage slid out when I finished, the kind buried so deep you didn't know it was there. Latent. It arrived with my tears of aggravation. Restless, my God, that's what it was. I was so fucking restless. Twitchy and scratchy and movey (it should be a word) and frustrated. I didn't realize I'd become so abrasive and miserable until the sexual release cleaved me like a peach, revealing the hard center of a stone fruit. It needed to be coaxed from its lodge and roots.

Even masturbation left me feeling wrong about everything, and I'm not even Catholic. I am, however, a glutton for punishment, so the next morning I went shopping for a new pair of jeans. Kidding. I wasn't looking for Hell, just Purgatory. So I hit the streets with my camera and headed for Crapass Central, yet again. This time I was prepared. I had gloves, tissues, and *my*Pod cranked to Nina Simone's "I Shall Be Released".

When I got to the part where she sees her own reflection on the walls and her life shining I mouthed the words, *any day now*. It wasn't working, any of it. Coffee would help, certainly. I like my coffee burnt and sweet, like flan syrup.

"Grandeskimnowhipgingerbreadlatte at the bar."

"Thank you," I mumbled.

"No, thank *you*, ma'am." Swell, now I was a ma'am. When did that happen? I fucking hate life and your green apron. What was she smiling about? How was she so happy grinding it out, putting white lids on white cups, pumping syrup and addictive stimulants into the lives of strangers?

"May I ask you a question?" I said plainly, pulling the Pod buds from my ears.

"You sure can."

"Are you, are you happy?"

"I am today," she said.

Maybe that's what really mattered? Living in the now, and all that crap about the past being over? The future hasn't happened, and today is forever? These aren't the kinds of statements that belonged beside question marks.

"You've got great hair. Surely that's reason enough to be happy," she added, in a twirl, as I began to suck foam from my coffee. Everyone around me was twirling lately. She got my order wrong. I didn't order Comfort and Joy with a side of Pep and Glee in my latte—I wanted it in my life.

She was right about the hair. I was wearing it curly again. I felt the chaos inside and couldn't be bothered trying to tame it. It was too much work. Besides, I was too busy "working on me." Days prior, I'd schlepped to the park to photograph old people and bridges. It wasn't helping and only felt like I was trying to pass the time until someone new entered the picture. "Work on yourself. Love yourself." Ew. Enough! I'd done that. I'd done that. I'd DONE THAT! I had the damn list to prove it. If I heard myself tell one more person about my hobbies and friends and job and dog, I was going to—

I hate when I do that.

I threatened just there. Did you see that? If I heard one more . . . yeah, big talker, what were you gonna do about it? I hated that I was empty threats, even to myself. And, more importantly, I hated the word *hobbies*. I still do. It's terrible and reminds me of Tyler Hobbes, a fat, freckled kid from my childhood who ate boxes full of toothpicks, and who, even in sixth grade, did the comb-over. I think of wooden hobby-horses. I was ill over the selling of my life. Maybe that's what was making me sick. I was out there working it, selling myself, really, telling people about my interests, about how nice it was to finally focus on being single. I'd done it in the park, in Jaimee's arms. Pointed to my camera and called it my baby. Who was I fooling? The worst bit of it was, I wasn't just try-ing to convince her. I'd been peddling "I'm happy now" to myself.

I'd built a thick, heavy wall of funny stories and interests around my heart. I didn't know how to let anyone in anymore. And the most un-comfortable I got was when someone asked me how I was while looking me in the eye, pausing in a stare, waiting for a reply. I looked away, and then looked back, ensuring I made eye contact so they wouldn't ask again. I'd lie to their face. Convincingly. "I'm good. Really good." I shook my head between good and really. "Yeah." They'd smile back, and I'd want to hide in a dark closet for days.

I was not fine. I was despondent. I felt myself hardening. I used to be so much softer than the cold armor of a woman I saw in the reflection of the coffee shop window.

"Be patient with yourself," I said aloud as I pushed the ear buds back in. "It's not going to happen overnight. Change takes time. You'll get there." It was how I comforted myself. It didn't come in an orange cylin-der from Duane Reade. My salve wasn't over the counter—it was be-neath all my bitching about misery. It was there trying to surface through my thick sob story. I didn't need a ball game or my father's closet. I needed me. I just had to sit still long enough to hear what I had to say. It was exactly where I should have been focusing.

fourteen

MANUAL FOCUS

ONE OF THE BELOVED ITEMS IN MY BEDROOM IS A MONO-grammed desk chair I purchased when I'd first moved in. A gold, cursive K is embroidered on the back of the linen slipcover. It has a kick-pleat skirt that dusts the floor, more of a dining-room chair than something suitable for a desk. In its own small way, seeing that K every day makes me feel stronger. "That's you, Stephanie," I remind myself. Then I shut up, sit in it, and begin to write.

Writing a list of my happiest moments wasn't as easy as I'd expected. Others might conjure images of their wedding days, births of their children. I couldn't. Sure, I'd witnessed the happy, quiet moments of others, watching a young girl pull the brass ring from the carousel, waving it in delight for her mother to see. But when I drew within myself to my happiest moments in life, they weren't about what I'd observed. They were about what I'd accomplished.

At ten years old, I'd spent the summer swimming at my parents' club. I timed myself in fifty-yard increments. Breathless. Waterlogged. Laps until it hurt to hoist myself from the pool. "You're just wasting your time," my cousin Electra chided from the edge of the pool. "You're too fat to be fast." Then she skipped away to the shuffleboard area to gorge on Italian sausages and yellow rice by the plateful.

At a formal end-of-summer awards night ceremony, I sat with the other children my age waiting for our swim coach to be invited to the podium. The swimming awards were saved for last, after they'd covered golf, tennis, and diving. When our coach announced the final award, my eyes were closed tight in prayer, fingers crossed. I was so busy chanting, *Please say it. Stephanie Klein. Please*, that I didn't hear him say my name.

"Stephanie, don't just sit there," Electra hooted over the rising applause. Was that right? Had I really received the most prestigious swimming award of the night?

"You've worked really hard to earn this," my coach said into my shoulder as he hugged me. "You should feel very proud."

STEPHANIE KLEIN: MOST VALUABLE PLAYER was engraved on a shiny golden trophy the size of my torso. I'd been undefeated that summer, earning our club more points than any other competitor. I needed both hands to carry the trophy back to my table. They're the first tears of joy I remember shedding. When I got home that night, I put the trophy on my nightstand and awoke several times to touch it in the dark. I nestled into my sheets, smiling and gripping my covers, as I fell back asleep.

As I got older, achievement continued to fuel me. I'd rehearse solos and choreograph dance steps in my socks, slipping on the living room floors, practicing each night. Seeing my name printed on the school bulletin board beside the leading role in *Oklahoma!* charged me with an intense yet contained sense of accomplishment. Over dinner, I spoke with a Southern accent. "Why yeeeeeees. Some more peas would be just love-LY, Ma'am." I walked differently, pulling my shoulders back, my hands balled into fists. YES!

When other kids were at Friendly's dipping French fries into their sundaes, I was home working on the next academic assignment, striving for good grades. When the thick acceptance letters to the colleges I really wanted to attend arrived in the mail, I hugged them. I raced to my bedroom, threw myself onto my bed, and kicked my feet wildly as I squealed into my pillows.

The moments that gave me the most joy were the culmination of work, suffering, and sacrifice. The harder something was for me, the more adamantly I was told I couldn't do it, the tastier the victory was when I finally did. If it took courage, perseverance, or strength, it meant more when the validation arrived.

I'd grown to associate accomplishment with joy, even when it was for others. I volunteered to tutor Aidina, a young girl living in a family homeless shelter who'd been classified as "slow." Teaching her to read was a long, arduous journey for both of us, but the day she read her first words aloud, all by herself, I felt a profound smile commandeer my face. She looked up after she read them, her mouth agape. We stared at each other in fixed astonishment, as if we weren't sure it was real. I looked over my shoulder. Did that really just happen? I grabbed Aidina by the arm and yanked her through the house, making each person we came across listen to her read. She and I jumped up and down, hugging tightly in all the rooms of the house. Seeing her radiate confidence made me euphoric.

Remembering these pointed moments as I wrote them from my K chair turned me into a blubbering mush, and I've never been one to want anything having to do with blubber. I couldn't stop smiling as I wrote the list, even when I wiped the stray tears from the corners of my eyes. My muscles collapsed, and I could linger on each memory, knowing no one could ever take it from me. It was mine. Something I'd earned. A permanent fixture in my core. But I had to work hard for each of those items on the list before I came to value my achievement. It's exactly what I thought love was, what a relationship was. I associated strife as something that would always lead to happiness. A labor of love. If the relationship came easily, it didn't seem worthy.

Then Linus pawed at my thigh, indicating he wanted up on my lap. "Come on up," I said in the baby voice I used when I spoke with him. I flipped him onto his back, cradling him in my arm as I rubbed his warm belly. This was love, too. I remembered the first night I'd taken him home with me. He fell asleep on my chest, his warm puppy breath in my face. I loved his Woodstock yawn, the smell of his corn chip paws, the sounds he made as he crunched his food. This wasn't earned. I added his name to the list. My love for him extended beyond a mere moment of recognition. There had to be others. I was resolved to find them.

I phoned Dulce. "I love *you*. I just added your name to the list. I needed to say that."

"And I love you. How's it going?"

"Eh. This shit doesn't happen overnight, right? So I guess I'm good today. That's enough. It sucks that it takes so long, but whatever. It's better than it has been. Want to know the worst part? I'm now that girl who says 'one day at a time.' Just kill me now, for real."

"You'll be fine," Dulce yawned.

"Goodnight, love."

It was the first time I'd said "I love you" to a friend.

Growing up I heard Lea say it constantly to anyone who'd listen. I remember overhearing her tell one of her camp friends, "I love you," over the phone and thinking, "Oh my God. She tells her friends she loves them?" I envied it. In contrast, I never touched my friends or expressed any of my feelings toward them. Telling a friend "I love you" was like having sex for the first time. It was a big deal for me.

Today, it's hard to keep me off my friends. I now tell them I love them aloud, not often, but purposefully. I'm not afraid they won't know how to respond. It's not about vulnerability, about who says it first, as it had been for me with men. The only fear I feel now is that they won't know their worth to me. It's why I make a point of saying it.

For some, the L-word means marriage, babies, and always. It means you're ready to spend forever together, with a drawer of mismatched socks, compromising vacation plans, beside someone who'll always tell you the truth, even when it hurts like a snapped bone. For me, "I love you" means I want to work on preserving this, right now. The only guarantee I have faith in is within myself, knowing whatever happens to me, no matter who leaves, I will be okay. And I don't need a trophy to validate that because I know it through me, the way you know hot from cold.

I KNEW FROM COLD AND RESOLUTIONS IN JANUARY. THE Valentine's Day cards were in their slots at the ready. My father's wife Carol invited an estate lawyer to their home to negotiate her parents' wills. It was an act of love. On the somber occasion, along with the raspberry Linzer tart cookies and Huggy Bear Tea, she offered the lawyer her "trophy" friend, Lulu.

"She's single and fabulous, and here's her most flattering misleading photo. She's really older and much more zaftig in person, and that light-ing is a godsend." Okay, that might have been her inner monologue pulling overtime. Carol thrust Lulu's photo into his lap as if her friend were a classic seven apartment, new on the market. Lulu had been single, without one offer to buy, for four-plus years. You could almost hear the *Fiddler on the Roof* soundtrack.

I imagine he flashed an ingratiating smile and tucked her number into his inner pocket with a false promise to phone Lulu later in the week. But when later in the week arrived, flowers were delivered . . . to my father's house. A note was affixed to the cellophane-wrapped arrange-ment: "Thank you for introducing me to such a fantastic woman."

My father and Carol were dumbfounded. Carol kept rereading the card, rubbing her manicured thumb over the words. She played yenta, calling each of her friends whom she'd tried (and failed) to set up previ-ously. "Ya see," she boasted, "I'm not wrong all the time." Yeah, and the sun shines on a dog's ass every once in a while.

"Stephanie, that's what you need," she phoned me to say, "a man with class." Yes, I needed a great many things, but looking for it hadn't been working. "Who needs to look? I have a few very nice ones for you." No way. I don't do blind dates. It's bad enough that the two being set up suffer, but now there's a third who gets dragged into the misery. Even if I had been agreeable to a set-up, Carol's idea of "very nice" meant an "oy"ster who had a Lexus SUV lease on life. I could never enjoy foreplay with a guy who said "fakakta."

"Thanks, but no thanks. I thought Dad told you I'm off the sauce."

"What do you mean? You're not dating?"

"No. I've resolved to work on myself for right now. I still have guys e-mailing me through the online dating sites, but it's just not a good idea. You know I haven't been on a date since I broke things off with Oliver over two months ago?" I said it more as a realization than a declaration. "I'm proud of myself, actually."

"Well, good for you." If it were her own daughter saying she was swearing off men, she'd have mentioned a clock and eggs while tapping her wristwatch. But with me, she said it—I was sure—because of what my father must have communicated to her about me. The way some parents live vicariously through their child's wedding or education, my father wanted me to be fulfilled without a relationship, for the both of us. Because we're the same that way. I didn't just inherit his mannerisms, red hair, or affinity for storytelling. I am emotionally built the way he is. Needy. That's why it's so easy for us to communicate with each other. He knows exactly how I operate because he thinks the way I do. He wants me to outgrow it for the both of us. So do I.

"Well, when you are ready again, you just let us know. I'm telling ya, classy guys." Oh, yes. I was sure. My idea of class was a bit different from Carol's. Mine was of the 101 variety.

I WAS SIGNED UP BUT NOT AT ALL READY FOR MY PRINCIPLES of Black-and-White & Color class at the International Center of Photography. I had the SLR camera but needed to purchase the textbook, which meant a swing-by at Barnes & Noble.

Normally, a tramp through the bookstore felt lovely and delicious, as if I'd come at pudding time. I was dressed to absorb time there, settling in, cozy amid the rows of thick, glossy photography books. I wrapped an oversized stone cashmere cable-knit 'round my waist, giving the hand to the "never wrap a sweater around your waist 'cause it adds ten pounds to your ass" theory. I was ready to enjoy the exploration behind corners and between turns. I loved how the bookstore housed the ability to discover and learn something new, the capacity to be inspired, to latch onto a blooming interest, to want more.

It was close to impossible for me to walk into that empire and not want to touch every table, drink a latte, and see just how much of my wardrobe had made it to the "not" side of the *What's Hot & Not* sections of the latest magazines. I picked up a thick issue of *InStyle*, warmed my hands for the ready, and made an intentional crease, past the first twenty pages of advertisements. And damn it, the January issue went there, like everyone does.

If you're single-without-prospects, do yourself a favor: don't open any magazines through January and February. March, if you read the from-our-last-issue letters. Especially the cooking ones. Beets cut into the shape of hearts, pink peppercorns, roasted red pepper sauce. Everything becomes pink. Sometimes people ask me what my favorite color is, and I've always wondered, what kind of question is that? I mean, who really has a favorite color after the second grade? Well, let me tell you something. I'm beginning to get it. Because, if there are favorites where colors are concerned, then PINK is my favorite color to HATE. Any magazine I thumbed through had red pages with pink hearts, even those tattoo, fishing, and trucker's magazines were going there. For the love of God and all things black and moody, go away. Taunt someone else.

I hate hearts. Chocolate. All the dumb cards. Leave me alone. Want to hear the worst part? Barnes & Noble had actual display TABLES that made me want to shit out all my tenderness. The displays were littered with hearts in many colors, though they all taste the same: like chalk. Books of *New Yorker* cartoons, sexual foods, then the red devil pens and heart key chains. Pink glossy gift bags with fuchsia feather handles. Oh, it was official. It was that time of month for the next two months. I didn't think it could get worse.

Love coupons. That was worse. Since when did we get so cheap about sex? Now they make coupons for it? I didn't use coupons for waffles or toilet paper, soap even, but I'd tear one out for sex? Prophylactics, yes. Perforated, no. That's just so wrong. The coupons weren't just for nights of triple Bs: beer, backrub, and blow job. They promised enslavement to laundry, dishes, and taking out the garbage. Aren't you supposed to do these things for each other without coupons? Yet, there they sat for consumption on the romantic table at Barnes & Noble. I didn't always feel this way. I'm sure I liked the holiday in fourth grade when they gave us something fun to color. Doilies to glue. *Candy.* Valentine's Day isn't for adults. It's for teenagers and children, for restaurants, florists, and lingerie sales. Adults should show and share love, daily, not when the magazines and card stores say so. It just so disingenuous, and I've had enough of that in my romantic relationships, thank you.

So I was a wee bit bitter. Okay, a lot bitter. But, don't get me wrong—I love a good bargain. I'm all about the savings card. It's like found money, but I'm no coupon girl. They get you, first, by leading you to their store for your shopping expedition. Now you're not just their customer, you're their bitch, buying things you wouldn't ordinarily purchase because who can say no to two dollars off? You go home with products you'll never use, stashing the Flex shampoo under the sink, and maneuvering the twenty-pound bags of long-grain rice behind the boxes of lasagna noodles. Now you have assorted meat varieties of soup and a Sara Lee ham with no home. When your apartment lease is up, you'll move and feel good about all the clutter you've just banished from under and behind things. Coupons lead to Under, Between, and Behind. You shouldn't need coupons to get under and between things during sex, and don't get me started with behind. That's a whole 'nother chapter.

"I'M GOING TO JUST ASSUME YOU'LL READ THE TEXTBOOK chapters on your own because we're not going to cover them in class. And I trust you've all read the first three chapters for today as the syllabus instructed." I had nerd-up'd her and completed the first five.

Class met on Wednesday nights at 6 P.M. in a square glass cube of a building, the kind I'd always imagined when I heard the word *modern*. I felt important being there, sliding my ID card past security with a smile and a nod that looked routine. I clutched my strap and drew the body of my camera closer to my core as I pressed through the halls of framed photos toward my classroom.

The halls were my favorite part of arriving each week. I'd read the small off-white rectangles beside each student's work to see what they'd named their prints. Grainy black-and-white silver gelatin prints of people sleeping: *REM*. The sheen of an empty unmade bed: *Insomnia*. A foot peeking out from a lip of sheet: *Sunday*. Each photograph told a story. I wondered what mine would be and if I'd need more than one word to tell it.

I felt invigorated in the contemporary building where creative minds and hands met, a more organized, clean, and inspired version of myself. "I'm going to be good at this," I thought as I took my seat.

My professor's name was Kimberlee, despite being a Canadian woman in her midforties who pronounced *batteries* as "batt-rees." I was mesmerized by her voice. It was smooth and oozy, like a smear of Camembert on a round paddle knife.

"Yes, I have a question about something I read in the textbook," a balding man with a long ponytail who looked like an employee at Hogs & Heifers said hesitantly. Her eyebrows lifted and chin pointed toward him, signaling he should continue with his question. "Is it really possible to set the camera to manual focus while it's in the automatic program mode?"

"Yes, of course," she responded. Her eyes looked like broad butter beans. "The two have nothing to do with each other. The program mode of a single lens reflex camera, or SLR, is like asking your camera to behave as if it were a point and shoot. There's no thinking involved. There's no customization or accommodation for aperture or shutter speed in that mode. You'd have to turn the dial to aperture priority, shutter speed priority, or manual for that type of control. Now, the focus setting, on the other hand, has nothing to do with exposure. You can switch focus to either manual or automatic. Can anyone think of a situation where you'd want to turn your focus to manual?" She was standing behind me now. She smelled like what I imagined cardamom smelled like.

We all looked cautiously at one another across the table. I raised my hand half-staff, unsure of what I'd say, my answer still forming. "Because sometimes you aren't sure what your focus should be until you really look around."

"Very good. Another reason to use manual focus is sometimes our cameras hunt for a subject when the lighting isn't good. It's hard for the camera to focus in the dark." I felt as if she were talking about my life. "Any more questions before I begin with the slides?"

She took our silence as a "no," flipped off the lights, and switched on a slide projector packed with her travel photography. She clicked through tribal images, gray ash on skin, paint, feathers, and fire, without a word on where we ought to focus. She just clicked through images, slowly at first, with a metered rhythm. Then at frenetic speeds, where my eyes weren't sure of the story it ought to construct. A boy in underwear, his legs propped up on a sofa. Etchings on a cave wall. A ski cap revealing an eye stitched closed. A goldfish dangling from the pinch of two fingers. My mind filled in blanks. Vietnam rice hats, a modern crop on a woman's hand holding a rooster, pink light on weathered skin. This is what I wanted to do, to explore, to be where she'd been. To capture gestures and evoke emotion.

"Rites of passage," she said on a blank dark slide. "Every culture has them, whether it's swallowing a live goldfish in college or being forced to drink the creamy blood of your father." Ew, man, she just said creamy blood, and I was still listening? "We all remember our own passages with some element of clarity." I remembered when my best friend from high school was slapped in the face by her mother when she'd first gotten her period. It was their tradition. My house didn't have any. My rite of passage happened, and I cried. Then my mother handed me a maxi pad and promised she wouldn't tell my father after I'd pleaded with her in a red-faced tantrum. Not exactly the behavior of a woman.

"Circumcision," she continued. "Knocking out teeth. They're rites, painful transformations reminding us we cannot go back. It's time to stow our childish delights away to accommodate new responsibilities." When she said *new*, a black-and-white studio shot of an engagement ring appeared on screen.

I'd undergone the ceremonial ritual of marriage before fully coming into my own as a whole woman.

"In Joseph Campbell's conversation with Bill Moyers, he discusses the aborigines in Australia and their celebrated rite of passage," she continued, now on a slide of a naked man's torso covered in white down. "Campbell spoke of naked men using blood as glue to decorate their bodies in thin strips of white feathers. The men would surround a young boy, cowering in his mother's embrace, and cleave him from her arms. They'd then force him to drink the blood of men to polarize the effects of the breast milk he'd fed on for years. He's no longer his mother's son. Now he's his father's son."

Gabe needed to feed on blood to grow up. If I'd only known! "In Catholicism, it's confirmation." An image of Jesus on the crucifix appeared. "The Jews have bar mitzvahs." The Hamesh Hand dangled from a gold chain, sandwiched in cleavage. "These puberty rights served to prepare adolescents for their new role in life." She flipped on the lights. "Now is your chance, each of you, to explore the rites you've been given, the freedoms you enjoy, and to find your voice through photography while you're still adolescents on the subject. What will your creative expression be?"

I was suddenly struck by an intense desire to kiss her. Her passion excited me. I couldn't stop staring. I clung to her words. It was a girl crush. I was in awe of her dedication and passion, the way the words formed as they left her mouth. I wanted everything she saw, to capture things the way she had. I was mesmerized by her fervor and lust for life. Her images were rich and saturated with pigment. I couldn't imagine ever being depressed around a woman like this. My God, this was what I wanted to become, to find in myself.

Yes, I wanted a man to share all my "new" with, but I had a strong sense I wouldn't be ready for a relationship until I became a professional at handling the manual controls of my life. Later that night, though, once I arrived home, I received another nerve.com e-mail from AperturePriority. It seemed he wouldn't take "rain check" for an answer. He countered with a poem by David Miller, "The Quiet Ways of Water," and attached a black-and-white photograph of a window pane enhanced by beads of rain.

No, Stephanie. Don't even think about it. I was tempted because what if he were as passionate as my photography instructor? I thanked him again for his offer but decided, for the time being, I'd sit back and do my thing, enjoying my moments, camera in hand. It didn't stop us from e-mailing and instant messaging daily as friends, but it did allow me to spend more time rounding new corners, exploring the city through my lens, like a kid peeking beneath a heavy rock.

In the two-plus months that passed since I ended things with Oliver and embraced the dreaded "alone," I enjoyed exploring the city by myself without having to apologize for wanting to stay late or leave early. I circled live music events in the About Town sections of magazines with the fervor of a college graduate in pursuit of a job. I'd go alone to prove I could, that it would be okay. Once I realized alone was a choice, not something about which to be embarrassed, I embraced it in more intimate settings. I'd try a new restaurant, something with linen and a notable wine list. I tumbled into random plays. Cooking classes! *Look, Mom, no hands!*

In the past, when I was involved in relationships, I didn't realize I could get that need for "new" satiated without involving myself with a man. I adored learning about people, following their gestures, and lingering on their observations, but as soon as I entered a relationship, that learning process was stymied. I associated "new" with flirting and mischief and wasn't aware it could exist outside a romantic relationship. Now I've learned new can come from friendships. From volunteering. From reading and a host of classes. From sitting at a bar, observing, listening, overhearing other dramas. From meeting other women—imagine? Out alone!—at a bar and hearing their stories and what they'd been through. It didn't just come in the body of a classy gentleman. It came from creating a rich life for myself, filling my time with activities that satisfied my needs.

Wandering the city, with camera in tow, was my first stab at a journey with an unknown destination—well, if you don't count life itself.

Photography fit. It was storytelling and let me leave my own crowded head and enjoy the moment. Instead of crafting a story through information architecture and advertising web design alone, I could express my stories with photographs, in stops of light. In those quiet orange evenings of observation, I became more aware of mannerisms, behavior, the way we flirt with napkins and eyes. Drinking through straws. It became about capturing a moment with a snap and click of a shutter curtain. In that small stop of time, I could explain what I'd seen and felt without having to articulate a word.

fifteen

RED

YES WAS THE WORD I FINALLY USED MID-MARCH TO RE-
spond to AperturePriority's e-mail.

> You know, I don't want to think of you as just a pen pal anymore, Ms.
> Klein. Meet me after your photography class, so I can, at the very least,
> think of you as a regular pal.—Stephen

Screw it. He was right. In our weeks of e-mails, phone calls, and daily instant messages, I'd grown to refer to Stephen as my *friendboy*, not to be
confused with boyfriend. I might as well meet the guy.

"Well, as long as our meeting isn't a date, then fine."

"Give it whatever name you'd like. I'd just like to see this unbalanced
redhead I've gotten to almost know these past few . . ."

"Yes." And that was that.

After my class, I met him at 'Cesca on the Upper West Side. He was
broader than his photo had hinted. His eyes bluer. His smile affection-
ately boyish. His hair decidedly more salt than pepper. He smelled like
warm laundry. We folded into comfortable conversation with ease, sharing an order of polenta with wild mushrooms, taking turns swiping
crusty hunks of sourdough through our bowl. I was still hungry.

"You're still hungry, aren't you?" I liked him, right there, in that moment. "God, me too!" He touched my leg. "Want to order the paella?"
No. I loved him, right there, in that moment. I touched his arm. His skin
was soft. I wanted to nap with him.

A lobster head sat between us, beads of yellow rice clinging to mussel shells. More wine. He walked me home. I texted him when I was finally upstairs and he was in a cab on his way home. "I really can't wait to see you again."

This was *bad*.

I WASN'T READY TO DATE! WHAT, YOU TAKE A FEW CLASSES and now you're this whole woman, full of esteem? Just like that? No! I knew I wasn't ready to date because I was still so desperate to do so. *Need*. So in the weeks that followed, when Stephen reached out, I spun away. We'd still meet for lunch or drinks, and sometimes we'd hit a movie on a Sunday afternoon, but I withdrew, serving up a litany of excuses. "I have to wake up early." "Linus is waiting for me." "My apartment's a mess." We were nondating, and he knew it.

I didn't have to make any excuses when Smelly invited me to the Scope Art Fair after-party, where emerging artists, curators, and dealers would be celebrating the close of the exhibition. "Come," she urged, "and bring your camera. There'll be a bunch of freaks there." I didn't need convincing. The party was on the roof of the not-yet-open Hotel Gansevoort. They'd converted the rooms of the hotel into galleries, showcasing the Scope art. I wondered how the interior decorator of the hotel determined the type of creative work used to adorn the suite room walls once the fair was over. I wondered aloud, actually, to one of the owners of the hotel. He was a friend of Smelly.

"Well, our interior designer is the wife of the hotel's architect, and I'm pretty sure she's still making decisions where the room art is concerned," he said after posing for a photograph with one of his partners. I'd learned never to travel without my camera, in fear of *needing* to photograph a moment and later kicking myself for not having it on me. "Just submit your portfolio, and I'm sure she'll get back to you one way or another." I thanked him, and two days later, I did just that.

How much of success comes down to what you know, whom you know, or how and when you do it? Would the wife of the architect be the hotel's interior designer if she weren't his wife? Did he simply open the door for her, and the follow-through was up to her? I'd found simply by pursuing my passions, unexpected opportunities were revealed. It wasn't a cocktail of two-thirds timing and a dash of whom you know. All of it played a part, and it seemed that mine was taking a risk, assembling a portfolio, and submitting it for review. I'd exhausted weekend hours dodging and burning in the photography lab. During the week, I worked past dawn, noodling with Photoshop filters and adjusting hues. It never felt like work. So the very last thing I thought about while attending the Scope party was "working the room." Opportunities presented themselves like a fanned-out deck of cards.

The evening of the Scope party, Patrick McMullen had approached me. I didn't know who he was, only that he liked my hair and wanted me to attend a Saint Patrick's Day party he'd be hosting. He flipped me his card and urged me to come. "With that red hair," he'd said while inspecting one of my locks, "you must come." When I showed his card to Smelly later that night, she gasped.

"Steph, that's the famous fashion photographer! I mean, he does fashion week, Bryant Park, the whole deal. Are you going to go?"

Of course I'd go. *The* Patrick McMullen was personally inviting me to his party. He was doing exactly what I hoped to be doing one day: making a living by pursuing his passion.

Gay Max and I attended Patrick's shindig days later. I hoped I'd have a chance to speak with him again. Perhaps he had an opening for a photographer to join his staff. It couldn't hurt to ask. Once I arrived at the party, though, I realized any "asking" would have to be done in a shout. His party was hardly jazz and candlelight. Green stout, paper shamrocks, grunge rocker musicians, and oodles of photographers, cameras in tow, flooded the "no cameras permitted" venue.

"How did you snag an invite to this?" Gay Max asked, eyeing me with a look of amusement.

"Heh. I knew you'd love it, even if it is fancy shmancy," I mocked. "The host invited me because of my red hair," I said with a toss of it. "Oh, don't ask. It's not like I know him."

"What, he thought you were Irish or sumtin'?"

I rolled my eyes and raised my apple martini. "Here's to green adult beverages and to being a Quarterican Jew who looks Irish."

"And to models!" Max added as his head turned to follow the direction of a sultry brunette.

We clinked glasses and pecked at our drinks, watching beautiful people not eat. "I'll be back," Max said while balancing his martini. "I've got to go tinkle." In his absence, I surveyed the scene through my telephoto lens. Spike-haired men in funky T-shirts and canvas shoes looked just past everyone they passed. Waifs applied waitress-red lipstick and pouted, afraid to smudge any on their teeth with a smile. The "under twenty-one" boy-candy himbos must've known someone working the door. They feigned older with the aid of some gum, chewing hard to compensate for their undeveloped jaw lines. Then there were the older gentlemen whose only chance of meeting women was to attend to the forty-five-year-old urban cougars, too botoxed to give 'em the eye. Still, one of the ascot-clad gents wasn't exactly shy about approaching me.

"So, how are ya dare?" A silver-haired, tangerine-faced man asked thickly as he licked milky beer foam from his upper lip.

"I'm good, and you?"

"Fine. Fine." He raised his voice over the din of the band. "I was just wondrin' if you've got a red carpet," the Oompa-Loompa slurred.

"What?" Maybe I'd heard wrong. "Do I shoot the red carpet?"

"No. No, dearie." He waved his hand in the air then leaned in closer, articulating into my face with forty-proof breath. "I asked if yer curtains match yer carpet." Before he could read a response in my withdrawn smile, he bowed into my hair, inhaling audibly. It wasn't just gross, it was alarming.

That's the best way I know how to put it: alarming. There is something shocking about being a redhead. Mostly, it's the people you meet being one. The old lad wasn't the first to have whiffed my head, imagining strawberry blonde must smell of "Strawberry Fields Forever." Usually after complimenting me on my curly locks, a man plucked a tendril from the mass and cradled in his hand, lifting it to his nose. He'd eye me tentatively while inhaling deeply. Then his eyes would close as if he were trying to discern peach from pear notes in his head. He'd open his eyes again, unsure of what he smelled but certain it was foreign and rare. Alarming. I told you.

There's no explanation for this desire for the rare and unknown. It's akin to the surprise experienced upon hearing I get my red hair from both my parents. No one expects my father to have red hair. We never think of men and their hair. Think of a famous redhead, and you don't think of Woody Allen or Vincent van Gogh. You think of Lucille, Julianne, and Nicole.

In cartoons, the redhead is the bully or the brain. In mythology, we're likened to venom, the underground, and Hades. Up here on Earth, we're likened to vixens. When I was born, it wasn't, "Oh what a cute angel." I was "quite the little devil." I've been associated with mischief and underhanded behavior. So, what the hell? Bring it. Pigeonhole me as you will. I could live up to the stereotype, and why not? I'd throw in the Irish temper for good measure.

The old-timer alluded to the fire crotch, shifting things beyond alarming and moving them into abusive. This brought out my abrasive. Before I had the opportunity to unleash it, we were interrupted. A young party promoter with a face that reminded me of a cherub touched me on the arm. "I'm sorry to interrupt, but did I hear right? You shoot red carpet events?" I felt myself staring at his cheeks, wondering if he wore rouge.

"Well, I . . ."

"So who do you work for?" he asked, eyeing my camera. Apparently, I was still staring, as he had to repeat himself. "Hello? Who do you work for?" he enunciated.

I shook my head, as if the act of doing so would stop me from wanting to pinch his face. "Oh, you know. I'm freelance mostly."

"Cool. Who invited you tonight?"

"Patrick," I replied, as if Patrick would actually remember my name at all.

"Listen," he took me by the arm, steering me away from Doom-Pa-

Dee-Do Man. "I have an event coming up. Would you be interested in covering it?" Gee, let me think. Come hang out, drink, and photograph people having fun? Nah. Not for me.

"Sure." And that's exactly what I did. My red carpet and I covered our first red carpet event. Others followed. Events and opportunities began to unfold for the redheaded stepchild, including a call from the Gansevoort's interior designer.

"After seeing your portfolio, we really think your style complements the vocabulary of the neighborhood. We'd like to hire you to photograph the surrounding area, but there's not much time. When can you start?"

I began that day and became responsible for photographing and choosing every piece of art in the hotel rooms and corridors, the combinations, representations of fashion, nightlife, restaurants, graffiti, and architectural elements. Environmental portraits of transvestites. I was actually paid money to tell a story, to explain what I'd seen, through a lens, in exposures and stops of light. People wanted to see what I did. I felt extraordinarily blessed. And busy.

By the time the hotel opened in April, I was putting the final touches on the web site I'd designed for them, examining the last of the prints (aka Quality Control), and trying in vain to secure myself a guest pass for the rooftop pool. I was also working a full-time job in advertising by day and photographing red carpet events by night. I needed to relax. Alcohol and a rooftop party would certainly suffice.

My friend Matt, a glorified chore whore at his PR firm, invited me to meet him at the Abercrombie & Fitch *Vanity Fair* party, where redheads seemed to be the new blonde. Three percent of the world is naturally redheaded, yet on the Gansevoort rooftop it seemed to be the trend. It was strange, like seeing a black person at a Dido concert. If redheads had a theme song, it would be by AC/DC, and pole dancing would be involved. Of course, everyone was beautiful, the kind of beauty that makes you want to touch things and hold in your stomach. I talked to everyone, and surprisingly all the gorgeous faces had genuine smiles. I was sure they'd spent enough time to roast a twenty-pound bird, making themselves look like they hadn't spent any time at all, using products with "Plump" and

"Bed" in their names. Yet, I couldn't see or hear the vanity. It seemed everyone there had grown into their own.

I grew tired come A.M. and decided I needed bed more than Bacardi. I yawned good-bye to Matt and headed curbside to hail a cab home. A swatch of male models approached me. Of *course* they were models, and okay, I don't know if "approached" is the right word. They watched me extend my arm for a cab, then asked where I was going. "Home to sleep," I replied.

"But you haven't taken our photograph yet," a trendy-bald man said.

"So get your act together, boys." I turned on the camera and adjusted my strap. "Put on your pissed off I'm-going-to-devour-the-camera faces, and let me do my job." It wasn't a job—it was my pleasure. I felt like a vixen. After snapping a few photos, Luke, Cole, and Rain (oh yes, Rain) invited me to join them at the nightclub PM. Four-letter-named men were inviting *me* to hang out with them!

Big. Fucking. Deal.

In the past, that would have done it for me. I would have squealed to my friends the next morning. Models. Gorgeous. Oh my God! But I've grown into myself, and there's more to life than pretty faces. I've learned that P.M. means bedtime and Linus, not beautiful boys and a nightclub. Call me crazy. Call me a redhead.

AT HOME I SLIPPED INTO MY SWEATSHORTS, SOCKS, AND 'beater, then drunk-dialed Stephen. No answer. I signed onto my instant messenger client to see if he was on. I happened to be a drunken dialer in the worst way. Worst way meaning, it extended beyond drunk dialing and became drunk IMing coupled with the dialing, like layering a scented lotion beneath perfume. I really shouldn't have been permitted near the Internet when sloppy. I needed a parental lock on my communication equipment that prohibited me from communicating with the opposite sex. A digital chastity belt.

Instead of putting metal around my lovely wares, I needed to take preventative measures, like keeping the number of the guy that mattered out of the cell phone to avoid a "morning-after disaster." But Stephen wasn't *that* guy. He was my friend. Why was I even calling Stephen?

I tried phoning him again. It was 3:20 A.M.

"Stephen?" His hello was a sleeping one. "I know it's late, but I'd like to ask you something."

"Okay . . ."

"Do you still like me?" Alcohol brings out the middle school in me.

"Who is this?" I panicked. What the fuck? Who is this? "Stephanie," I responded in a small tentative voice.

"I'm kidding. Stephanie, I've never stopped, but there's only—"

"Okay, so will you go out on a date with me tomorrow?" I sounded like a seventeen-year-old boy. I didn't care.

"You're calling me now to ask me this? Didn't we just have drinks together two nights ago? Wasn't that a date?" He was awake now.

"No, that wasn't a date. It was a nondate."

Stephen knew my theory on nondates: how men ask unavailable women out for a nondate hoping to change her mind. She'll go home hoping to awake with a voice mail asking for the next time he can *not* take her out. And if it doesn't come until two days later, she'll want to see him again, just to learn why he's the type of guy who waits two days.

It's extremes. I'd tried both. I'd gone months without dating, focusing on self-help books, my photography, friends, just enjoying myself without any anxiety. It was easier to be alone, not dating, with the thoughts of a "someday when I least expect it he'll show up" keeping me warm. That way, I wasn't frantic, I wasn't on the watch. I could breathe and realize life doesn't revolve around one person of the opposite sex. Then I could go back to my self-help book. That way, though, I was hiding. Just as I'd advised Smelly with Dude Ranch Boy, if someone says they don't date, it means they're not ready. When I wasn't dating, I didn't have to get hurt. There was no vulnerable in my vocabulary and no fear of failure. I didn't even go there. You can't win the game if your cards stay in your pocket.

"Stephen, I want a real date."

"Okay, you're insane. You know that, right?" I imagined he was now sitting upright. "We *have* been dating. We've been dating for months. I don't care what you want to call it. We have talked every single day since January, have we not? January! We go to dinner, parties, movies. You even shared your nasty movie nachos with me, and I know what a big deal that is for you. We spend the day together, like the whole day, from brunch to dinner, don't we?"

"Yeah." An unconscious smile slipped across my face.

"Frickin' right, yeah! So now you want to call me in the middle of the night and declare that you now want it to be dating instead of nondating, is that what I'm hearing?" I didn't want to say "Yeah" again. "Stephanie," he lowered his voice, "you can call it whatever you want." We were both quiet. "As long as it means I get to see more of YOU, okay?"

I didn't know whether to laugh or cry. I did a little of both, then argued, "My point, Stephen—"

"Oh, boy, let's hear this!" He laughed.

"If you'd let me speak, my point is, I want to get closer to you and spend more frickin' time with you." I was yelling. "I want to really do this."

"Do you mean that?"

"Yes!"

"Well, quit being a brat about it, and do something." Did he want me to come over? "That's right. And as far as I'm concerned, I think it's about time we step things up. We should do something special on this so-called *non* nondate of ours, don't you think?"

I thought for a moment, wondering if I'd really succumb to sado-masochism. We'd already photographed the city together, done restaurants, sporting events, musicals. What else was there? I knew he had a plan. "Okay," I hesitated, waiting to hear what it was.

"Good." He clapped. "So how does a ride out to Queens and an afternoon at the cemetery grab you?" I wasn't the crazy one. "Stephanie, I told you tomorrow I have to attend my grandmother's interment." Tournament? "An interment is when we bury her ashes in the same plot as her husband." Oy. "Stephanie, it's not a big deal at all. I didn't even know her, and it will be very small. Besides, you'll get to meet my family, and that's really the point." Yeah, okay, words *so* not to say to Stephanie: Meet. My. Family.

"Um . . ."

"Oh, come on. Don't *um* me. Just do it."

"Um, the thing is, yes. I want to go," I said, as if it just occurred to me. "I want to meet them." Besides, if there's ever a good time to meet any man's family, it's when the focus is not on you. This would work—they'd already be mourning.

The next morning, Stephen began our day on a sarcastic note.

"I love how you're always late," he said, while holding his car door open for me.

"Yes, I know you do, especially when I look this good doing it." I was being facetious right back. I looked like ass. It was the brumous frizz weather, the perfect bleak backdrop for a day at the plots.

He stared at me and lingered near the door before closing it. "Stephanie, you gotta know how beautiful you are." In the past, I hated when people said this. *You must know,* as if it's math. What the hell? In comparison to what? Some days, sure; others; stomach bloat, a new pimple that hurts, and fat that's nearly crippling. Beautiful isn't a town with its own train station; it's a voyage. How would I even answer that?

"Yes, I do know." Then a teasing smile peeped out. "I mean, thank you, Stephen." Then the worst bit followed: Stephanie Klein giggled. Oh, dear God! My smile faded a little when he looked at me. I was shy about letting him see how happy I was.

"You're welcome, Stephanie," he whined back with the *I know you are but what am I?* tone. Once he was in the car, he kissed me on the nose.

"At what age do you start reading the obituaries?" I asked without waiting for an answer. "I swear I'd be clueless about who died without my father. He reads them every day on the toilet."

"Yeah, well, when you get up there in age, they start dropping, so you pay attention."

"When did your grandmother actually die?" This wasn't a funeral but an interment.

"A year ago, but I didn't have to read about it in the obits. She was sick for a long time."

I remember when I learned Gabe's grandmother had died. We were no longer married. My father had called to tell me he'd read it in the paper. It was a strange feeling, knowing his family so intimately, yet being so estranged. As much as I hated Gabe at times, I still had a life with him. I picked up his socks, petted his head when he was sick, traveled with him, borrowed his ties for belts, slept in his shirts, shared a toothbrush from time to time, definitely his razor, and I loved him very much. We had a full, real life together. His grandmother was always kind to me, but I didn't belong at the funeral. Not one impulse in my body told me to go. It wasn't my life anymore. I was no longer a comfort to any of them, and I didn't want to be. I knew Gabe didn't need my comfort, and I wasn't sure I could even give it. I was surprised that I cared. I guess I still love Gabe, but I also hate him for his venal recklessness.

"Stephen, relationships should have obituaries, so everyone knows what happened in a succinct line or two."

"Where'd that come from?"

"I dunno. Wanna know what I do know? I'm totally screwed when I die."

"How's that?"

"We've got no more land in my family. I mean, the Kleins, all their space is taken and accounted for. I have to find my own family to get buried with." I wanted to grip the words from the air and swallow them quickly. What the fuck was I saying?

"I tell you what. On our first wedding anniversary, my gift to you will be burial plots together."

"So that's our first anniversary, ya? Hmm. Not exactly paper, now, is it? And not exactly uplifting."

"Well, neither is a first *non* nondate at a gravesite, but what the hell, Red."

He called me Red. If I were standing, I would have swooned.

HIS MOTHER HUGGED ME UPON SIGHT. "STEPHANIE, I'M so glad you could come today." She smelled of scented candles and pencil shavings. "It's just so nice to meet you." She was warm and hugged like she meant it. Quiet hellos were exchanged with his father, Paul, and sister, Ilyse, in the parking lot before we all made our way to the funeral plot. The ashes of Stephen's grandmother had been FedExed to his father's office. Not exactly theater tickets or a new corduroy blazer from J. Crew. "Hey, this is the business of death. It's part of life, just as much as anything else," Stephen's father said while holding the white cardboard box with both hands. I expected him to scatter the ashes, a sprinkling on a bush or tree. Dramatic movements, a story about her last wishes. Instead, he looked at the box, mentioned something about health-code violations, and nodded his head as if to say, what's done is done, then put the box in the hole, a square peg in a round hole. "Okay, we're done." He wiped his hands on his thighs.

"Shouldn't we, I don't know, say something?" Stephen replied to his father.

"Look, I said my good-byes to her a long time ago. Nothing is permanent. We hold onto what we can, when we can. That's it. We try to cherish our family while we can, but then that's it. Permanence doesn't exist until you're dead."

We took a moment of silence. I watched the grave diggers watch us, looked at the sky and the impending silver threat of a storm. Then I looked at Stephen, who was looking down at the hole in the ground. He noticed I was looking at him and squeezed my hand. I looked down, too. Was that right? Wait a minute. Was I seeing things? Right there, carved into the stone at our feet were our names. STEPHEN & STEPHANIE. Paul's parents were Stephen and Stephanie, too—the exact spelling, right down to the ph's.

We were at an ending with a new beginning.

ALL OF US MADE OUR WAY BACK TO THE PARKING LOT IN silence, then hugged and kissed our good-byes with promises of again and soon.

Once Stephen and I were behind the closed doors of his car, he turned off the radio.

"Stephanie," he said, "that was really freaky, you know?"

"I know. I mean we were just talking about it on the ride here."

"Not that I need a sign, Stephanie—you know I KNOW you're the one—but damn if I did, that had to be it." He grabbed my hand and rubbed it with his thumb while his eyes turned glassy. "I am so head over heels crazy about you." I smiled back and pulled a stray tear off my cheek with the back of my hand. I believed it was a sign, too. Even if it weren't, the fact that we both wanted to believe it was a sign said enough. We drove the rest of the way back to Manhattan listening to Rhett Miller, holding hands.

"I really liked meeting your family, Stephen," I said as we pulled up to my apartment building. "They are such warm people."

"And I'm sure they liked you too. But you know, even if they couldn't stand you, which is hardly possible, I'd still love to argue with you." He kissed me quickly on the lips, then smiled. "Okay, Red, I'm off to the gym. I will talk to you later and see what you're in the mood for. Maybe you'll let me play the guitar for you?"

"You so want to get laid." I kissed him and skipped into my apartment lobby. Skipped!

I ARRIVED HOME TO THE NOTORIOUS D.O.G., AND I REALized, I am happy with my life. "Do you know, baby, that it would be okay if it were just us? Go lick my blister. Go on, right there. Yeah, that's my good moo shoo." This is still my life—my coming home to my furkid, curled into a comma, ears pinned back, going to town on my blisters, healing them with his magical canine saliva. It hurt but felt strangely like it was working.

I always believed the best medicines hurt. I used to pour the brown bottle of fizz on my open wounds, despite being told not to apply hydrogen peroxide directly. If it hurt, it meant it was working. When I have a sore throat, I drink grapefruit juice. If it stings, it's healing something. Of course, intellectually I know none of this is true, but it feels true.

When Linus finished licking my salty wounds, he climbed onto my stomach and looked up at me. "It really would be okay, you know, if it ended with just us, Linus." It won't, but it's nice to know that I'd still be okay if it did.

I'm perfectly satiated living with my dog, photographing, and story-telling, coming home to those ears and that FACE. Linus looked like an old man, and for a moment, I was certain he was about to either say something profound or tell me the secret ingredient of his famous baked bean recipe. Instead, he pawed at me, indicating he wanted more love.

Even if there weren't a man across time or town waiting for me to meet up with him, I'd still be happy. I feel fulfilled, as if someone just irrigated my wounds and kissed me where it hurt.

I got hungry and decided to grab a lamburger at my local watering hole Compass, journal in tow. I frequent there for the Parmesan bread-sticks and first-date watching. It's the kind of place that caters to "new." Rutilant light casts a soft glow over faces meeting for the first time. The bar area is staffed with small, round candlelit tables and polite, unobtru-sive service. It's always just empty enough where it's not dead or con-gested. I dipped into a seat along the red banquette wall, beside a couple clearly in the newer stages of dating each other. A hobbit of a man with a birthmark below his jaw that resembled a molar spoke quickly and seemed rushed, fidgeting with his cuffs, removing bits of lint from his blazer lapel. He struck me as the type of man who, in the spirit of effi-ciency, folded his pizza slices before eating them.

When he began to order their fries well done, he stopped himself, asking his date, "do you mind?" In the next beat, he mentioned his ex-girlfriend while huffing clouds of breath onto his metal-framed eye-glasses. I watched for her reaction, expecting her knee to bounce beneath the table, for her to cross her arms, to withdraw. Instead, she smiled warmly, touched his hand, and offered, "Would you like to try some of my soup?" She fed him from her spoon.

Had she mentioned her compassion and willingness to share in her online dating profile? Or was he lured there by her beach photographs, the one of her in a bikini, a dusting of freckles on her shoulders. Had he lied about his smoking habits or zodiac sign in his? I wondered why they chose to date each other, what the deciding factor was in their agreeing to break bread. Something seemed to work between them. Maybe it was the lighting. Though I think it was more.

According to Phone Therapist, there's a subliminal fabric that ties us to people. It's beyond attraction. We're drawn to those who push our buttons and who will hopefully create a safe environment for us to work on our issues. I wondered why I was drawn to Stephen.

He was a pain in the ass, for one. He gave me my way, most of the time, but he made me work for it. Stephen challenged me when I acted out or pouted unfairly. We debated often, which usually led to teasing, which later I would learn sometimes led to sex. Verbal foreplay. But it was more than that. Part of what made us was the timing. I finally knew my worth, believed in myself, and didn't need some guy to tell me how great I was to believe it, so I could see Stephen for Stephen, not for how much he liked me. It was no longer about need and became about want.

It wasn't about the charming Jewish doctor with the Ivy League education and George Clooney looks. That's what you look for in a guy when you're incomplete. With Stephen, I realized it's about a man who's my equal and best friend, a man who loves me most when I leave him at the bar to chase down a stranger to get the photograph. For the first time in a long time, he was someone I wanted to make happy. I wanted to be the best person I could, for myself, and for him. And that would take work. It would mean opening the wounds that hurt and taking a chance.

My cell phone buzzed with a text. I knew it was Stephen before I opened my phone. When I looked at the screen, though, I saw it was a text message from Alexandra:

> *Dulce, Adele, and I are at Pastis having yumsies and drinksies. Scene is rye-dic!*
> *Get your loverly ass here, my pritts.*

I'd have jumped at the opportunity to be out, prowling once upon a time, but I was staying put. I still love to love my friends, but I punctuate those moments with solitude. In the past, sitting by myself at Compass, watching the couple beside me, would have instigated tears. I'd have scoured the pages of my journal, stared at my "life list," and panicked about how off-track I'd become, chanting *But, I want that, and I'm running out of time.* I would have worried I was failing myself.

But now, sitting at Compass, I realized it's about abandoning your stupid wristwatch and giving your compass a flick to make sure the needle still moves . . . having the courage to follow in the direction to which it points. I opened my journal to a blank page. I still do want that: the husband, babies, and house in the suburbs, but I'm no longer envious because I know I can have it, all of it, with Stephen or any other man. Success isn't about crossing things off life's to-do list. It's having the grace and fortitude to move through change, curls intact, and smiling. I certainly didn't need to craft a new "designs for life" list because the blank page of my journal wasn't about what I didn't have. It was possibility. The plan should be learning how to live without one, or how to carry a big fat eraser in your petite handbag. It's comfortable to have plans, but you've got to be loose enough to accept change. Plans get revised, new blueprints get drafted to accommodate the expansive garden. And nowadays, I'm planting my own, even if it is in crapass Central Park. I'm digging my feet into the warm soil, retaining and nourishing everything I've got left—and that's a lot.

My cell phone buzzed again, this time with a text message from Stephen reading: *So, whatcha wearin', Red?*

I laughed and responded: *A smile.*

Acknowledgments

COUNTLESS THANKS ARE DUE MY PUBLISHER, JUDITH REGAN, first and foremost, for her vision, belief, and boldness. Thank you.

I'd like to express my gratitude to my agents, Diane Bartoli and Joe Veltre, for seeing what could be before it was, and for really, at the end of the day, making me excited to write with each interaction. Thanks to Diane for walking me through it all, setting me at ease, and letting me know when my writing was getting in the way of my writing. She championed my work and believed in it when I needed it most. Thanks to my editor, Maureen O'Neal, whose diligence, guidance, and complete adeptness helped carry this book, and to Marc Chamlin, Beth Silfin, and Francine Wachtell for their expertise and dedication.

I have learned so much from the helpful members of my New York JCC writing workshops, especially Charles Salzberg. Sally Koslow, Sharon Gurwitz, Ellen Schecter, Marian Nash, and Vivian Conan were my daily editors, who "got" my work. Barbara Cole and Kimberlee Auerbach are more than writing peers; they are my providers of white light and laughter. The group's feedback and encouragement helped me grow as a writer and person.

My heartfelt thanks to Kimberly Gilman, Jennifer Hanser, and Kelly Wick for shouldering burdens, sharing tears, and becoming my middle of the night over the years. For reading that shite over and over, for bickering over the car radio, for squeezing my hand through the scary bits, and for reminding me of the good, sing-out-loud parts, not just in the book, but in life. True friends help you celebrate your successes; these are my truest.

My deep appreciation extends to Michael Pryor for reading version after version and making me laugh through each one, to Chris Di-Clerico for encouraging me to write publicly (and come to terms with it), to Jennifer Barako, Amy Bellotte, Monique Ellenbogen, Jaimee Loewy, Erin Maunder, and Yasmin Mehrain for the important girl moments involving adult beverages, instant messages, and my anxiety, and to Heather Hunter for commiserating and cheering so often. I would be remiss without properly thanking AT for adding so much to my life, and to my teachers Colin Harrison, Mary Gordon, Faith Toperoff, and Katy Roberts for their profound inspiration, wisdom, and encouragement.

While writing this book, my blog kept me committed to writing, especially when I didn't feel like it. I never imagined receiving such a gift of making so many friends from all points of the world. Their wishes, insightful observations, and camaraderie are immensely appreciated. It is through their daily involvement that I've come to learn the true successes in life have nothing to do with praise or criticism and everything to do with inspiring change. I'm thankful for the readers who've reached out and made me realize this.

My deepest gratitude is reserved for my family: my mother, for reminding me how young I started, for saying, "I always knew," for homemade rice pudding, for being the nicest person I've ever known; Lea, for making me laugh until I snort, for her laugh and heart, for being my memory and friend; Carol, Erica, and Amanda, for always making me feel at home beside them; Ted, Barbara, Hollis, and Mikayla for their warmth and open arms; my grandfather, Samuel, who has supported and encouraged me and offered wisdom at the hardest times; and to my father, Donald Klein, who deserves his own page. He has taught me to live a life of worth and integrity. To live straight up. And when things were at their most solemn, he urged me to "write it all down."

Finally, to Philip Beer, my family by choice, who, by now, knows every word by heart and has mine. He transcends language and improves everything, especially me.